A+ CERTIFICATION COURSE

MINDWORKS STUDY MANUAL

VERSION 5.X

Core Hardware

MINDWORKS
4141 N. Granite Reef Road, Suite 101
Scottsdale, AZ 85251
www.mindwork.com

Publisher:	MINDWORKS
Executive Editors:	Jim Gardner, Ron Brown
Editor:	Carol Hartwig
Technical Editor:	Dan Waldo
Page Layout/Design:	Carol Hartwig
Layout & Graphics:	Jim Knott
Cover Design:	Tom Hagen, Jim Gardner
Author:	Tom Hagen
Supported By:	The Entire Staff at Mindworks

THIS BOOK IS DEDICATED TO ALL OF OUR VALUED STUDENTS AND CUSTOMERS WITHOUT WHOSE SUPPORT THIS BOOK WOULD NOT BE POSSIBLE.

THANK YOU!

Table of Contents

What is A+ Certification?

A+ Certification is a nationally recognized standard that certifies a benchmark level of competency in the microcomputer industry. This certification will be a valuable addition to your résumé. This certification sets a standard for those working in the personal computer industry as technicians, help desk and support staff.

Many computer resellers and service companies today are required by hardware vendors to have A+ Certified personnel on staff to ensure that these businesses are capable of providing high-quality, authorized service for their clients. Because of this requirement and because of the high standard set for attaining *A+ Certification*, employers often require that their personnel become A+ Certified. *A+ Certification* has become one of the most sought-after certifications in the computer industry.

Who Sponsors A+ Certification?

The *A+ Certification* program was established by the Computing Technology Industry Association (CompTIA, *www.comptia.org*) and is sponsored by many of the largest PC vendors in the industry, including IBM, Hewlett-Packard, and COMPAQ.

What are the Requirements for A+ Certification?

A candidate must pass two tests.

- The first required test is the **Core Hardware** exam, which covers basic microcomputer hardware, configuration, installation, upgrading, diagnostics, repair and basic networking.
- The second test is the **Operating System Technologies** exam, which covers the installation, configuration, diagnosing and troubleshooting of the Windows 95/98 and Windows NT/2000 Operating Systems as well as Internet and networking technologies relating to software.

To obtain more detailed information, or to register to take the exams in your area, call *Prometric* at (800) 77 MICRO and ask for the A+ Registrar or your can visit them on the Web at **www.2test.com**, or contact VUE at (877) 551-PLUS or visit them on the Web at **www.vue.com.**

The A+ Core Hardware Course

Introduction

The *MindWorks A+* Core Hardware Course is designed to provide an in-depth study of the various areas that are related to servicing microcomputers and peripheral PC devices. Because the expectations and knowledge level of customers are higher than ever before, a good customer service representative must have the skills necessary to meet the challenges of the market place.

This course will prepare you for the *A+ Certification* exam, and will also be a useful resource to anyone wanting to gain more knowledge about PCs and related hardware. The course is not intended to create hardware experts. Rather, the *MindWorks A+* Core Hardware Course will provide you with a solid base understanding of PC hardware, DOS, networking, printers and troubleshooting. Expertise in these areas will come from experience and continued study.

Objectives

When you've completed this course, you will have a thorough understanding of these subject areas:

- Basics of computer electronics
- Safety when performing maintenance on computer equipment
- Identification and knowledge of computer hardware
- Assembly and disassembly of PCs
- Installation and use of basic DOS commands
- Configuration and optimization of the DOS environment
- Configuration of computer equipment
- Diagnosing and troubleshooting problems with peripherals
- Proper use and troubleshooting of different printers
- Familiarity with LANs and their basic components
- Implementing a preventive maintenance program
- Knowledge of basic hardware troubleshooting steps and potential causes for common problems, error codes and messages
- Essentials of good customer service

Section 1

A Brief History of Computing

Section 1: A Brief History of Computing

Introduction

The remarkable thing about the Computer Age is just how much has happened in a relatively short span of time. The major advances that have allowed the computer to evolve from extremely large, expensive machines, to portable, affordable PCs have occurred over a fifty-year period. The rapid advances occurring in the Computer Age can be directly tied to three major technological milestones: the vacuum tube, the transistor and the development of the integrated circuit. Each of these individual developments has had a drastic effect on computer equipment and how we as users interface with them.

Objectives

When you have completed this section, you will be able to:

- Discuss the use of vacuum tubes and the creation of the first computers
- Describe the advantages of transistors
- Identify the importance of the invention of Integrated Circuits
- Understand the function of the microprocessor
- Identify the key developments in the creation of the Personal Computer

In the Beginning

The beginning of the modern Computer Age can be traced back to June of 1951. This was the introduction date of the first **UNIVAC** (Universal Automatic Computer.) The first client to purchase and use such a colossal computing machine was none other than the U.S. Government.

The U.S. Bureau of Census purchased the **UNIVAC** to tabulate the previous year's census. This in itself was a milestone in that this was the first time a computer was used and built for data processing applications rather than for military or scientific use. Actually the **UNIVAC** was a non-military version of the **ENIAC** (Electronic Numerical Integrator and Computer), a machine that was built to rapidly calculate the trajectory of missiles. Work on the **ENIAC** began in the early forties with the intent to use the machine to aid in the War effort. Despite the fact that scientists worked on it around the clock for three years, it was not finished before the end of the War.

The Vacuum Tube

This first generation of computers was built around the use of the vacuum tube. These tubes were about the size of a light bulb and were the primary internal computing component for these early machines. Thousands of tubes were required to operate these early computers. Consequently, these machines required a tremendous amount of space and generated a great deal of heat. This meant that large rooms with special air conditioning equipment were required to house them.

Because vacuum tubes had a relatively short life span (an average of 3000 hours) bulbs would burn out nearly every fifteen minutes. The large number of tubes that these machines used meant that it took considerable time to find the problem tubes.

Another problem with these early machines was that the language they used was machine-language based, which emphasized the use of numbers as opposed to higher-level languages which use simple, English-based commands, such as *go to*, *put*, *if then*, etc.

For all of these reasons, these machines were fairly impractical for widespread, general use.

The Transistor

In 1947, John Bardeen, Walter Brattain and William Shockley, three Bell Lab scientists, were awarded the Nobel prize for developing the **transistor**. The transistor was designed to perform the same function as the vacuum tube, but offered several advantages. Unlike the vacuum tube, the transistor was relatively small. It was approximately one-hundredth the size of a vacuum tube or about the size of a pencil eraser. At the same time, because they conducted electricity faster and more efficiently, a single transistor could perform the equivalent workload of 40 vacuum tubes. In addition, transistors gave off very little heat and were much less expensive to produce.

The development of the transistor was a key step in the computer revolution. Machines that used transistors as their primary internal component were faster, smaller, less expensive and more reliable than their predecessors. These improvements led to the first use of a computer outside of the government. In 1960 the Bethlehem Steel company used a transistor-based computer for orders, inventory and production management. However, it is important to note that these machines were still large, expensive and required too much manpower for all but the largest organizations to be able to use them. During this time, computers were used primarily in governmental agencies, universities or large businesses and had not yet been adopted for widespread, general use. The next step in the development of the computer would prove to drastically revolutionize and popularize the computer.

The Integrated Circuit

Two men, Robert Noyce of the Fairfield Corporation and Jack Kilby of Texas Instruments, independently discovered that they could pack a large number of transistors onto a single, extremely small, wafer of silicon. Silicon is one of the most abundant earthly substances and is therefore relatively inexpensive. Besides its availability, silicon is valuable because of its semiconductor qualities. As a semiconductor, silicon conducts electricity when treated with certain chemicals. **Integrated Circuits (ICs)**, which are sometimes referred to as semiconductor chips, can house incredible numbers of transistors on a single silicon wafer.

ICs provided several key benefits that built on transistor technology. First, they were much smaller than transistors. Second, they were much less expensive. Third, they were more reliable: chip technology could be used over and over again and failed on average once every 33 million hours. And finally, the miniaturization of circuits meant lower power requirements.

The ICs initially developed by Fairfield and Texas Instruments incorporated multiple transistors on a single chip. In the early 1970s, technology was introduced that allowed for thousands of transistors to be placed on a quarter-inch of silicon. This was known as Large Scale Integration (LSI). Today's technology uses Monolithic Integrated Circuits, which have extended the number of transistors that can be placed on a chip into the millions. This number continues to grow exponentially. In fact, since the invention of the Integrated Circuit, the number of transistors that can be placed on a single chip has doubled every two years!

The Microprocessor

Once the technology was developed that enabled millions of transistors to be placed on a single chip, it was possible to place all of the computing logic and power onto a single processor. The microprocessor is made up of many Integrated Circuits. It is essentially one single chip that can perform all of the processing of a full-scale computer. The first microprocessor was developed by an Intel design team led by Ted Hoff and was first commercially available in 1971. It was the invention of the microprocessor that led to the creation of the microcomputer or, at it is better know today, the Personal Computer (PC). Today's common, off-the-shelf PC is hundreds of times smaller, and much more powerful, than the original UNIAC.

The Personal Computer (PC)

While there are many computers that may vie for the title of the first Personal Computer, the Altair 8800, produced and marketed by a company called MITS in 1974, is considered by many to be the first computer widely accepted for personal use. The Altair was based on an Intel microprocessor and was sold as a kit that could be assembled to create a Personal Computer. While these first PCs allowed individuals to own computers, they did not provide much in the way of practical, everyday use. They were awkward to work with, requiring programming by means of toggles and switches.

In 1975 Microsoft was founded with the purpose of making computers more generally accessible. In 1976, Apple Computer was founded with the same purpose. However, while Microsoft focused strictly on **software** (one of their first products was an interpreter for the Altair), Apple developed its own proprietary **hardware** and **operating system** as well as a proprietary set of **desktop applications**.

Apple was the brainchild of co-founders Steve Wozniak and Steven Jobs. After introducing the Apple I at a local computer club in California, ten retail stores were selling them by the end of that year.

The Apple computer was extremely successful, much more so than any other computer previously designed for personal use. The success of the Apple computer was due in large part to the fact that the hardware and software were extremely user-friendly and useful. From the very beginning, Apple computers came with integrated software tools such as word processing, databases, spreadsheets and even games.

Then in 1977, Apple introduced its Apple II, a fully-assembled computer with a whopping 4K RAM for under $1300.00. Its open systems platform allowed third-party vendors to manufacture hardware enhancements. This, coupled with new sound and color graphics, quickly catapulted the Apple II computer to become the most widely used computer in the school and home market place. About this same time frame, Apple was also gaining notice in the business workplace primarily for the innovative VisiCalc software that was developed to run on its computers.

In 1983 after much success, Apple released the **Lisa** computer. The Lisa line was specifically aimed at the corporate market place. The Lisa was short lived and was eventually replaced by the more popular **Macintosh**. The MAC entered the market place poised as a low cost desktop publishing solution. However, while it did receive high marks for its ease of use it was limited by its relatively slow speed and small monochrome monitor. In 1987, the Mac II was released offering higher speeds and a much larger color screen.

The IBM Personal Computer

In 1981, IBM released its own PC, equipped with a basic operating system licensed from Microsoft. IBM took a different approach to their Personal Computer. For the most part, IBM focused on hardware development and encouraged other third-parties to write programs to perform functions such as word processing and spreadsheets.

At the time of its release to the world, most computers were still processing 8 bits of information per clock cycle. IBM's new PC revolutionized the industry by hitting the streets with a then new computer based on Intel's 8088 processor, which was compatible with 8-bit computers but processed information internally at 16-bits per clock cycle. The IBM PC also featured a design, known as "open architecture", which made it possible for users and technicians to add features via expansion slots without replacing the whole computer.

The original IBM Personal Computer, the model **5150,** came out of the box with 16K of RAM, that was expandable to 64K of RAM on the motherboard. It also came standard with a green-on-black Monochrome Monitor (**Model 5151**). The power supply was rated at 63.5 Watts, a far cry from today's 250 watt plus power supplies. Other features included a Monochrome Graphics Adapter, a 25-pin female parallel printer port, a 25-pin Serial Port with 25-pin male interface (perhaps the first in the industry), 2 full-height drive bays, 1 full-height floppy diskette drive capable of using single- and double-sided, single- and double-density disks and IBM PC-DOS v1.1. The 1.0 version was found to be a bit "buggy" for use and was quickly replaced by version 2.0. Because of its open architecture, third-party manufacturers quickly started selling hard drives that could be used to add mass storage capability to the IBM PC.

In March of 1983, IBM released the Personal Computer XT (e**X**tended **T**echnology), or simply the XT. It came equipped out of the box with a 10 megabyte Full-Height Hard Disk Drive, was expandable to 640K of RAM on the Motherboard and came with a new version of the operating system (MS-DOS v2.1), which supported directories and subdirectories. It also came with one or two half-height 5 1/4 inch floppy drives. Shortly thereafter the XT was available with a 20 megabyte Half-Height Hard Disk Drive. The expansion bus also contained eight slots instead of the original five. This offered users greater flexibility in the addition of peripherals devices. Because the XT became very popular very fast, many other manufacturers began copying IBM's design. These copies were referred to as "**clones**."

In today's computer world, the IBM or "clone" machines built to match IBM's specifications, and the Apple Macintosh are essentially the two types of personal computers available.

An important note: Computer terminology can be very tricky and must be used carefully. Today, the term PC is most commonly used to refer to an IBM-style computer, while Apple systems are referred to as "Macs". It is also important to note that the term "Personal Computer" is no longer a completely accurate description of these machines since they are used pervasively throughout the business community as well as in governmental and academic circles.

Interesting Note: *Original Price:* ***$7,545.00*** *(according to IBM price list)*

Exercise 1.1: History Recap

DIRECTIONS

In the space provided answer the following questions by writing a brief paragraph.

1. Why did the early computers like the ENIAC and the UNIVAC generate so much heat?

2. What characteristics of transistors made them a better choice than the vacuum tubes in the production of computers and other related equipment?

Summary

The development of the computer has occurred over a relatively short period of time. The major advances that have allowed the computer to evolve from extremely large, expensive machines, to portable, affordable PCs have occurred over a fifty-year period. The three major technological milestones fueling these advances were: the vacuum tube, the transistor and the development of the integrated circuit. In this section, we discussed the use of vacuum tubes and the creation of the first computers, the invention of and advantages of transistors, the development of Integrated Circuits and the importance of the microprocessor in the creation of the PC.

Review Questions

1. What does UNIVAC stand for?

   A. Universal International Academic Computer
   B. Universal Automatic Computer
   C. Unified Versatile Atomic Computer
   D. Uniform Verification Analog Computer

2. What company created the transistor?

   A. Texas Instruments
   B. Intel
   C. IBM
   D. Bell Labs

3. Which of the following was introduced first?

   A. Powerbook
   B. IBM PC
   C. Altair 8800
   D. Macintosh

4. An Integrated Circuit contains thousands of:

   A. Transistors
   B. Wafers
   C. Tubes
   D. Microprocessors

5. Which company created the microprocessor?

   A. Texas Instruments
   B. Intel
   C. IBM
   D. Bell Labs

Section 2

Basic Computer Electronics

Section 2: Basic Computer Electronics

Introduction

Computing would be impossible without electricity. Therefore, in order to understand how computers and computer components function, it is important to understand the basics of computer electronics. In this section we will discuss the basics of electricity and how they relate to PCs. We will conduct an overview of the various terms that define the ways in which electricity flows and is controlled. Then we will identify the two main types of electrical power and how these relate to the functioning of computers.

Objectives

When you have completed this section, you will be able to:

- Define electricity
- Understand the concepts of voltage, current, resistance, capacitance and watts
- Know the difference between Alternating Current (AC) and Direct Current (DC)
- Understand the basics of AC/DC conversion

What is Electricity?

Electricity is a form of energy that occurs at an atomic level. The atom is composed of three parts: protons, neutrons and electrons. Each atom is formed by a core or center that contains at least one proton and one neutron. At least one electron travels around the atom's center at a very high speed. Electricity is created when electrons are forced from one atom to another.

In more basic terms: ***Electricity is simply the movement of charges.***

Computers use electricity in various ways. For example, electricity supplies power to the monitor and hard disks as well as to peripheral devices such as printers, modems, etc. In computers, electricity flows mainly through wires and printed circuitry. In reality, electricity, in one form or another, flows through each essential component of the computer.

Let's begin by defining the following key terms relating to electricity.

- Voltage
- Current
- Resistance
- Capacitance
- Watts

Voltage

In technical terms, voltage is defined as the electron moving force (EMF, sometimes also referred to as electromotive force) or the potential difference. More simply stated, voltage is the push that causes the flow of electricity. To better understand voltage, think about water being forced through a hose: the greater the pressure (voltage), the greater the flow of water (current.)

Standard outlets in the U.S. supply 120 volts (V), while the European standard is 230V. The PC power supply converts from these voltages and utilizes several voltage ranges. The most common PC voltages are +12V, -12V, +5V, -5V and 0V. The latest low-power consumption chips can operate on voltages as low as 2.5.

Current (Amps)

The flow of electrons caused by voltage is known as the current. Again, think of the water hose: as the pressure increases (voltage), the amount of water passing through the hose increases (current.) Current is measured in terms of amperes (amps) and reflects the number of electrons per second that pass a given point. The more current that flows through a circuit, the higher the amps.

Higher currents equate to increased energy. Energy also relates directly to heat. This is why an appliance designed to generate heat, such as an electric blanket, would have a relatively high amp rating. In the PC world, heat may damage or destroy components. For this reason, most PC electronics use currents in the very lowest ranges, normally milli-amps (1/1000th of an amp) and micro-amps (1/1,000,000th of an amp.)

Resistance

Resistance is defined as the opposition to the flow of electrons through a material. Some materials such as glass, rubber and plastic display a high level of resistance. Such substances are known as **insulators** or **non-conductors**, because they impede or resist the flow of electric currents. Other materials such as silver, copper and gold show a low level of resistance. These substances are known as **conductors**, because they encourage the flow of electric currents. This is why if you examine a typical electrical cord, you will find that it is composed of a metallic center (such as copper) to induce electric flow inside the cord and is encased in rubber (a non-conductor or insulator) to shield the flow of electricity outside the cord.

Resistance also defines another kind of substance crucial to the PC: the **semiconductor**. A semiconductor is a material that allows a current to flow, but in a limited or controlled fashion. Examples of semiconductors are silicon and geranium. Silicon (which gives its name to Silicon Valley) is normally a very poor conductor. However, when it is treated with certain other substances it easily passes a current in one direction, while prohibiting flow in the opposite direction. This unique property of silicon has made it the basis of the computer and electronics industry.

The unit of measurement for resistance is the Ohm. This unit is defined by Ohm's Law which states that resistance is determined by dividing the Voltage by Amps. Ohm's law can therefore be defined as the relationship between voltage, current and resistance. This law can be represented mathematically in three different ways, depending on what you need to calculate.

To calculate voltage:

Voltage = Amps x Resistance

To calculate current:

Amps = Volts ÷ Ohms

To calculate resistance:

Ohms = Volts ÷ Amps

Capacitance

To understand the concept of capacitance, let's first define a capacitor. A capacitor is an electronic device that has the ability to temporarily store an electrical charge. The amount or size of this charge is capacitance. In other words, capacitance is the capacity of a device to hold a charge. This capacity is measured in units called Farads. The Farad is a relatively large unit of measure. Most PC power supply capacitors are rated at approximately 4,700 uF (uF stands for micro-Farad or $1/1,000,000^{th}$ of a farad.)

Capacitors are found in a variety of PC components because of their ability to act as power reservoirs. The two most notable PC components containing capacitors are monitors and power supplies. The main component of a computer monitor is the tube (also known as a Cathode Ray Tube or CRT). The tube, which is filled with inert gases, acts as a capacitor and can store thousands of volts of electricity after being turned off and unplugged. Power supplies also use capacitors, although in a much smaller version than monitors. Capacitors are used in power supplies to help to even out the flow of electricity.

Watts

A Watt is a measure of electrical power. We have already discussed amps and volts. Watts are the product of the amp rating times the voltage. This is expressed mathematically as:

Amp x Volt = Watts

Light bulbs are a common device rated in terms of Watts. Since standard U.S. outlets supply 120 volts, the wattage of a light bulb in the U.S. might be expressed as the following:

1/2 Amp x 120 Volts = 60 Watts

Watts are used in the PC world to rate a variety of components. For example, wattage is often a consideration when choosing a power supply. Most PC power supplies today typically are rated in the 200-300 Watt range, although you may see ratings that are much higher for power supplies designed for high-end systems. With higher wattage, power supplies gain greater ability to power a larger number of PC components. This is important in today's systems that come equipped with a variety of peripherals.

The following table should help to summarize our basic review of important terms relating to electricity:

Term	Definition	Unit of Measure	Symbol
Voltage	The push that causes the flow of electricity	Volt	V
Current	The flow of electrons caused by voltage	Ampere (or Amp)	A
Resistance	Opposition to the flow of electrons through a material	Ohm	Ω
Capacitance	The capacity to store an electric charge	Farad	F
Watts	Measure of electrical power	Watt	W

Alternating Current (AC) vs. Direct Current (DC)

When we introduced the concept of voltage, we mentioned that standard outlets in the U.S. supply power at 120V. We also said that PC power supplies convert this power, providing voltages to the internal PC circuitry from 12V to 2.5V. While the electricity that utility companies provide is delivered as an Alternating Current (AC) the PC uses Direct Current (DC). Let's briefly examine the difference between these two types of power and how it relates to computer electronics.

Direct Current (DC)

Direct Current is the simpler of the two types of electricity. It flows in a circuit in one direction and always in one polarity (positive or negative). A Direct Current may be fixed at a specific voltage, or it may vary. A Direct Current may also be constant or it may start and stop. Regardless, the current will always flow in the same direction and will always be either positive or negative. Most battery-powered devices use DC. Portable CD players, flashlights and mobile phones are all examples of devices that use DC power. Generally speaking, DC circuits usually operate at fairly low voltages. As we have said, the PC uses DC power in voltages ranging from 2.5V to 12V. This is normally the higher end of the voltage commonly used by DC powered devices today. Most computers and electronics require DC voltage in the range of 1.5V to 13.5V.

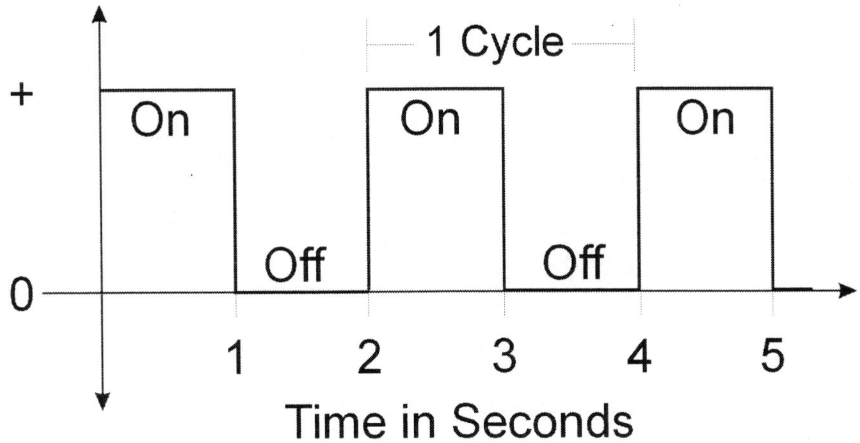

Direct Current (DC)

Alternating Current (AC)

Alternating Current is more complex than Direct Current. While DC always flows in one direction and at one polarity, AC flows in alternate directions and at alternate polarities. AC voltage flows in one direction for a short period and then in the opposite direction for another short period. The polarity of an Alternating Current also reverses every so often, alternating between positive and negative. As we have said, the power delivered by utility companies that we access through power outlets is AC power. Most electrical appliances that we plug into these outlets use AC power. Refrigerators, electric stoves and vacuum cleaners are examples of appliances that use AC.

In the United States, most AC power is delivered at approximately 120V. This standard voltage is also often rated at 110V or 115V. One of the reasons for the different ratings is the more complex nature of calculating the voltage of an Alternating Current. An Alternating Current is measured as a waveform which represents its alternating movement in direction and polarity. In order to determine the voltage of an AC, the Root Mean Square (RMS) average of the wave is calculated. This calculation is somewhat complex, but it represents a fairly simple idea: it is intended to represent the same voltage that a Direct Current generating the same mount of energy would produce.

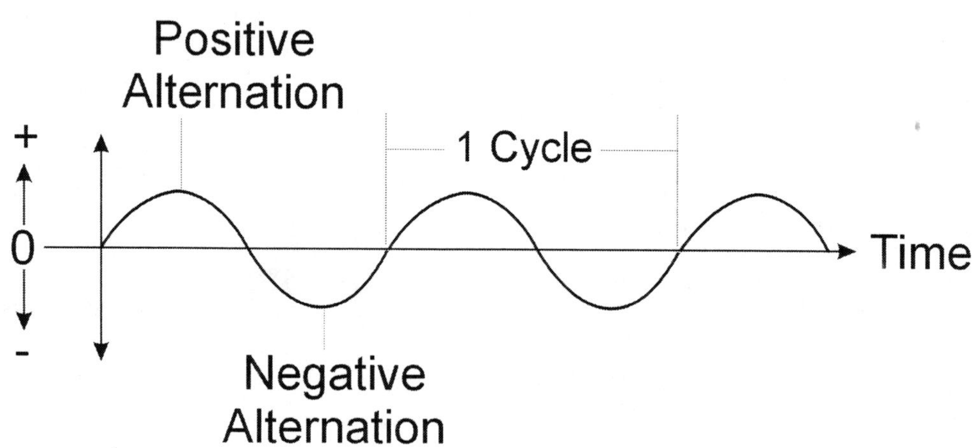

ALTERNATING CURRENT (AC)

AC/DC Conversion

In order for a PC to use the AC power from an electrical outlet, this power must be converted to DC. The primary function of a PC power supply is to convert AC to DC power. In addition, because the internal circuitry of the PC requires voltages that are much lower than 120V, another important function of the PC power supply is to provide power at a variety of different voltages. In a later section we will discuss power supplies in more detail. For now, let's cover the basics of AC/DC power conversion.

Most of us are familiar with AC adapters. These are the electrical cords that have what appears to a "battery pack", either as part of the plug, or at some point along the cord and that allow us to plug battery-powered devices into an AC outlet. AC adapters are known as **linear** power supplies. These kinds of power supplies are relatively simple and inexpensive. However, they have one main problem: they are extremely inefficient. AC adapters typically waste half the energy that they take in, and expend this energy as heat. This is why AC adapters become so warm to the touch after they have been plugged in for a while.

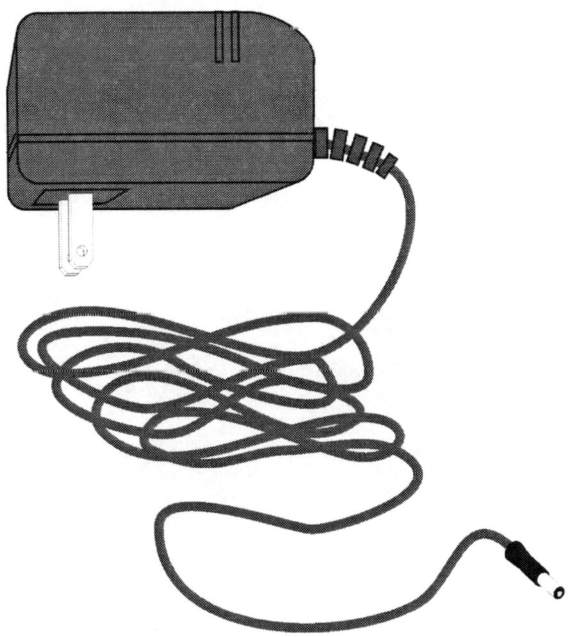

AC/DC CONVERTER

PC Power Supply

The PC power supply is a **switching** as opposed to a linear power supply. A switching power supply is able to regulate the power that it receives from an outlet. This allows the power supply to draw only the amount of energy it needs to create the necessary DC output. The ability of a switching power supply to regulate power in this way not only saves energy, it also creates less heat. This is very important in the PC environment where excessive heat can damage or destroy components. There is one important drawback to switching power supplies, however. Because of the way they convert power, switching power supplies create high-frequency signals that can interfere with other electronic devices, causing them to malfunction. This is why PC power supplies are always encased in metal to shield other devices.

Summary

Electricity is essential to computing for a variety of reasons. In this section, we reviewed the basic concepts key to understanding electricity as it relates to the PC. We defined electricity and concepts such as voltage, current, resistance, capacitance and watts, which describe the movement and flow of electricity. Then we identified the difference between the two kinds of electrical power: Direct Current (DC) and Alternating Current (AC). We learned that the power that is provided by utilities throughout the world is delivered as AC and that computers use DC. Then we reviewed the basics of AC/DC conversion which make it possible for computers to use AC power.

Review Questions

1. The flow of electrons caused by voltage is know as:

   A. Resistance
   B. Impedance
   C. Watts
   D. Current

2. Resistance is measured in terms of which of the following?

   A. Ohms
   B. Amps
   C. Volts
   D. Farads

3. The following graphic represents which kind of current?

   A. Alternating Current
   B. Direct Current

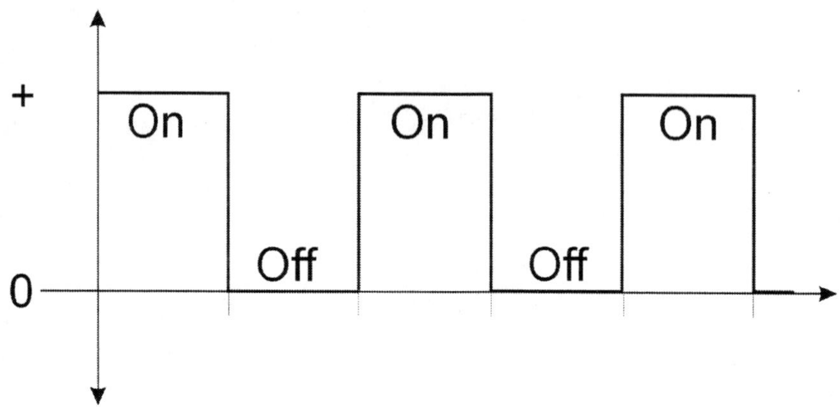

4. Electricity in a Direct Current can only flow at a specific, fixed voltage.

   A. TRUE
   B. FALSE

5. Which of the following is NOT a valid definition of voltage?

   A. Electron Moving Force
   B. Opposition to the flow of electrons through a material
   C. Electromotive Force
   D. Potential difference

6. Current is measured in which of the following?

   A. Volts
   B. Watts
   C. Amperes
   D. Farads

7. Which of the following exhibits the lowest level of resistance?

   A. Rubber
   B. Copper
   C. Plastic
   D. Glass

8. Capacitance is measured in which of the following?

   A. Farads
   B. Amperes
   C. Volts
   D. Ohms

9. A watt is defined as:

   A. Capacity to store an electric charge
   B. Measure of electrical power
   C. Opposition to the flow of electrons
   D. Push that causes flow of electricity

10. Which kind of power supply does a PC use to convert AC to DC?

    A. Linear
    B. Vertical
    C. Regulatory
    D. Switching

Section 3

Computer Safety

Section 3: Computer Safety

Introduction

During this course, you will work hands-on with various microcomputing components. You will disassemble and reassemble a Personal Computer and learn how to configure the various components that are integral to the system. It is important that we first discuss some basics for safety when working with personal computers. There is serious potential for injury if you do not observe basic safety rules when working with computer equipment. You must take precautions to protect yourself against physical harm, especially when working with the internal computer components. At the same time, when you service a computer the potential exists for harming or destroying the computer components themselves. You must also take steps to protect the components you handle. In this section we will also discuss the ways in which you can protect the equipment you work with as well as yourself.

Objectives

When you've completed this section, you will be able to do the following:

- Know how to protect against injury when working with computer equipment
- Understand how to protect components from being damaged or destroyed by Electrostatic Discharges (ESD)
- Understand Electromagnetic Interference (EMI) and how to prevent it from affecting system performance
- Explain the environmental concerns associated with the disposal of computer equipment

Potential Health Hazards

Electrical Shock

While computers would be useless without electricity, it can be hazardous both to the people that service them as well as to the individual computer components. As we learned in our discussion of electricity, the flow of an electric current is pushed by voltage through materials that show the least amount of resistance (conductors.) For the technician working with electric components, this means that the greatest danger occurs when working with high voltages and when the environment makes the technician a good conductor.

For the most part, computer components operate at a voltage of 12V or less and are relatively harmless. (Monitors and power supplies, which we will address next, are a couple of key exceptions.) However, it is still important to be careful when working with **any** electrical device. One important rule for your safety and the safety of the components is to **always turn off the power** before opening a computer case. You should never attempt to adjust wires or cables or to remove peripheral cards when a system is still powered on and electricity is running through these parts.

There are also a couple of easy steps you can take to reduce the likelihood that a stray electric charge will choose you as a good conductor. First, always make sure that you do not have wet hands and keep liquids away from an open computer case. Water is a very good conductor. It is also a good idea to wear insulated shoes or to stand on an insulated mat when possible. If the surface you are standing on is insulated, this will discourage electric charges from flowing through you. Remember, “insulator” is another word for “non-conductor”.

Monitors and Power Supplies

The main health hazards relating to servicing computers are posed by monitors and power supplies. Both of these devices contain capacitors, which store electric charges even when unplugged. These charges can be very dangerous. For this reason before working with any of these components, it is best to discharge the capacitors. However, the act of discharging a capacitor is also potentially dangerous and should most often be left to experts who are specifically trained to service these electrical components.

- **Monitors**: The monitor screen (which is also known as a Cathode Ray Tube or CRT) is a big bulb filled with inert gases. CRTs act as large capacitors and may hold charges of over 30,000 volts, even after they are turned off and unplugged. Wearing a grounding wire around an exposed CRT is an open invitation for those charges to use you as their ticket to freedom. The experience could literally kill you. For this reason, it is not a good idea to remove the cover from or attempt to service a monitor, unless you have received special training to do so. The fact that monitors today are so affordable often makes them less expensive to replace than repair. This is another good reason not to risk your health attempting to service a monitor.

- **Power Supplies:** Most power supplies display a warning on the case to prevent you from trying to perform maintenance on them. Power supplies are outfitted with internal capacitors, so that they also hold a charge when turned off and unplugged. Again, unless you have been trained to perform maintenance on a specific power supply it is best not to attempt it.

Electrical Fires

While somewhat rare, a PC or one of its components could, for various reasons, catch on fire. For your safety, as well as the PC's well-being, it's important to know what type of fire extinguisher would be the best choice for an electrical fire.

Not all fires are the same and if you use the wrong type of fire extinguisher on the wrong type of fuel, you can make matters worse. It is very important to understand the four different classifications of fuel:

Class A Wood, paper, cloth, trash, plastics.
Solid combustible materials that are not metals.

Class B Flammable liquids: gasoline, oil, grease, acetone.
Any non-metal in a liquid state, on fire.

Class C **Electrical: Computers and printers.**
As long as it's "plugged in," it would be considered a Class C fire.

Class D Metals: potassium, sodium, aluminum, magnesium.
Unless you work in a laboratory or in an industry that uses these materials, it is unlikely you'll have to deal with a Class D fire.

Most fire extinguishers will have a pictograph label telling you which fuels the extinguisher is designed to fight. For example, a simple water extinguisher might have a label indicating that it should only be used on Class A fires.

Additional Safety Considerations

While the charges present in monitors and power supplies may pose a serious threat to your health, there are other less imposing, but equally real health hazards related to computers.

Lasers

Because of the intense nature of the light that some lasers emit, they can cause damage to the skin or the eyes if exposed. A variety of computer peripheral devices use lasers. Among them are printers, CD drives and DVDs. When in regular use, these peripherals are built to shield the lasers. If you need to disassemble a CD or open a laser printer for maintenance, take care not to disable any safety mechanisms designed to shield the laser light. It is also important to remember that you should never look into a laser beam or allow a laser beam to point in a direction that might affect someone else's vision.

Handling Cases and Components

One area of PC safety that is sometimes overlooked is the potential for injury when opening a PC case and handling internal components. While cases are designed for safety externally, many have sharp metal edges when opened. Internal components may also have sharp edges or pieces that can cause cuts. It is always a good idea to handle all internal parts of the PC with care to avoid any injury to yourself or the computer.

Laser Printers

In addition to the potential health hazard associated with lasers, there are a couple of other precautions to take when working with laser printers. If you have ever overworked a laser printer, especially when it is located in a confined space, you may have noticed that it gave off a funny smell. During the printing process, laser printers create ozone gas. If this gas exceeds certain levels it can act as an irritant and become potentially dangerous. For this reason, it is always important to place laser printers in well-ventilated, open areas and to take precautions to prevent their overuse.

The toner used in laser print cartridges is another potentially harmful substance. As we will learn in more detail in a later section, laser printers create images by using heat to fuse toner to paper. If you are servicing a laser printer and accidentally spill toner, do not use hot water, an electric vacuum cleaner or anything else that might generate a lot of heat. Heat may cause the toner to adhere to your skin, the carpet, or whatever surface it contacts.

Chemicals and Material Safety Data Sheets (MSDSs)

There may be occasions when you use certain chemicals, such as solvents to clean or service computer components. Whenever working with these kinds of substances it is important to understand the rules for their safe use. All potentially dangerous materials should come in containers that are labeled with warnings against improper use. In addition, the U.S. government requires that Material Safety Data Sheets be created for all hazardous materials. These sheets provide information regarding the following:

- Melting point
- Boiling point
- Flash point
- Toxicity
- Health effects
- First aid
- Storage
- Disposal
- Protective equipment
- Spill/leak procedures

You should be able to find MSDSs in the following places:

- You should receive an MSDS with any substance that requires it. These data sheets should be kept on file somewhere for ease of access to anyone who will be working with these hazardous chemicals.
- The manufacturer and/or distributor should be able to provide you with a copy of the appropriate MSDS. If you cannot locate the copy you received with the product, contact the manufacturer or distributor.
- The Internet provides a wide range of resources for locating MSDSs. You might be able to quickly find what you are looking for by searching on the Web.

Potential Hazards to Components

Now that we have identified the potential health hazards associated with servicing a PC, let's review two kinds of electrical hazards that may harm the PC components themselves. One of these hazards, Electrostatic Discharge (ESD) has the potential to damage or destroy electronic components, while the other, Electromagnetic Interference (EMI) can cause equipment to malfunction.

Electrostatic Discharges (ESD)

What Causes Them?

An electrostatic discharge is an energy flow between two objects with different electrostatic potential.

Imagine two containers filled with water to different levels. If you connect the two containers through a small hose at the bottom, water will flow from one to the other until the water level in both containers is the same.

An electrostatic discharge occurs in the same way; higher potential seeks to come into balance with lower potential. If no safe path is provided for this flow to occur, energy is released in the form of a spark (light and heat) as the objects come into close proximity.

Static potential is constantly generated by every move we make. Driving a car, walking across a carpeted room or simply taking off a jacket will increase your static potential.

Preventing ESD

The human body will notice discharges above 2000 volts, but charges as low as 20 volts may damage sensitive electronic equipment. Personal computers are comprised of many components which are ESD sensitive. All Integrated Circuits (ICs or "chips") are very susceptible to damage caused by electrostatic discharge. RAM and CMOS chips are especially vulnerable. Damage could occur even when you don't feel it.

How can you prevent damaging electronic components? You need to constantly remain in electrostatic potential balance with the equipment you are working on. The following recommendations will help you accomplish this:

1. When you are ready to disassemble the computer, turn it off, but leave the power supply cord attached to the AC outlet. The AC outlet provides the most reliable path to ground for any electrostatic potential to discharge.
2. Stand on a anti-static mat. Wear an *anti-static wrist strap.* The typical wrist grounding strap is composed of a strap and a wire that connects to a resistor and a metal clip. The strap uses the clip to attach to a known good ground. One good ground source is to attach this clip to the metal frame of the computer case itself.

ANTI-STATIC WRIST STRAP

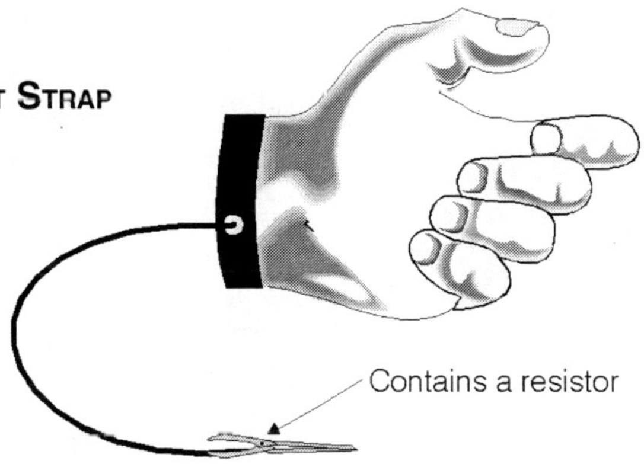

3. Apply anti-static spray to the floor surrounding the area where you are working. This will help reduce the electrostatic potential in the area. A solution of fabric softener and water works well as an anti-static spray.

Now let's say you are properly grounded: the power supply cord is plugged into the AC outlet; you are wearing a wrist-strap adequately secured to the computer case; you are standing on a rubber mat; you even applied some anti-static spray to the floor around you. Can anything go wrong? You bet!!! Depending on how carefully you handle your equipment, a kink or a fray in the grounding cable may prevent it from carrying electrostatic discharges. A periodic resistance check on your grounding wire will assure you it is working properly.

Components of a Good ESD Prevention Program

To prevent ESD damage to components as you work on personal computers, ensure that you always follow these steps:

- Maintain humidity levels between 70 and 90 percent. The greatest risk for static discharge is in low humidity.
- Always wear a wrist-strap before working with ESD-sensitive components.
- Never touch components by their electrical contacts.
- Anytime you are shipping ESD-sensitive components, make sure to enclose them in an anti-static shipping bag. This will prevent them from getting damaged during handling.
- Avoid nonconductors in areas around an open computer.

When is Grounding Necessary?

Grounding is necessary to prevent ESD damage to sensitive electronic equipment. This means that you need to be grounded any time you handle boards, chips or other electronic material. Sources for ground may include the center connector on the AC wall outlet or any known earth ground.

However, there are situations when wearing a anti-static wrist strap is not a good idea, such as if you are working near exposed monitors.

The Electronic Symbol for ground is: 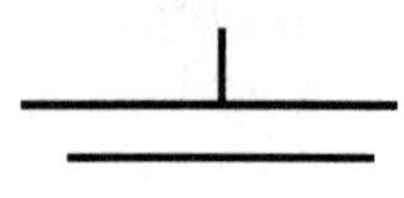

Electromagnetic Interference (EMI)

Electromagnetic interference is another potential problem for computer equipment. A common example of EMI would be running a network communication cable too close to an electric motor or across fluorescent lights in the ceiling. The motor or the lights will cause interference with the electronic signals passing through the network cable. This will cause the PC to malfunction when attempting to communicate with other parts of the network.

Similar problems can occur when a monitor is placed too close to another powerful electrical device. The interference from the device will disrupt the monitor's performance.

The major difference between EMI and an ESD event is that EMI is recoverable. In the above examples, the cables or monitor merely need to be moved away from the interfering device. However, static damage is permanent and sometimes fatal to components.

Environmental Safety and Computer Component Disposal

There is one more important topic regarding computer safety. This topic is computer component disposal. Regardless of the quality of your ESD program, or the care that you take with computer equipment, components will inevitably break down and need to be replaced. In addition, some components, or even entire systems, may become outdated and unable to perform up to necessary standards. When this happens, you will need to have a plan for dealing with your broken or unneeded computer equipment.

Computer components contain various parts or elements that pose environmental hazards. We have discussed many of these parts already in this section. For example, **CRTs** contain gases which, if released, could be potentially harmful. For this reason, monitors should not be placed in the trash in order to be taken to the dump. At a landfill they might be crushed, releasing these dangerous gases. There are other reasons for not throwing away computer monitors. Most of the parts contained in a monitor are not biodegradable, so it would take hundreds, even thousands of years for these components to decompose. In addition, some of these parts also contain **batteries** that contain cadmium, lithium and mercury, which are all environmentally harmful. The disposal of batteries is regulated by the Federal government in the U.S. and certain strict guidelines must be followed.

Many other computer components pose the same kinds of environmental threats. Most computer parts are non-biodegradable, and many contain batteries. Many components contain other hazardous chemicals as well. For example, monitors, as well as some peripheral cards and circuit boards, contain lead. Capacitors contain PCBs. It is important not to throw any computer equipment in the trash.

So, what should be done with broken or obsolete computer equipment? There are a variety of options available today for proper computer component disposal.

Recycling

The best option for disposing of unwanted computer equipment is recycling. In today's market, there are many different options available for computer recycling. Both profit and non-profit organizations exist that conduct computer recycling on a variety of levels.

You may have seen advertisements for businesses that buy used computer equipment, refurbish and then resell it. This is obviously only an option for equipment that has the potential for reasonable repair and would not apply if, for example, you needed to dispose of a large quantity of outdated video cards.

There are also a variety of non-profit organizations that reuse computer equipment. Many schools, special community groups and other charitable organizations will eagerly accept unwanted computer equipment. The advantage to giving to these groups is that you may be able to deduct some of the value of the equipment as a charitable donation. Like the for-profit recyclers, most of these groups will only be interested in equipment that can be reasonably repaired.

Reclamation

Reclamation is the best option for those components that are beyond repair. Reclamation is the salvaging of certain materials, such as gold, silver, platinum, and even plastic, from computer components. These materials are recycled and resold by companies that specialize in this kind of reclamation. While these companies do profit from your used computer parts, don't expect them to pay much, if anything, for them. In fact, depending on the kind of parts, and the quantity, they may not even be willing to make the effort to come pick up your unwanted equipment. In this case, you may have to find a way to get the equipment to them in order to dispose of it.

Removal

In some areas there may be a final option for disposing of computer equipment. Some local environmental agencies may sponsor, or be aware of, programs for the removal and proper disposal of computer components. In order to find out if such a program exists in your area, call your local environmental agency.

Summary

In this section, we discussed the potential for physical injury when working with computers. We emphasized that the most significant health hazard is the possibility of electric shock when working with monitors and power supplies, as well as with other components. We then discussed various other safety hazards including lasers, cases and components, laser printers and various chemicals. In addition to our personal safety, we also learned about the dangers that threaten to damage or disrupt the equipment with which we work. We learned that Electrostatic Discharges (ESD) can irreparably damage computer components, while Electromagnetic Interference (EMI) can disrupt equipment. Finally, we conducted a brief overview of the issues related to environmental safety and the disposal of computer equipment.

Review Questions

1. The following symbol represents 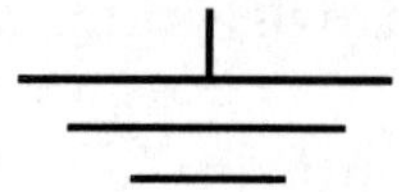

   A. Diode
   B. Ground
   C. Capacitor
   D. A wrist strap

2. An ESD (static) event is recoverable.

   A. True
   B. False

3. An EMI event is non-recoverable.

   A. True
   B. False

4. When servicing a monitor, you should always wear a wrist strap.

   A. True
   B. False

5. A typical computer monitor can hold a potentially harmful charge, even after being unplugged.

   A. True
   B. False

6. What class of fire extinguishers would you use for an electrical fire involving computer equipment?

   A. Class C
   B. Class D
   C. Class A
   D. Class E

7. MSDSs provide information regarding the handling of which of the following?

   A. Sharp, plastic objects
   B. Chemicals
   C. Software
   D. Hard Disks

8. The laser printing process creates which potentially harmful gas?

   A. Nitrogen
   B. Mustard
   C. Chlorine
   D. Ozone

9. Which of the following is NOT an environmentally safe means of disposing of computer equipment?

   A. Discard in local landfill
   B. Give to charitable organization
   C. Deliver to reclamation firm
   D. Sell to recycler

10. It is not necessary to turn off a computer before opening the case for service.

   A. True
   B. False

Section 4

PC Hardware, Components & Tools

Section 4: PC Hardware, Components & Tools

Introduction

To understand something as complex as a computer, it helps to first understand the various parts that form the whole. In this section, the various components that make up today's PC will be discussed.

To successfully repair, assemble or disassemble a computer, a technician must be able to identify the different PC components and understand the relationships between them.

Objectives

When you've completed this section, you will be able to explain and identify the following:

- Basic PC computer terms
- Basic PC tool kit
- Connectors and buses
- Microprocessors (CPUs)
- Memory
- Power supplies
- Disk drives
- Input/output devices
- Portable systems

Repair Tools

There are two types of tools that you need when working with personal computers: hardware tools and software tools.

Hardware Tools

- **Screwdrivers -** Most minor maintenance work will require only a pair of screwdrivers. A size 1 Phillips will fit most screws. A much more involved repair job may require that you have various sizes of both Phillips, straight-slot and Torx screwdrivers. Apple computers and Compaq utilize Torx screws on their machines.
- **Anti-Static Wrist Strap/Grounding Wrist Strap** - This is a very important tool for your tool kit. There are several types. One of them plugs in directly to the ground port of the AC outlet. A different type has an alligator clip that should be attached to any non-painted metal surface on the computer case. There is also another type of grounding wrist-strap that plugs directly to a port on the power supply box.
- **Anti-Static Mat** - Anything that helps you eliminate the possibility of static discharge is a good addition to your tool set. It is important to make sure that any mat you use is full rubber and not a rubberized carpet.
- **Flashlight** - Flashlights are always useful in locations that are poorly lit. Consider also carrying a spare set of batteries.
- **Mirror and Magnifying Glass** - A small mirror (the best type is a dentist mirror) and a magnifying glass make it much easier to work with hard-to-see components.
- **Extractors -** Extractors are used to remove chips from their sockets. This tool can sometimes be relatively expensive, but not having one could cost you a lot more in the long run. Chips will damage easily if you don't use the proper tools.
- **Tweezers** - A set of tweezers may be used to remove small parts that have fallen in places that your fingers can't reach. Any tool with a magnet is not recommended since you could erase the magnetic data contained in the hard drive or floppy diskette.
- **Compressed Air Cans** -Compressed air cans are very useful for blowing dust or small debris from any surface. They are especially useful on keyboards and power supplies.

Software Tools

- **Diagnostics Disk** - Diagnostics disks are great tools for troubleshooting purposes. Some of the best diagnostics software on the market are *Norton Utilities* or *PC Tools*.
- **Operating System Emergency Diskette** - This diskette comes in handy when the computer locks up and does not allow you access to the data on the hard drive. Additionally, you should create bootable DOS diskettes for every version of DOS you work with. The emergency diskette could include utilities like **FORMAT**, **FDISK, SYS**, and other key utilities from that particular DOS version.
- **Anti-Virus Software** - Anti-virus software is useful for detecting and cleaning viral infections. Some of the best known programs are *Norton Anti-Virus, McAfee's Anti-Virus and Cheyenne's InocuLAN.* Anti-virus software must be continuously updated to keep up with newly created viruses. It is important to maintain the most current versions of this software.

Specialty Tools

Most of the tools discussed so far have been fairly straightforward in their usage, however the **multimeter (Volt/OHM Meter)** requires more discussion.

A multimeter is a hand-held instrument that is typically used to measure voltages, both AC (Alternating Current) and DC (Direct Current). It is important to remember, when using the multimeter to measure DC voltages the proper polarity must be maintained. Usually this means that the black test probe will go to ground and the red test probe to the positive side of the circuit. When using the meter to measure AC voltages, it is not necessary to maintain polarity.

Multimeters usually come in two types: analog (with a needle on a scale) or digital. The digital meters tend to be more precise and require less expertise by the user. Another common use of the multimeter is to measure for resistance or continuity. This is very helpful when checking the value of a resistor or checking for a potential break in a wire or cable.

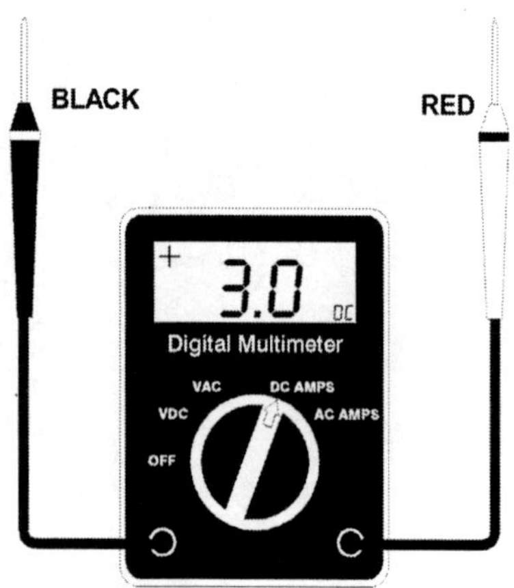

The following checklist should be helpful when using a multimeter:

- When checking unknown voltages, always start with your meter on the highest setting.

- When checking a resistor set your meter for the OHMs scale.
- Capacitors are measured in Farads.
- Be careful. Since the multimeter contains a battery, use caution when testing sensitive components. The very current from the meter itself could damage some integrated circuits.

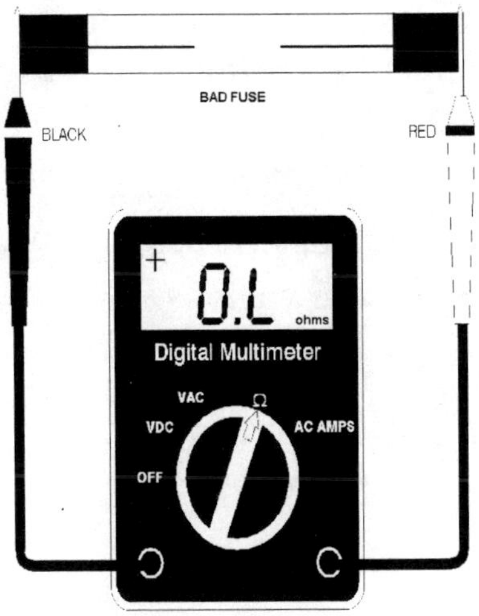

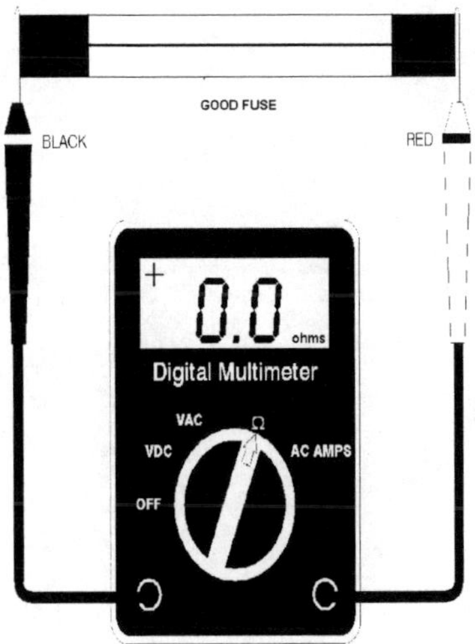

NOTE: **THE READINGS ON INDIVIDUAL METERS WILL VARY, HOWEVER, A GOOD FUSE SHOULD READ 0.0 OHMS AND THE BAD FUSE WILL TYPICALLY READ 0.L. GENERALLY, THE 0.L IS DISPLAYED IF THE INPUT SIGNAL STAYS EITHER HIGH OR LOW. (SOME METERS MAY JUST FLASH.)**

Basics

A computer is a collection of electronic parts (hardware) that gathers, processes and relays information. Some of the parts can be separated into two categories: **input** and **output** devices.

- **Input devices**, such as the keyboard, mouse, light pen, etc., collect information provided by the user and convert it into electronic signals for further processing.
- **Output devices**, such as the monitor, a speaker, or a printer, convert electronic information into some kind of format that the user understands. Outputs take the form of images on the screen or paper, or sounds.

Inputs are converted into electronic signals, which are sent to the CPU or Central Processing Unit (CPU) for processing. The CPU processes **all** communication among the various components of the PC. Once the task is completed, the CPU relays information to the user by means of an output device and waits for more input. This cycle is repeated continuously.

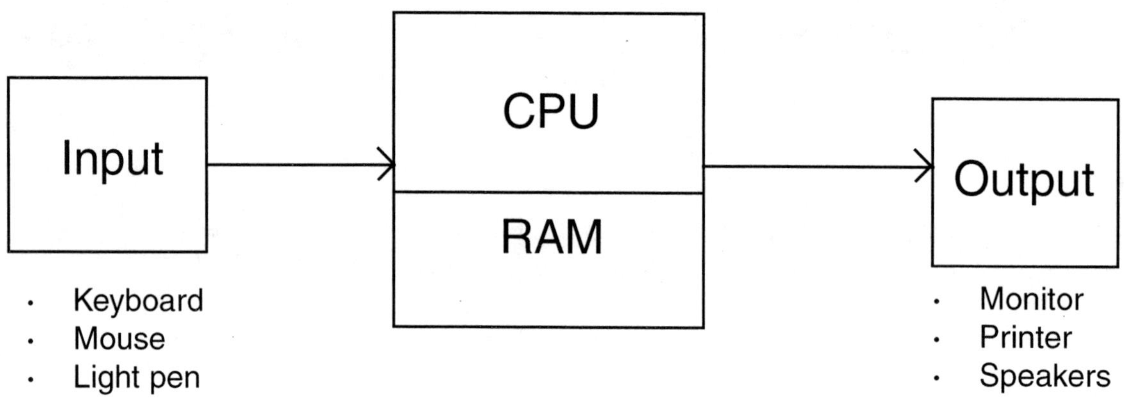

Bits and Bytes

The CPU and many other electronic components are considered **integrated circuits**. They contain thousands of microscopic digital switches (transistors), which continually produce two voltage states, high and low.

A computer uses a binary system to count. This means that the computer understands only two numbers: one and zero. These 0s and 1s are called bits or binary digits. A grouping of eight bits will form a byte. As a general rule, it takes one byte or eight bits to represent a character, symbol or a number.

These values are used often in the computer world to reference such things as measurements for storage devices, such as disks, files and databases.

The following is a list of the most commonly used terms and their associated values:

Bit

A **bit** (**BI**nary digi**T**) is the smallest unit of computer storage. It is a single digit in a binary number (0 or 1). Computers represent bits by using electrical signals that can either be **on** or **off**. These states represent the bits, with **off** indicating a 0 (zero) and **on** indicating a 1 (one). Groupings of bits make up storage units in the computer, called "characters".

A bit is typically represented by a lower case "**b**" and is often used in units of one thousand bits or a **Kb** (**K**ilo**b**it). This is technically equivalent to **1,024 bits.**

Byte

The **byte** (**B**inar**Y** **T**abl**E**) is the most common unit of computer storage from the mainframe to the PC. It is made up of eight binary digits (bits). So it could be restated to say 8 bits make one byte. A byte (8 bits) holds the equivalent of a single character in computer storage. This character could be a letter of the alphabet like the letter "b" or it could be used to represent a character like a "period" or a "comma".

In the case of numbers, a byte can hold a single **decimal** digit (0 to 9) or a number ranging from 0 to 255 (binary numbers). You will learn more about binary numbers later in this section.

A computer byte is represented by an uppercase "**B"** and is typically used in units of one thousand. This is referred to as a **KB** (**K**ilo**B**yte). In computer terms it is technically 1,024 bytes. The **K** is used as shorthand notation for $2^{10 \text{ power}}$ or the equivalent of 1,024.

Nibble

The nibble is a unit of measurement that is not used very often, but that is worth the describing. A **nibble** represents a unit equal to a half of byte (4 bits). The nibble is sometimes used to make an eight-bit number (a byte) easier to read, by grouping it into two separate pieces.

Megabyte

A **megabyte** is approximately equal to one million bytes, technically $2^{20 \text{ power}}$ or 1,048,576 bytes. It is represented by **MB** (**M**ega**B**yte). In terms of computer related measurements, a 500 MB hard disk could technically store 524,288,000 bytes of information.

Gigabyte

A **gigabyte** is approximately equal to one billion bytes, technically $2^{30 \text{ power}}$ or 1,073,741,824 bytes. It is represented by **GB** (**G**iga**B**yte). Most hard disks that are manufactured today are measured in gigabytes.

Terabyte

A **terabyte** is approximately equal to one trillion bytes, technically $2^{40 \text{ power}}$ or 1,099,511,627,776 bytes. It is represented by **TB** (**T**era**B**yte).

ASCII Codes

The method of combining 1s and 0s to form character sets has become the industry standard and is referred to as ASCII (American Standard Code for Information Exchange).

The code originally used only seven of the eight bits, which allowed for 128 different combinations of characters. The remaining eighth bit was used for error checking.

Later, the IBM Corporation developed a character code that used all eight bits, which created additional characters (256 total). This was referred to as EBCDIC.

Binary Representation	ASCII Character
01000001	A
11000001	a
10000010	B
11000010	b

The Binary Primer

Whenever two or more people communicate with each other, they do so by using a common language. That language might be English or Spanish or German. Whatever the case, the key is that it is common to all the people that are involved in the conversation.

When computers communicate with each other, they use a language called **binary**. Everything that you input, send, output or retrieve is all converted to the computer's default language (binary).

Binary is a numbering system. In fact, as the name would imply, it is a Base 2 numbering system. A Base 2 numbering system only uses two numbers, 1 and 0, to represent numerical values equal to our Base 10 system of numbers. The more familiar system of Base 10 uses 10 numbers, 0 through 9, in various combinations. An example of an eight bit binary representation of the number 148 would appear as the following:

10010100

Now, let's take a look at how the computer actually uses the binary numbering system to represent data, words and numbers. One single binary 0 or 1 is referred to as a **bit**. A bit is actually an abbreviated version of "**b**inary dig**it**". It should be noted here that computers use electrical signals that can either be **on** or **off.** These on/off states can then be used to represent a binary 1 or 0.

When you take a series of eight (8) bits and string them together, you now have what is commonly referred to as a **byte**. One byte can represent any decimal value between 0 and 255. This adds up to 256 unique values. Every possible character on a English keyboard can be represented with less than 128 characters. This 128 character set is called the **ASCII code set.** It takes 8 bits or 1 byte to represent a single letter of the alphabet. The following is an example of an upper case "A" in a one byte, binary format:

01000001

Reading Binary Numbers

Let's review. A **byte** is made up of 8 **bits**, these bits can either be a **1** or a **0**. When you are trying to determine the value of a byte (an eight bit binary number), do not think of the 1 or the 0 as a value in and of itself, but rather as an indicator to determine if that place holder is relevant to the final result. Confused yet? Let's see if the following example helps:

Before trying to decipher an eight bit binary number like **(10010100)**, it's often easier to first create a table like the one below:

128	64	32	16	8	4	2	1
—	—	—	—	—	—	—	—

Now, notice the least significant bit (low order) furthest to the right has a value of 1. The next low order bit has a value of 2 and so on up to a value of 128. Remember, a binary number can be one of two states (on or off) represented by a 1 for On and 0 for Off.

128	64	32	16	8	4	2	1
1	**0**	**0**	**1**	**0**	**1**	**0**	**0**

To determine the value of the eight bit binary number, you need to find the sum of the relevant placeholders. To do this, add only those positions that have a 1:

128+16+4 = 148

*A value of 1 (on) will indicate that the corresponding placeholder is relevant. A value of 0 (off) indicates that the corresponding placeholder is not relevant and should not be considered in the value.

Let's try that again finding the binary equivalent to the number 224.

128	64	32	16	8	4	2	1
1	1	1	0	0	0	0	0

128+64+32 = 224

What would be the decimal equivalent to the following binary number?

11111111

128	64	32	16	8	4	2	1
1	1	1	1	1	1	1	1

128+64+32+16+8+4+2+1 = 255

What would be the decimal equivalent to the following binary number?

00000111

______________________________________.

System Board

From the beginning, most PCs have had, as a central component, the **system board.** The system board is also commonly referred to as the **motherboard** or **planar board.**

The system board is a printed circuit board that provides a common platform for attaching the chips and other devices that make the PC functional. The system board also provides output and input connections to the computer.

The key function of the system board is to provide a central "home" for the CPU and the input/output cards. Math functions, sometimes referred to as floating point functions, are built into the CPU. CPUs have had math capabilities built into the chip since the advent of the Intel 486 chip. Prior to the 486, a separate math co-processor chip handled the math functions of the PC.

All system components are connected to the system board and rely on their connection here to communicate with each other. Communication takes place on the system board through its Bus connectors.

AT Motherboard Design

The original AT style motherboard was designed for use in the original IBM XT computer. After Intel released the 80286 processor, in 1984, they redesigned the board slightly to accommodate the new processor. The resulting processor/ motherboard became known as the AT style PC. The boards dimensions were approximately 12" x 13". In an attempt to free up a user desk space, a smaller computer enclosure was required. This mandate resulted in what became known as the Baby AT system board. It was very similar to the original except that it fitted into a much smaller case.

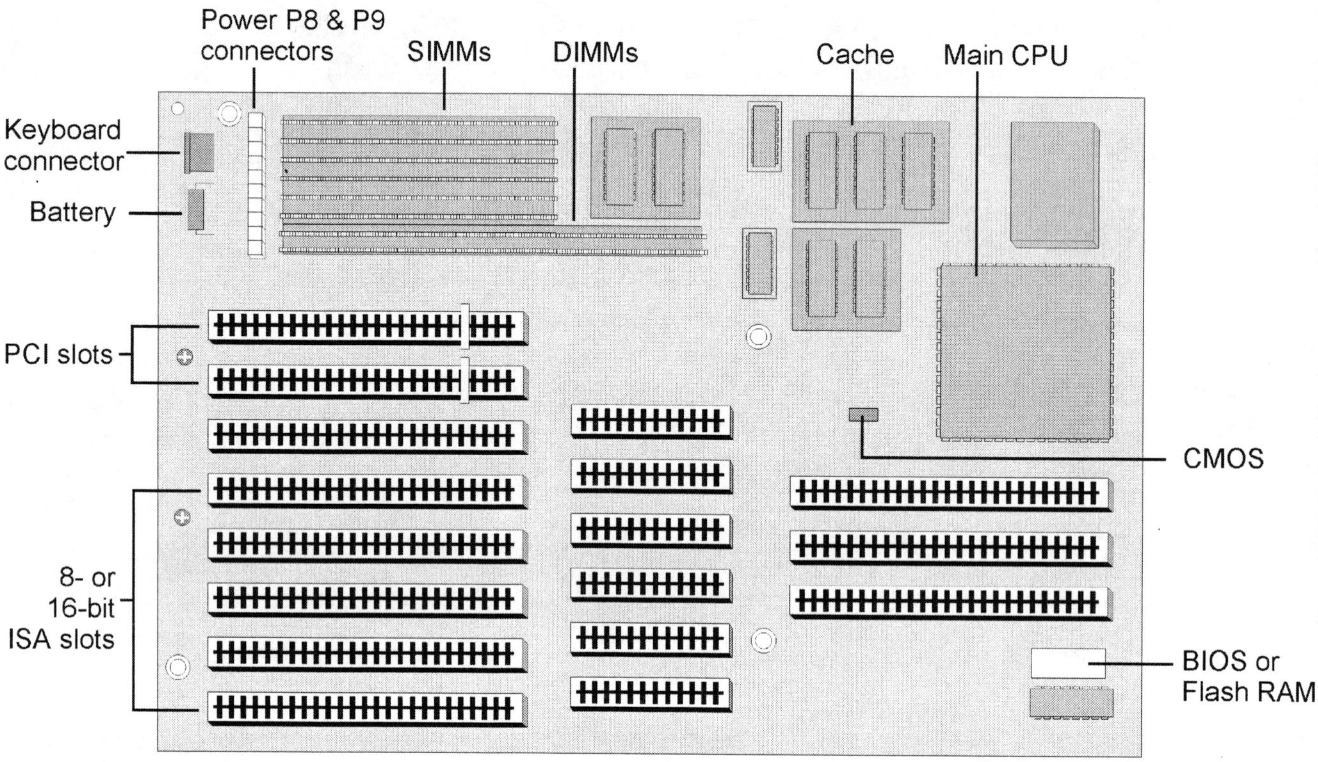

TYPICAL AT STYLE MOTHERBOARD

ATX Motherboard Design

The ATX system board design is an industry standard for desktop computer motherboards. The ATX design is based on the older AT standard. The improvements made by the ATX board relate primarily to design and functionality rather than speed and performance. One of the major differences between the older AT board and the newer ATX design is that the microprocessor and expansion slots have been rotated 90 degrees on the ATX. This design allows for fewer cables and more space for full-length expansion cards.

Almost all the major PC manufacturers have incorporated the design including: IBM, Compaq and Apple based computers.

Another major difference in the look and feel of the ATX board are the power supply configuration and cables. Many of the ATX systems now have two power switches. One is located on the power supply itself. The other is mounted on the case. The switch on the power supply is the primary power switch, shutting down power to the entire computer. The case mounted switch is used to supply power to the motherboard. When you turn on the main switch located on the power supply you may hear the fan turn on. This simply means that the motherboard is receiving power but has not yet received the signal from secondary switch located on the case. The look of the cables has also changed. The **P8** and **P9** power cables used on the AT have been replaced by a single **20** pin connector, called a **P1** connector, which plugs into the mother board.

In addition, the ATX motherboard has a software controlled power-off switch. You may notice in the following graphic that many ATX boards have both ATX (P1) and AT (P8 and P9) connectors

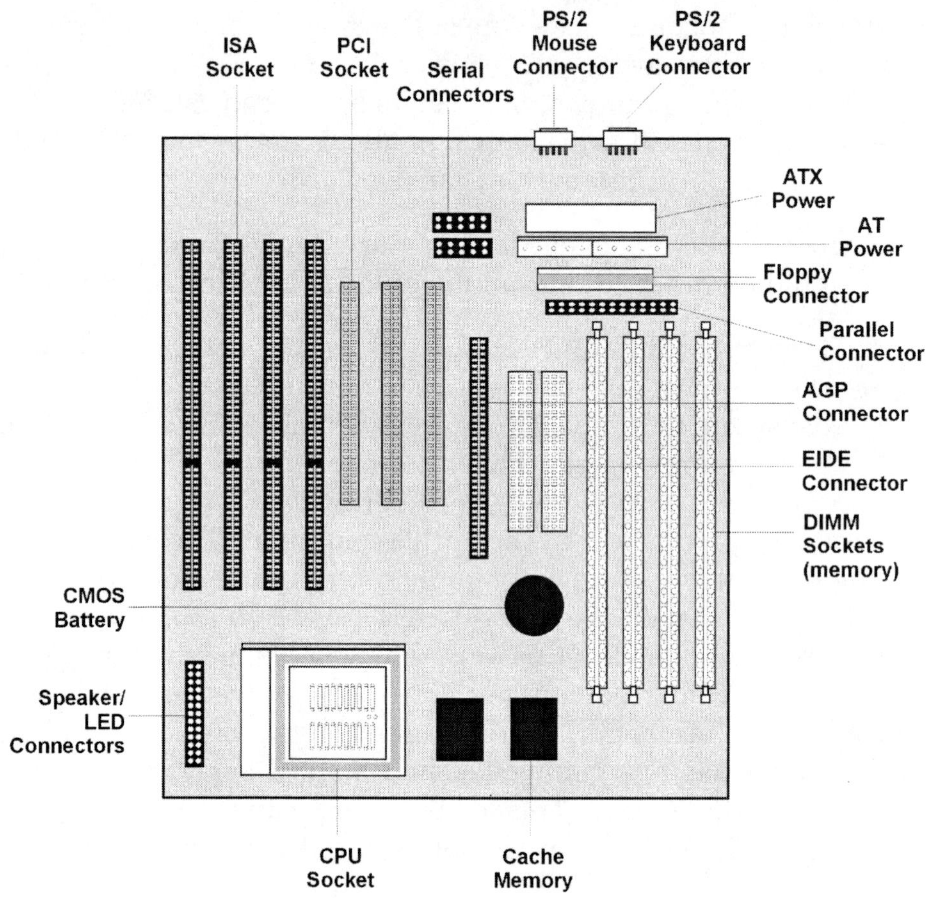

TYPICAL ATX SYSTEM BOARD

NLX Motherboard Design

The NLX is a new very low profile motherboard designed specifically to meet the demands for today's design market trends. The following list summarizes some of the advantages of the NLX system board:

- Supports most current and future processor technologies.
- Supports new AGP (Accelerated Graphics Port).
- Provides more system level design and flexibility. The new design allows designers to implement a system board that can be removed quickly, in some cases without removing screws, lowering the PC's total cost of ownership.
- It provides support for tall memory technology.

The graphic below shows an example of an NLX board and riser:

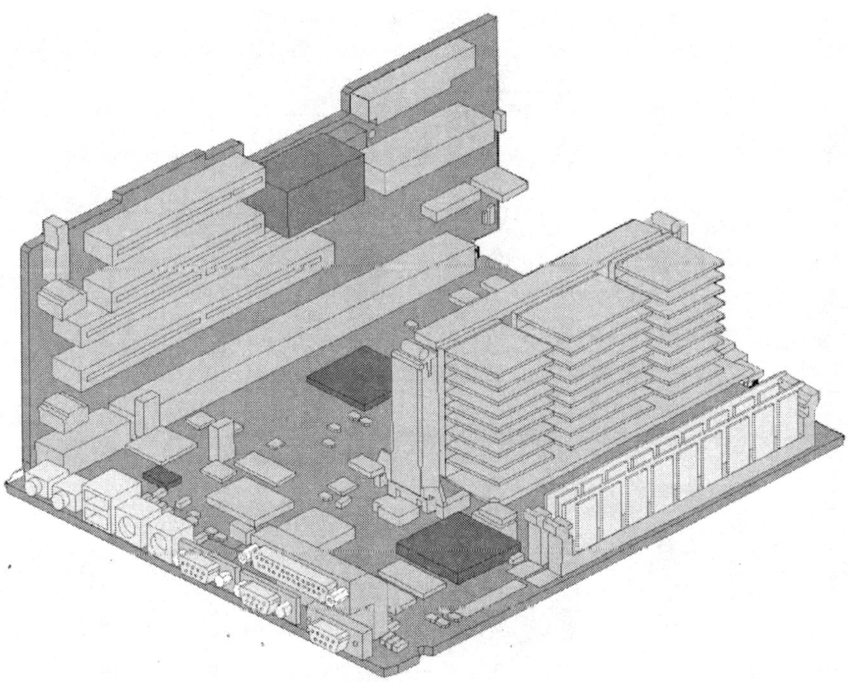

TYPICAL NLX MOTHERBOARD

Many of the major PC vendors throughout the world have jointly gathered to work on the NLX design. NLX is a public specification, with the intent that it will be adopted for widespread use in a variety of systems.

Case Styles

Now that some of the different system board designs have been discussed, it's time to take a brief look at the various types of cases (enclosures) used in the industry. The original IBM PCs took up a lot of precious space on your desktop. There is even a phrase that was coined to refer to the space consumed by your computer, the **footprint**. The smaller the case design, the smaller the footprint or actual desktop space taken by that PC. Over the years many different case designs have been developed; some to maximize space, others to facilitate a specific need.

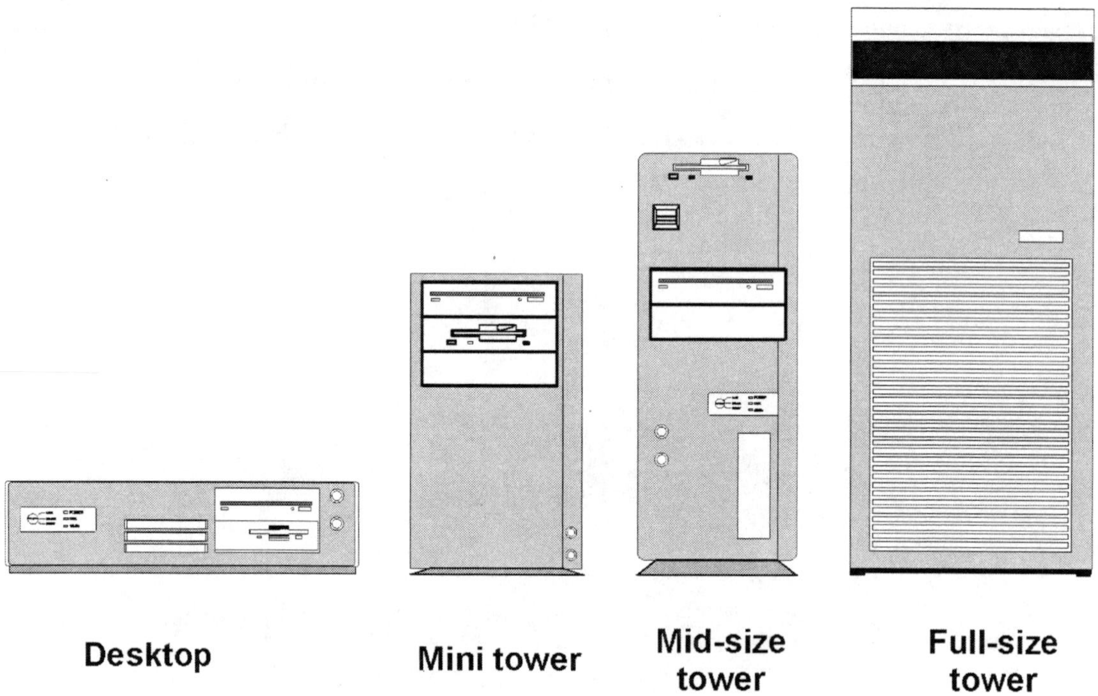

TYPICAL INDUSTRY STANDARD CASES

The choice of the case design, desktop or tower, is completely up to you. The desktop designs allow you to place a monitor on top of the case. The Mini-Tower cases permit the PC to be self-standing (vertical). However, their size (Mini) does not permit much in the way of expandability. Both The Mid-size tower and the Full-size tower cases offer enhanced expandability to accommodate devices like tape backup units and more and larger disk arrays. For this reason, you will generally see these cases being used in network server environments. Whatever your choice, it is important that you not only consider your immediate needs but also take into consideration any future expansion you may need down the road.

Bus Design

Before the different types of Bus designs are discussed, it is first necessary to understand the meaning of a "Bus."

The CPU (Central Processing Unit) is the heart and soul of the computer, and as such, needs the ability to talk to the other components of the computer system. These other components are devices like the keyboard, expansion boards and memory modules. All of these pieces need to be connected to the CPU. This connection is accomplished through what is referred to as **Bus connectors**, or adapter slots.

The adapter slots are wired to the CPU via a series of small traces (those shiny thin metal strips that are on the system board). These adapter slots allow for an access point to the system. Following is a list and description of the most popular type of Bus designs:

PC or XT Bus

IBM developed the XT Bus around the 8088 processor. The 8088 processor had an 8-bit data path, so it comes as no surprise that the adapter slots were called 8-bit slots. Actually, there were 62 separate lines feeding into the connectors, but only eight of these were used for the actual data transfer.

AT (ISA) Bus

When development on the AT computer started, IBM decided to create a new Bus architecture to exploit the new 80286 processor which supported a 16-bit data path, twice that of the XT system. AT system boards also contained at least two of the older 8-bit slots to ensure backwards compatibility.

While the ISA design gave the computer a wider highway to move data, the speed at which the data could move was still the same as before: 8MHz. The implication here was that even if the CPU could perform internal instructions at 25MHz, the data could only move across the Bus at the 8MHz speed. Attempts to boost the speed limit beyond 8MHz on the AT-type Bus created noise and tended to be unworkable. This was a drawback on the ISA Bus that would be addressed in future Bus designs.

The MCA Bus Architecture

Early in 1987, IBM announced its PS/2 line of computers. To facilitate a faster data transfer rate and to clean up the noise levels that plagued the ISA Bus at higher speeds, IBM developed a new Bus design. The new architecture was call MCA (Micro Channel Architecture). The design was completely new and did not offer any backwards compatibility with older designs like the XT or ISA expansion boards. IBM introduced the MCA architecture in both 16-bit and 32-bit versions.

The MCA design also included a new feature: POS (Programmable Option Select). This feature allowed expansion boards to be smarter and more interactive in attaching to and communicating with the rest of the computer. This feature also simplified the configuration of the boards and lessened the dependencies on switches and jumper settings.

EISA Bus

The industry response to IBM's very proprietary MCA design was the EISA Bus (Extended Industry Standard Architecture). The industry in this case was actually a group of companies known as the "Gang of Nine." Included in the group were Compaq, Tandy, AST, Zenith, AT&T, Olivetti and a few others. This joint effort took the best features of the MCA design without giving up the backwards compatibility with the older AT (ISA) Bus.

The EISA architecture features a full 32-bit data path and supported speeds up to about 20MHz. EISA also incorporated the POS type features found in the MCA system. While the EISA and MCA Bus designs increased Bus speeds, they still could not match the speed of the CPUs.

VESA Local Bus

In 1992, the VESA Local Bus was introduced. This design is sometimes referred to as VL Bus. The designers of the VL Bus created a special type of high-speed slot on the system board which could operate at speeds equal to the speed of the CPU. As would be expected, this slot only accommodates cards designed specially for it. These special slots are called "Local" Bus slots. Local Bus slots currently support disk controllers, video and memory boards.

Note: *Beware! There are no standards for this design. Compatibility is a problem.*

PCI Local Bus (Intel)

The VESA Bus technology was an important step forward, but did not fully exploit the advantages of the newer CPUs. The VESA solution was essentially a beefed-up version of the old ISA technology. It did not allow for Bus mastering or software setup of boards like the MCA and EISA designs did.

The Intel Corporation was keenly aware of these shortcomings and developed an even faster and more flexible Bus slot called the PCI Bus. The PCI design used a 64-bit Bus that was more in line with the new Pentium processors. PCI still supported a 32-bit data path, making it a viable solution for high-end 486 systems.

The PCI Bus supports speeds up to 133MHz and also provides backward compatibility with ISA and EISA slots all on the same board. Like MCA and EISA, the PCI design supports Bus mastering and software configurable boards. The PCI architecture also conforms to the new Plug-and-Play standards defined by hardware vendors.

PCMCIA

The PCMCIA (Personal Computer Memory Card Industry Association) released in 1990 was designed to meet the special needs of laptop computing. The standard itself came from a group of Japanese vendors of memory-related products. While originally intended for memory products, the standard was also extended to support modems and hard disks. Because the design constraints are different for memory cards than they are for modems or hard disks, there are many different types of PCMCIA cards. There are three types of PCMCIA cards, each a different thickness:

Type 1 - 3.3 millimeters

Type 2 - 5.0 millimeters

Type 3 - 10.5 millimeters

Previously, PCMCIA cards supported only a 16-bit data path, although 32-bit versions are common today. The speed of the Bus is limited to a 33MHz clock rate.

Accelerated Graphics Port (AGP)

The Accelerated Graphics Port (AGP) is a high-speed interface that enables a typical PC to quickly display 3-D images. The AGP port is especially suited for displaying Web site graphics much more quickly than ever before. The enhanced performance is made possible through the use of the PC's main memory (RAM). The AGP interface uses the system RAM on a demand basis, meaning that when it is not being used by the interface for graphics it is returned to the operating system or other applications.

The Intel Corporation has been instrumental in the development of the AGP specifications. The newest and fastest Intel processors are designed to exploit the benefits of the AGP chipsets.

Universal Serial Bus (USB)

This is a new connection interface for all types of peripheral devices. USB replaces all the different kinds of serial and parallel connectors with one standard plug and port combination. The USB specification was developed by the Intel Corporation, for communication between a PC and external peripherals over an inexpensive cable using bi-directional-serial transmission. The USB transfers data at 12MBps and supports up to **127 devices** with both synchronous and asynchronous data transfers.

Because of its relatively low speed, USB is intended to replace existing serial ports, parallel ports, keyboard and monitor connectors and be used with keyboards, mice, monitors, printers, and possibly some low-speed scanners and removable hard drives. For faster devices, existing IDE or SCSI interfaces can be used.

Perhaps one of the most exciting features of the USB specification is the "hot swap" capability, which allows you to attach a new device and have the PC detect it without restarting your machine.

USB ports can also provide power to certain devices if desired. This feature greatly enhances the Plug-and-Play capabilities of the latest versions of Windows. Ideally, if Plug-and Play works as designed, a USB device can be installed on a Windows 9x or Windows 2000 system while it is still running. The system should recognize the device, automatically install the device and then activate the device. It is important to note that Windows 95a, and Windows NT did not support USB. The first version of Windows to support USB was Windows 95 OSR 2.2.

USB Cables

There are two types of USB cables. Those that are attached permanently to a device are called **TYPE A** connectors. Those that require a separate cable are referred to as **TYPE B** connectors.

Examples of TYPE A and TYPE B cables and connectors are shown below:

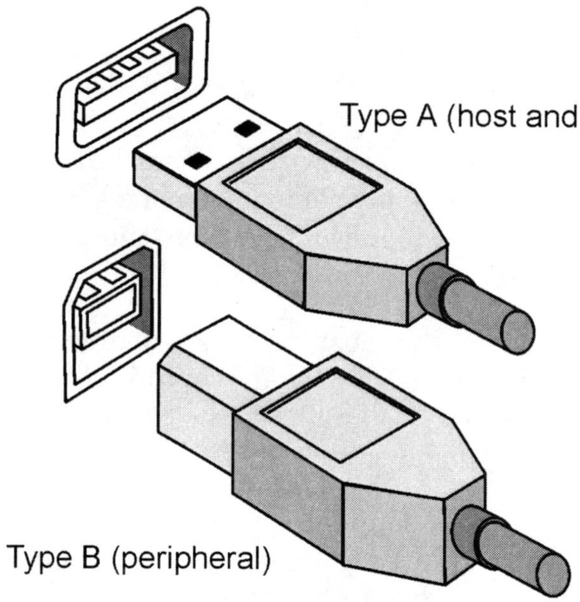

USB CONNECTORS

FireWire (IEEE 1394)

FireWire is a high-speed serial bus interface that provides enhanced PC connectivity for a broad range of devices. These would include: A/V (audio/video), storage devices and other PC-related peripheral devices.

The FireWire standard has been adopted by the Consumer Electronics Industry and is expected to provide Plug-and-Play compatible expansion interfaces for the PC environment.

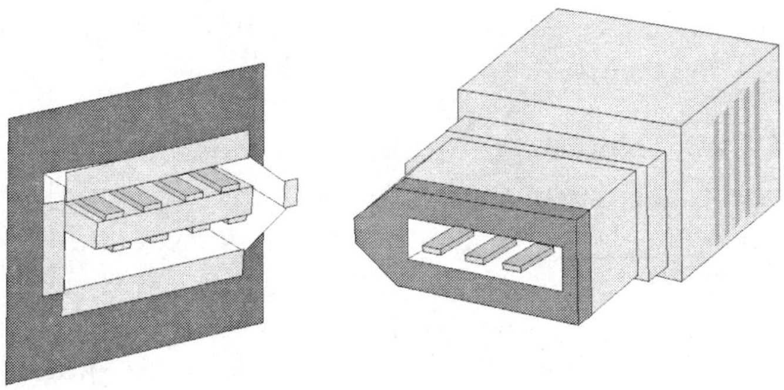

FIREWIRE CONNECTORS

Central Processing Unit (CPU)

The Central Processing Unit, which is often referred to as "the processor," is the heart and soul of the computer. Without this chip, no other function of the PC is possible. It is the CPU that understands commands, executes program instructions and does all the basic processing in the computer. The capabilities of the CPU will basically define the design of the computer.

The lead manufacturer and designer of processors for the personal computer is the Intel Corporation. Most of the material presented in this course is based on the Intel chip design. Other companies that manufacture processors are AMD, Cyrix and Motorola.

The PCs of today are built around the family of Intel processors, starting with the 8088. Every couple of years, a new chip is released. The 8088 was succeeded by the 8086, which was followed by the 80286 and then the 80386 chip. The new major leap came with the 486. The Pentium processor is the latest of the Intel line of chips. Each of these chips is more powerful than its predecessor, capable of performing more commands and dealing with data more quickly. Emphasis is also placed on backward compatibility. It is important that each chip has the ability to run software that was originally designed for the previous generation(s) of chips. There is some question as to whether this trend will continue in future design generations.

CPU Performance Factors

Clock Speed

Computers, like musicians, run or play to a beat. In music, the drummer must synchronize with the rest of the band in order for the music to sound right. In the computer world, the beat is controlled by a CPU clock. If the clock rate is too fast, malfunctions will occur. This would not result in actual damage to the chip. It would mean, however, that the PC would not function correctly.

The computer's speed or clock rate is integral to its overall design. The computer's clock rate is the frequency at which it can execute a set of instructions. Computer clock rates are measured in Megahertz (millions of clock ticks per second).

There are two types of speeds that should be considered when evaluating system performance:

- **internal clock speed** - The internal clock speed is the speed at which the processor can obtain information within the CPU itself. An example of internal clock speed would be the speed at which the chip communicates with its internal cache of memory or its registers.
- **external clock speed**. The external clock speed is the speed at which the CPU communicates with components outside itself, like the external memory (system RAM or external cache memory).

Cache Memory

Internal to the design of some processors is something referred to as "cache memory." This is very high speed memory that is actually built right into the chip itself. It supplies the processor with the instructions and data which can be accessed faster than instructions and data located in main memory. The more data the processor can access directly from cache memory, the faster the computer runs.

There are two levels of cache memory:

- **Internal Cache** (Primary or level 1 cache)
  Located inside the CPU chip. The function of the internal cache is to hold a copy of frequently used instructions that enhance CPU performance.

- **External Cache** (Secondary or level 2 cache)
  Located on the system board.

CPU performance is certainly instrumental in determining overall computer performance. It should be noted that other factors, such as speed, amount of system RAM, and types of Bus architecture, also influence the ultimate computer performance as well.

Intel Processors: Now and Then

There might come a time when you will have to replace or upgrade a processor in order to fix a problem. Listed below are details and characteristics of some of the most popular chips from Intel and other manufacturers.

8088

This is the chip found in most of the IBM XT-class machines. The 8088 came in a 40-pin DIP package. Translated, this means the 8088 is a small, rectangular chip with two rows of 20 pins each. The original speed of this chip was 5MHz. Later versions reached a top speed of about 8MHz.

80286

Introduced in 1981 by Intel, this chip became the mainstay of the AT-class computers. The chip itself was packaged in a square called a Pin Grid Array (PGA) instead of a rectangle. The chip contained about 130,000 transistors — about 100,000 more than the 8088.

80386

The 80386 was introduced to the market in 1985 and came in two different types: DX and SX. This chip was also packaged in the PGA configuration. The 80386 contained 250,000 transistors and also provided features like multitasking of DOS programs and a 32-bit data path. The 32-bit data path was available only in the DX version, while the SX version had a 16-bit data path. This made the SX more compatible with the 80286 computer and hardware.

80486

The 80486 chip was actually a "beefed-up" version of the 80386. The 486 processor was a composite of three other chips. The 80486 consisted of a 386 chip, a 385 cache controller and a 387 math co-processor. The 486 contained about 1.25 million transistors and 8K of internal cache memory. It provided a 32-bit data path and a built-in math co-processor. Like the 80386, the 80486 came in two types: the DX and SX. The 80486 SX had all the features of the DX version minus the math co-processor. Actually, the math co-processor was still on-board, but was disabled in the SX version.

80486DX2

To understand the 80486DX2, it is important to understand another Intel creation designed to increase system speed: the "Overdrive" chip. The Overdrive chip could run at two clock speeds simultaneously. If the chip was placed on a 486SX/ 25MHz system board, it was placed in the socket for the co-processor chip and took over for the 486SX chip. When data was passed through the Bus or memory, it was done at the speed of the processor; in this case 25MHz. This is referred to as the external clock speed. All the internal calculations were done at twice the 25MHz speed, at 50MHz. The 80486DX2 is very similar to the Overdrive chip in that it runs at a certain external speed "X MHz" but performs all internal calculations at "two times X."

80486DX4

The plot thickens. DX4 chips used a technology developed by IBM called Clock Tripler (nicknamed "Blue Lightning"). Under an agreement with Intel, IBM manufactured 486 chips using the Intel mask. Using their own Clock Tripler technology, IBM took an Intel 486DX 25MHz chip and increased its speed to approximately 75MHz.

Intel followed suit and announced the 80486DX/99MHz chip. This chip would run external speeds of 33MHz and perform internal calculations at 99MHz.

Pentium

In 1993 Intel introduced the Pentium processor. The initial market response was not overwhelming, but the Pentium has now become the standard for personal computers sold today. The Pentium processor contains over 3 million transistors and provides a 64-bit data path.

The first generation of Pentium chips were subject to heat problems. Computers not designed to deal with high temperatures tended to experience high failure rates. Newer versions of the Pentium chip were designed to run cooler. System boards and internal components were also designed to cope with the higher temperatures.

The Pentium chips will run both internal calculations and external processing at the same speed. Another unique feature of the Pentium chip is the cache. The Pentium has two 8KB caches: one that is used for program code and another used for data cache. The Pentium chip was also designed to be fault tolerant, something Intel refers to as "superscalar." This feature is only functional when the Pentium chip is installed on a system board that will support multiple processors. Fault tolerance simply means that when two processors are present on the system board, the second chip takes over if the first chip fails.

Pentium Pro

The Pentium Pro processor has a different look and design than the other chips. It is the first Intel processor to combine Level 1(L1) and Level 2 (L2) cache in the same package as the CPU. The Pentium Pro processor is a dual-chip configuration that houses the Pentium Pro CPU on one side of the dual-cavity package and the L2 cache memory on the other. According to Intel, this simplifies system design and saves space. The Pentium Pro processor has about 21 million transistors in total. The CPU core has 5.5 million transistors and the L2 cache has 15.5 million. The Pentium Pro was designed to support multiple Pentium Pro processors connected in parallel. The Pentium Pro is a true 32-bit processor. It operates at speeds of 200MHz.

MMX Technology

The MMX technology is based on a new set of instructions that are built into Intel's Pentium microprocessors. This new instruction set enables the chip to efficiently process video and audio data. Prior to the MMX technology, multimedia operations, in video and sound, had to be handled by separate components like sound cards and enhanced video boards. These same functions can now be managed by the processor.

MMX chips' internal memory (cache memory) has doubled in size (32KB). This is the area in memory that holds recently accessed data. It is designed to speed up subsequent requests to this data. This means that more instructions and data can be stored internally in the chip, reducing the number of times the processor has to access slower external memory. Most multimedia applications run dramatically faster and smoother. To really get the most out of the new MMX chip, you must run the enhanced MMX applications that have been written to exploit the true power of the technology.

Pentium II

The Pentium II processor is available in speeds from 233MHz to 450MHz. It utilizes the innovative 0.25 micron manufacturing process that enables these CPUs to include over 7.5 million transistors. This results in more power in less space. The processor core is packaged in the Single Edge Contact (SEC) cartridge enabling ease of design and flexible motherboard architecture. The processor also includes MMX technology. The Dual Independent Bus (DIB) architecture increases bandwidth and performance over single-bus processors.

Pentium III

The Intel Pentium III processor is groundbreaking in terms of graphics capabilities. The chip has been built to exploit many of the new and expanding 3-D graphic images and their manipulation. The following are some of the highlights of the Pentium III.

- Added 70 new instruction sets for enhanced graphics, video and sound. The Pentium III processor introduced a new processor instruction set called Streaming SIMD Extensions (SSE). Single-Instruction, Multiple-Data (SIMD) was the instruction set used by the MMX processor to improve multimedia performance. The Pentium III SSE instruction set was designed to further enhance multimedia performance.
- An embedded serial number to help companies with an inventory of computers. This feature will also enhance on-line security transactions. Although it also raises some very serious privacy concerns.
- Clock speeds in excess of 800 MHz.

Pentium 4

The Pentium 4 is Intel's latest processor in the Pentium family. It features NetBurst micro-architecture, which significantly improves processor performance. The Pentium 4 also uses an improved floating point and the Streaming SIMD Extension 2 (SSE2). These features enable lifelike video display and enhance gaming and multimedia performance. The Pentium 4 also improves system bus speed, boasting a rate of 400 MHz that provides a 3.2 Gigabyte per second transfer between the processor and the memory controller.

Celeron

The Celeron is Intel's entry into the low-end microprocessor market. It is based on the same architecture as the Pentium II. However, it lacks some of the performance features of the Pentium II family. The newest of the Celeron CPUs include an L1 and L2 on-board cache. This configuration means that the cache is actually accessed at the same clock speed as the processor operates. When comparing the Celeron's L2 cache to the Pentium II's cache you will find it somewhat smaller (128 KB) as compared to the Pentium II's (512 KB) cache. However, since the Celeron's cache is built in and the Pentium's is not, their effective L2 speeds are roughly the same. The Celeron processor supports clock speeds up to 466 MHz and can be mounted in a **Slot 1 motherboard**. Intel is marketing this chip for the entry level PC, capable of providing performance solutions geared to the home and light business use.

Itanium Processor

The Itanium processor, formerly known as the Merced IA-64, is unique with its Slot M configuration and L3 cache. The L3 cache is small in physical size and is not located on-board the chip itself but is bundled instead within the processor package.

Currently there are two flavors: the 800 MHz and 1000 MHz versions.

Motorola Chip Family

The Motorola chip set is not quite as well known in the PC market as Intel. For the most part, it is associated with the Apple computer line.

68000

Introduced in 1979, the 68000 chip is closely associated with the Apple computer. The 68000 chip employed a 32-bit design and used a 16-bit data Bus. The 68000 was far ahead of Intel's efforts at the time.

68010

In 1982, Motorola introduced the 68010 chip. The major difference between the 68000 and the 68010 was the addition of virtual memory support. This chip also incorporated internal cache which made the processing of sub-routines much faster. This chip did not find widespread use in the computer world but was used extensively in Motorola's component division.

68020

This chip was introduced in 1984 as the first full 32-bit chip in the Motorola line. The 68020 had the ability to access 4 GB of RAM and utilized floating point processing capabilities. It was used in the Macintosh II and found widespread use in minicomputers as well.

68030

Introduced to the market in 1987, the 68030 had all the features of the 68020 plus demand page memory management. Other enhancements to the chip also increased the speed of the chip. It was used most widely used in the Macintosh II series of computers.

68040

In 1989, Motorola's answer to Intel's 486 was the 68040. However, the 68040 did not gain the market share that Intel's 486 enjoyed.

Power PC

Apple, IBM and Motorola all joined together to develop the PowerPC family of chips. *PowerPC* stands for Performa2 Optimization with Enhanced RISC. Currently Apple incorporates the chip in its PowerMac series of computers. This chip can also be used in everything from laptops to computers functioning as servers.

Other Available Chips

Cyrix

Cyrix (SYE-rihks) is a family of low-end, low-cost microprocessors intended for personal computers and personal information devices. Cyrix competes with Intel in the low-cost, low-end market for PC microprocessors. Typically, Cyrix has been able to under-price Intel for comparable low-end microprocessors.

Cyrix began making semiconductors in 1988. Its first product was a math coprocessor. About 1992, it introduced its first microprocessors that would handle the instruction set specified by Intel's 486 microprocessors.

AMD K6

The AMD K6 is AMD's answer to the Intel Pentium series of microprocessors. Although it is considerably less expensive than the Pentium II processors, according to many industry based benchmarks the K6 has slightly better performance. The K6 has 64K of L1 and L2 cache. The K6 processor can be mounted in a Socket 7 based motherboard.

AMD offers multiple K6 versions which support a 66 MHz bus and operate at clock speeds starting at 166 MHz. There is also a 266 version, referred to as the K6+. The K6+ (266) operates at about 2.5 volts of power at a very low heat output making it an ideal candidate for the laptop computing market.

K7 (Athlon)

The K7 processor was the first AMD product to support a 200 MHz bus and to reach a 1 Gigahertz (one billion) clock speed. The K7 classification was actually the development name for the Athlon processor. Compaq and Gateway are among companies that manufacture computers that include the 1 GHz Athlon. As the successor to AMD's K6 microprocessor the K7 compares favorably to Intel's Pentium III. The K7 has a 128 KB L1 and L2 cache that is built into the chip itself, significantly increasing performance.

Processor Sockets and Slots

Motherboard sockets were originally designed to provide a place to insert the processor into the motherboard. Recently, Intel has defined standardized socket and slot specifications for use with various Intel processors. Intel is the primary manufacturer of PC processors. However, two of Intel's main competitors (AMD and Cyrix) have been able to use these same standards.

These standardized sockets allow motherboards to accommodate future processors that are designed to fit these sockets.

Processor (CPU) Classification	Slot/Socket Type
Pentium	Socket 7
Pentium MMX	Socket 7
Pentium II	Slot 1
Pentium III	Slot 1
Pentium Pro	Socket 8
AMD K6 II & III	Socket 7
AMD (K7) Athlon	Slot A
Xeon	Slot 1
Celeron	Slot 1
Intel Itanium	Slot M

Processor Classification	Working Voltage
486DX	5 V
486DX, SX	5 V
486DX, SX, DX2	5 V
60 or 66 MHz Pentium	5 V
Pentium	3 V
486DX4	3 V
Pentium Pro	3 V

Slot 1 and Slot 2 Configuration

Both Slot 1 and Slot 2 refer to the way Intel P6 based processors are mounted to a computer's system board. The Slot 1 and Slot 2 connectors were developed by Intel to replace the older ZIF (Zero Insertion Force) sockets. The most familiar of these was also referred to as the Socket 7 configuration used with the Pentium-based processors. When Intel introduced the Pentium II, a P6 based architecture, it also switched to the Slot 1 configuration. Unlike the ZIF sockets, which accepted the processor chip directly, the Pentium II chips are packaged on a card that is inserted into Slot 1 on the motherboard.

Intel currently refers to Slot 1 as its 242 contact slot connector and Slot 2 as its 330 contact slot connector. Besides the Pentium II, the **Celeron**, Intel's low-end processor, also uses the Slot 1 configuration.

AMD Slot A

When AMD introduced the K7, the industry was quick to notice the similarity to the Intel Pentium II packing. Like the Pentium II, the K7 is a processor mounted on a card. In addition, the slot for the card, referred to as Slot A, is physically identical to Slot 1 used by the Intel Pentium chip. By utilizing the Slot A design, AMD was able to hold down the production costs.

It should be noted, however, that while the Slot A is physically identical to Slot 1, it is not electrically compatible.

System Memory

RAM (Random Access Memory)

The most common type of memory installed in a computer is called RAM (Random Access Memory). This type of memory is also considered volatile. Volatile simply means it is not permanent and can be changed. This is an important characteristic of RAM. Anything that is written to RAM will be lost if the machine loses power or if the machine is turned off.

RAM can be broken down into two types: DRAM (Dynamic Random Access Memory) and Static RAM. DRAM memory chips need to have an electrical current supplied to maintain their electrical state. Static RAM chips do not need an electrical current for refresh purposes. Static RAM is much more expensive than DRAM.

Another key point to remember about RAM is that data stored in RAM in accessed much more quickly than data retrieved from a hard disk. Theoretically, data retrieved from RAM is accessed 100 to 300 times faster than the same information from a hard disk, optical drive, or floppy drive.

RAM is physically installed by adding chips to the motherboard. The most common configurations of these chips today are called:

- **SIMM (Single Inline Memory Modules)**. One of these modules actually contains either eight or nine separate RAM chips. The ninth chip is actually called the parity chip or parity bit. For each byte stored, the system adds the bits together. The parity bit determines whether the result is odd or even and is used for error checking. SIMM memory is configured with 30 and 72 pins.
- **DIMM (Dual Inline Memory Module)**. Typically DIMM is configured with 168 pins.

Besides SIMMs, other types of RAM are detailed below:

MEMORY	DESCRIPTION
EDO RAM (Extended Data Output RAM)	A faster type of pin-compatible RAM. If a system can accommodate this type of RAM, speed can be increased up to 25% without the need for static cache.
VRAM (Video RAM)	Special type of memory found on faster video boards.
WRAM (Windows RAM)	Windows RAM allows blocks of memory (in "windows") to be addressed in just a few commands. More expensive, but a good value in video boards.
DIMM (Dual In-Line Memory Module)	Small circuit boards carrying memory integrated circuits, with signal and power pins on both sides of the board. In SIMM memory, the pins are on both sides of the chips but are connected to the same memory chip. On DIMM, the connections on each side of the module connect to different chips

30-pin SIMM

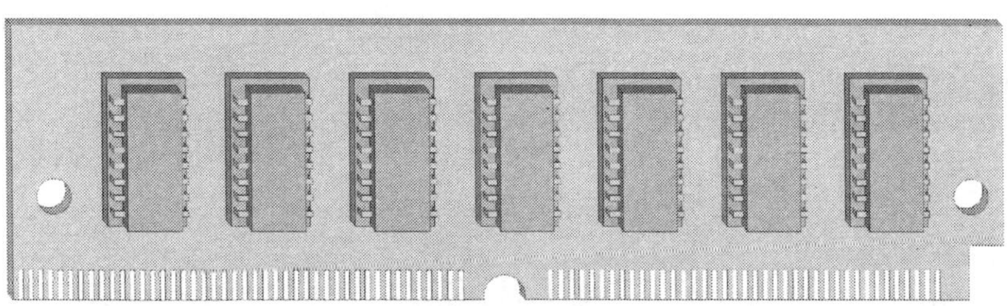

72-pin SIMM

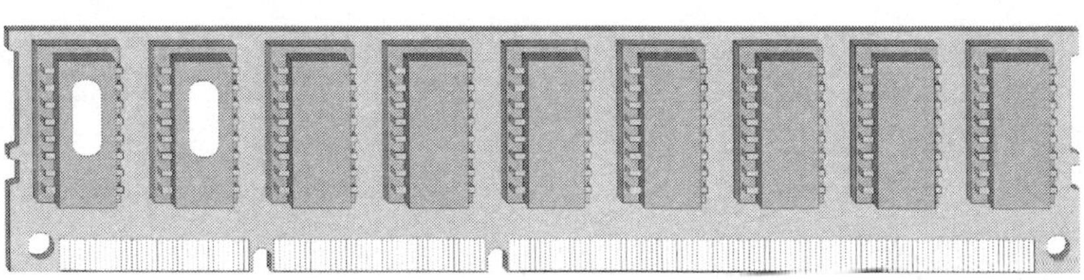

168-pin DIMM

INLINE MEMORY MODULES

Parity Vs. Non-Parity Memory

Before you can understand the concept of parity memory vs. Non-parity memory, you should understand the concept called **parity checking**. Parity checking is an error **detection** scheme that tests the integrity of digital data within a computer environment. To accomplish this, parity checking uses an extra ninth bit that retains a zero (0) or a one (1) depending on the data content of the byte. Every time a byte is transferred within the computer or transmitted across a network, the **parity bit** (9th bit) is tested. Notice that the word error detection is used... not correction. The parity technique will detect but not actually correct the error.

Parity Memory

Parity modules that have an extra chip that detects if data was correctly read or written by the memory module. However, a parity module will not correct the error.

Non-Parity Memory

Non-parity memory modules do not perform error detection or have error checking capabilities.

ECC Memory

ECC (Error Checking and Correcting) memory modules have an extra chip that not only detects if the data was correctly read or written by the memory module but that will also use the extra chip to correct errors in many cases, depending on the actual type of error.

Parity or No Parity?

I'm sure you could guess by now that parity memory modules are more expensive than non-parity modules. Many manufacturers are building desktop computers with non-parity memory to save costs. There is also a slight performance issue with ECC memory. Using ECC decreases your computer's performance by about 2%.

A good general rule of thumb if you are up-grading or adding memory to an existing system is to look at what's already installed in your system. If your machine does not support parity, a parity module will not operate in parity mode, and it can affect system performance or may not work at all.

If, on the other hand you're building or purchasing a new computer, the following guideline should prove helpful. If you plan to use your system as a server or other mission critical type machine, it is to your advantage to use parity or ECC. That extra protection in this type of environment is well worth the extra money!

Performance Note: *It is not advised to mix and match parity and non-parity memory modules.*

Power Supplies

In this section, we'll take a look at computer power supplies. The computer needs electrical power to operate. It is plugged into a wall outlet which is a 110 volt socket and uses AC (Alternating Current). Computers utilize 5 and 12 volt DC currents. Therefore, a device is required to convert the AC current from the wall outlet to the DC current required by the computer. This is the function of the computer power supply.

Computer power supplies come in all different sizes and shapes and are rated in different ways. The most common rating is in watts. A watt is a unit of measure for electrically powered devices and is determined by the amount of electricity that is passed through it. Because computer components are becoming increasingly more efficient and require less power, a 200-watt power supply is typically large enough for most systems.

The power supply itself is typically located in the rear corner inside the computer case. It will usually have several colored wires extending from it. These colored wires are called power connectors and are used to connect peripheral devices such as floppies, hard drives and tape backups. Another component of the power supply is the fan. The job of the fan is to maintain an internal temperature acceptable to the design of the particular power supply circuitry.

On a more technical note, the power supply takes the AC current from the wall and converts this to a DC or direct current. This DC output is split into four different voltages: +5 volts, -5 volts, +12 volts and -12 volts. **A positive 5 volts is the voltage used by PC board digital circuitry.** The power supply not only converts the AC voltage into these DC voltages, but also performs somewhat of a filtering function, ensuring that the flow of electricity into the computer circuitry takes place evenly.

Because PC power supplies are fairly complex and because of the different voltages, attempting to repair them is not recommended. The power supply is generally considered an FRU, a Field Replaceable Unit, and such replacement is the best option.

There are several important factors in choosing a power supply replacement. You must determine what voltage, ampere rating and wattage you need. You should also take into consideration the size and shape of the power supply as well as on/off switch placement. This will ensure that the new power supply will fit in the computer case.

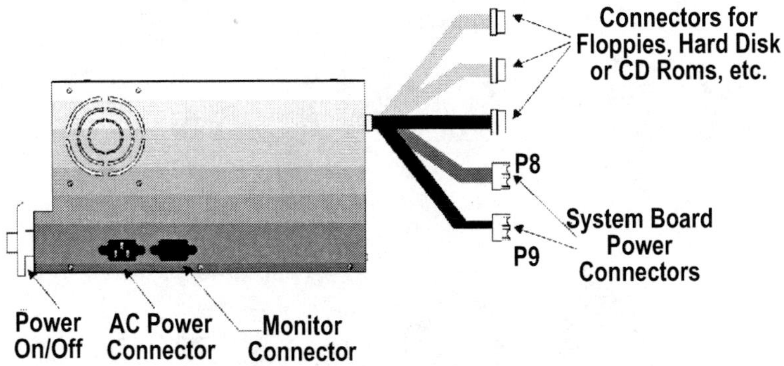

Typical AT PC Power Supply Configuration

Notice that the ATX power supply is very similar to the AT power supply. One major difference, however, is that the ATX power supply design has replaced the **P8** and **P9** system board connectors with a single 20 pin connector typically labeled **P1**. Other than the 20-pin power connector, the AT and ATX power supplies have similar connectors like standard drive connectors as well as 3.5" drive connectors.

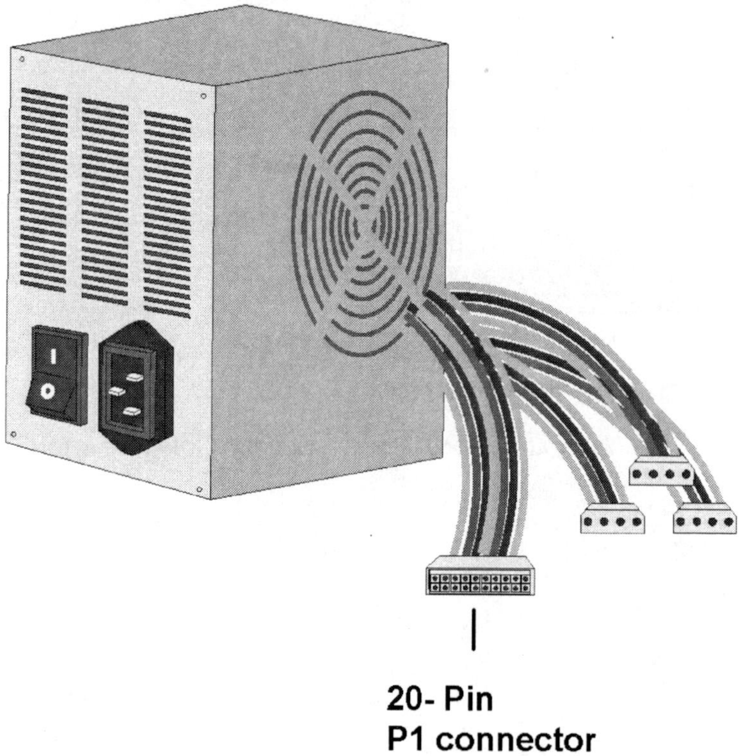

TYPICAL ATX POWER SUPPLY CONFIGURATION

Hard Disk Drive

The hard disk, or hard drive, stores large amounts of information for long term usage. The Random Access Memory (RAM) discussed in the last section is good for intermediate, temporary high-speed storage. But RAM loses its information when you turn the machine off and provides a limited amount of storage space.

The advantage of the hard disk drive is that it stores information magnetically on a metallic platter. As a result, information is retained even after the machine is turned off or loses power.

Hard disks are capable of storing large amounts of information, often hundreds of megabytes. In most cases, a typical user will keep all the programs and all the data they need on the hard disk. The major components of the hard drive are

Hard Disk

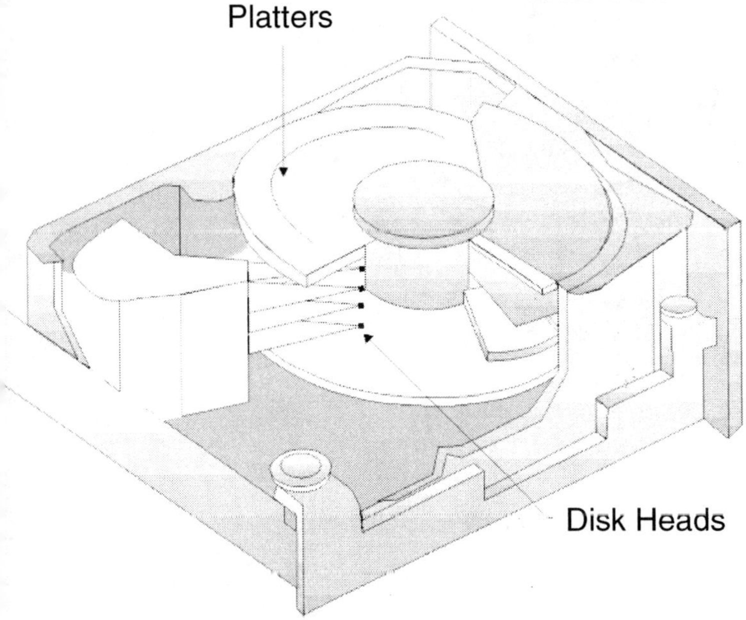

- The platter
- Read/write heads
- Head actuator
- Spindle

The **platter** is an aluminum disk that has been coated so it can accept magnetically recorded data. Multiple platters are then connected to a **spindle** which, in turn, is connected to an electrical motor that spins the platters. The rotation of the platters is somewhat like a record spinning on a turntable. Most modern hard disks are capable of 3,600-5,000 rotations per minute.

The mechanisms that allow data to be written to or read from the platters are called the **read/write heads**. The read/write heads have the ability to access both sides of the platter and to retrieve or write information to either side of the platter. The mechanism that allows the read/write heads to move back and forth across the platters is the **head actuator**.

HARDWARE / TOOLS

Hard Disk Layout

The information on the hard disk platter is recorded in a circular fashion in **tracks**. (The tracks are like tracks on a record.) Tracks are then subdivided into pie-like slices that are referred to as **sectors**. A **cylinder** is a vertical stack of these sectors. Finally, the minimum unit that DOS uses to store information is called a **cluster**. Clusters are formed from several sectors on the same track. Tracks and sectors are created on the hard drive during the low-level formatting process.

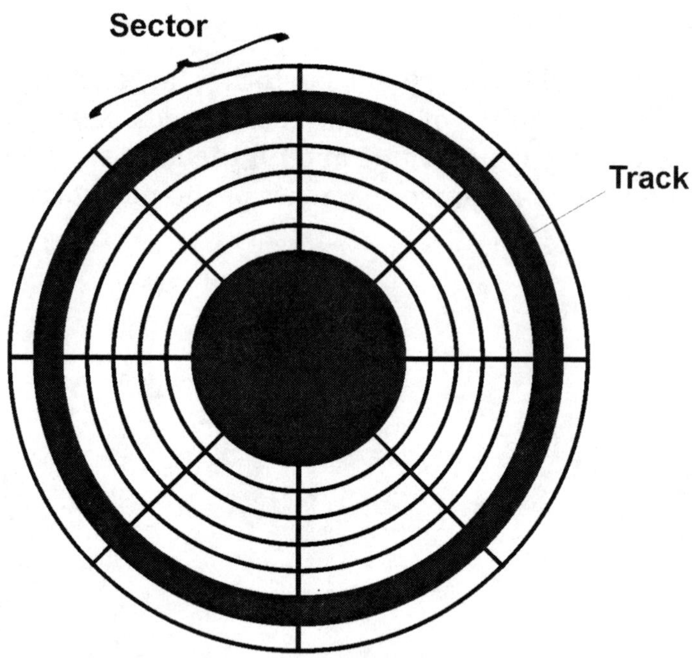

LAYOUT OF A HARD DRIVE

File Allocation Table

The File Allocation Table (FAT), is usually created at sector zero for DOS-based systems. The information recorded in the FAT keeps track of the location of each file on the hard disk. The File Allocation Table is automatically created when the hard disk is high-level formatted.

Encoding

There are many different methods that may be used to store data magnetically on the drives. These methods are called encoding techniques. The different encoding schemes determine how much data can be placed on a disk or how fast that data can be accessed. There are three major types of encoding schemes used for hard disks: MFM (Modified Frequency Modulation), RLL (Run Length Limited), and ARLL (Advanced RLL). A common characteristic to each of these encoding schemes is that they use **state changes** on the magnetic surface of the platter to indicate a binary 1, or binary 0.

Hard Drive Interfaces

The hard disk in and of itself cannot directly communicate with the CPU. For the hard disk to communicate with the computer, it depends on two more components: the **controller**, which links the drive to the computer and **Host Bus Adapter**, which converts the signals used by the hard drive to those used and understood by the computer.

Originally in older systems, all three of these were separate devices. As computers and computer components evolved, the controller and the Host Bus Adapter were combined on the same physical board. In some cases, this single board was actually built into the same housing as the hard disk itself. The hard disk interfaces determine how all of the individual devices work together.

There are four major interfaces: the ST-506, ESDI (Enhanced Standard Device Interface), IDE (Integrated Drive Electronics), and SCSI (Small Computer System Interface).

ST-506

The ST-506 was the original IBM PC interface. Two cables were used to connect the drive to a separate controller: a 20-pin data cable and a 34-pin control cable. The data was transferred on the cable via a serial format one bit at a time. This interface supported the following three encoding methods: MFM, RLL and ARLL.

ESDI

The ESDI interface was actually a hybrid ST-506 but was more efficient in translating and transferring the data. The ESDI interface used the RLL encoding scheme. The ESDI interface also supported much larger drive capacities than that of the old ST-506 interface. The interface used the same type of 20-pin data cable and the 34-pin control cable as the ST-506.

IDE

The IDE (**I**ntegrated **D**evelopment **E**nvironment) was the first interface to actually embed the controller within the housing of the hard drive itself. Because of the integration of the hard drive and controller in one unit, the cost of the drives also came down. This, along with its improved performance, has made the IDE drive a very popular selection for most personal computers sold today. Unlike the ST-506 interface and the ESDI interface, the IDE interface only requires a single 40-pin control and data cable, which connects the hard drive to the actual system board.

The IDE interface is officially referred to as the **ATA** (AT Attachment) specification.

When installing an IDE drive into a PC, the CMOS setting is usually set for type 47 or user-defined. The drive type setting is critical for proper functioning of the IDE drives. Some of the older BIOS versions may not work. If the PC has one of these older versions of the BIOS, it must be replaced with a compatible or new version. DOS relies on BIOS to issue commands to the hardware. BIOS is not loaded from the operating system. It is stored in ROM.

EIDE

An EIDE (**E**nhanced **IDE)** is an interface that supports the ATA-2 and ATAPI standards that provide for faster transfer rates and allow for multiple channels and can support two additional drives. The IDE interface supports two drives physically attached to the same cable, but one drive must be configured as the **master** (the **primary**) and the other as a **slave** (the **secondary**). This is done by setting the **master-slave** jumper on the second hard drive to slave. The master drive then performs the single decoding for both drives. A failure to the master drive renders the slave useless or inaccessible as well. Since about 1994, PCs have shipped with EIDE interfaces. Some of these interfaces are external and others are built into the mother board with support for a primary and secondary channel each supporting two IDE devices.

Auto-Detection

Most computers' BIOS today have an auto-detect feature, which means you can install the drive (IDE or EIDE) and the BIOS will detect the presence of the disk and auto-configure it for you. For some IDE drives (typically larger ones over 500 MB), you may be asked to select **LBA** (**L**ogical **B**lock **A**ddressing), which is nothing more than a method used to support IDE drives larger than 500 MB. LBA is also required for compatibility with FAT32 formatting. This will be discussed in more detail later in the course.

Installing an IDE Hard Disk

Installing an IDE or EIDE hard disk is a relatively simple process. Depending on the specific drive, it can usually be done in just a few steps. For most IDE drives you need to complete the following steps:

- Install the IDE controller or locate the IDE connectors on the system board.
- Configure the IDE drive.
- Install the IDE drive into the computer.
- Configure the computer's CMOS.
- Load the operating system.

Install the IDE Controller

Technically the IDE controller is built into the drive itself. However, there has to be some mechanism to attach the drive to the system board. This is usually done in one of two ways. One means of connecting a drive is via an expansion card, which is sometimes loosely referred to as the controller. (Although this is technically not correct.) This card can then be installed in any open IDE slot on the system board. Make sure that the expansion card is fully seated and secured in the expansion slot.

The other way to connect a drive is through an on-board controller. If the system uses an on-board controller then you must locate and identify the 40-pin IDE connector located on the system board itself. Remember that many system boards provide support for two IDE channels. In this case, you will be looking for the one that is typically labeled as the **primary**.

Configure the IDE Drive

Now that the expansion board has been installed or the on-board connectors identified, it is time to configure the drive. The typical IDE drive can be configured in one of three different ways:

- Configured as a single drive only
- Installed as the **master** (the boot disk) in a two drive configuration
- Installed as the **slave** (the non-boot disk) in a two drive configuration

This configuration is typically accomplished by physically setting a series of jumpers located on the drive itself. Consider the graphic below. A jumper placed on the first set of pins would configure it as a single (default) drive only. Jumping the second set of pins would configure the drive as the **master** (bootable) in a two drive configuration. A jumper placed across the third set of pins would configure the drive as the **slave** in a two disk configuration.

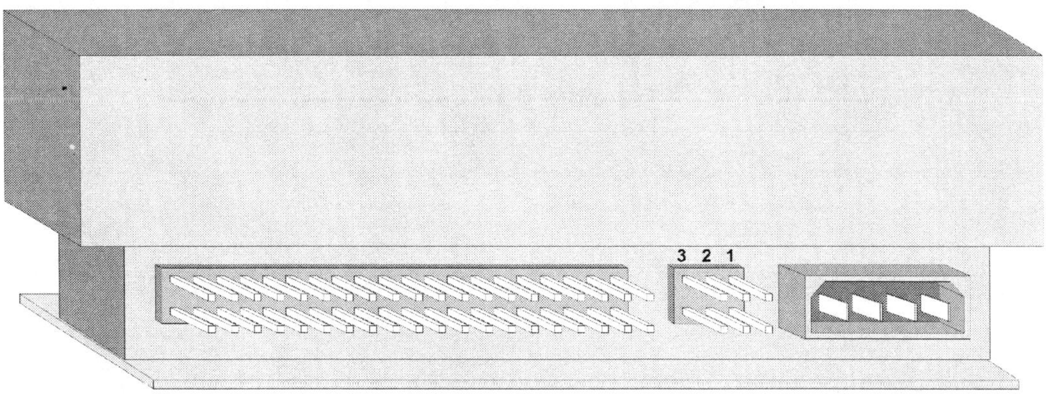

For exact configuration details you should always read the documentation that came with your specific disk.

Install and Configure the IDE Drive

Once you have the drive configured for master/slave, you can then physically mount the drive into the computer. Specific steps for this procedure will vary depending on the type of case (enclosure) you have. Typically you would locate an available drive bay opening in your system and install your drive. This may or may not require you to first attach separate mounting brackets or rails. Next, attach the 40-pin cable making sure that the red stripe (pin-1) is properly oriented and then attach the DC power connector (Molex connector) to rear of the hard drive.

Configure the Computer's CMOS

Once you have the drive physically configured, installed and cables attached, you are ready to power on the computer and configure the CMOS settings. Typically most PCs today will auto-detect the new disk and automatically configure the drive. Older systems may require you to manually configure the CMOS settings to match your specific drive type. You can do this by choosing the user defined type from the CMOS menu. Sometimes this is designated as **Type 47**. You should also record (document) these settings in case you ever have to restore them because the CMOS gets changed or erased due to a CMOS battery failure.

Load the Operating System

The final step of any drive installation is to prepare and load an operating system. This may or may not include creating partitions and pre-formatting the disk. These steps will depend on the type and version of the operating system installed.

Troubleshooting an IDE Drive Installation

Now you have installed the disk, configured the CMOS and nothing works… then what? Well the bad news is that it could be just about anything, including the possibility that the new drive itself is defective. You should always re-check items like:

- Are the cables all connected and securely seated?
- Are the cables properly oriented, pin 1 to pin 1, on the connector? Remember, the red stripe should always go to pin 1 on the connector.
- Have you attached the DC power connector?
- Have the drive(s) been configured correctly as single or master and slave?
- Is the CMOS configured for the proper drive type?

As mentioned previously, the list could go on and on. However, this list includes the most common types of problems that occur with a new installation.

SCSI

As the PC world started to blossom, there were an ever-growing number of peripheral devices that could be connected to a computer, and an ever-growing number of vendors who were trying to interface these devices to the individual PCs. This created somewhat of a problem in that there were no standards to specify how the interface was to take place.

One way to solve this problem would be to agree on a kind of computer Bus that would be used by all types of small computers. This Bus would need to provide an interface for a hard disk, but would also need to support other peripherals like CD-ROMs, WORM (Write Once, Read Many), optical disks, and other types of removable disk storage devices and optical scanners.

The standard that evolved from this mandate was called the **SCSI** interface (pronounced "scuzzy" from **S**mall **C**omputer **S**ystems **I**nterface). The SCSI is a system interface that is actually a complete expansion Bus. It allows up to 7 intelligent devices on a SCSI-1 or SCSI-2 system and up to 15 devices on a SCSI-3 system.

SCSI Device

The length of a SCSI cable is critical for proper operation. An exact SCSI cable length will vary between 1.5 meters and 12 meters depending on the type of SCSI interface as well as the number of devices attached to it. As you approach the length limit, errors will increase.

Technology Name	Maximum Cable Length (meters)	Maximum Cable Length (feet)	Maximum Speed (MBps)	Maximum Number of Devices
SCSI-1	6	19.7	5	8
SCSI-2	6	19.7	5-10	8 or 16
Fast SCSI-2	3	9.8	10-20	8
Wide SCSI-2	3	9.8	20	16
Ultra SCSI-3, 8-bit	1.5	4.9	20	8
Ultra SCSI-3, 16-bit	1.5	4.9	40	16
Ultra-2 SCSI	12	39.4	40	8
Wide Ultra-2 SCSI	12	39.4	80	16
Ultra-3 SCSI	12	39.4	160	16

SCSI Standards

SCSI Addressing

Every SCSI device that connects to the cable must have a unique address (identifier). This is what makes it possible for multiple SCSI devices to work together. These identifiers are generally referred to as the **SCSI IDs**. On a SCSI-1 device these IDs range from 0-7 and then from 8-15 on enhanced SCSI devices. The IDs are normally configured by flipping a set of rotary switches on external devices or by setting jumpers on internal devices.

When configuring SCSI devices, you must remember that each SCSI device must be set to use a unique SCSI ID. Most PCs will expect to find the bootable device located on SCSI ID 0. An example: Drive C (the bootable device) will be set to use SCSI ID 0. A second device or drive could then be set for SCSI ID 1. Any other SCSI devices could then be set to use any of the remaining addresses (2 through 7). You should remember the following rule of thumb:

The host adapter (**SCSI controller**) will typically default and use **SCSI ID 7**, which has the highest priority. The **hard disk** that will be the **bootable device** should be addressed as **0** (zero).

All of the SCSI devices are daisy-chained together using a straight ribbon cable with either a 50-pin or 68-pin connector. Macintosh systems are the exception to this rule. They may use a 50- or 25-pin D-Shell connector.

Based on the following graphic, assign a valid SCSI ID to each device:

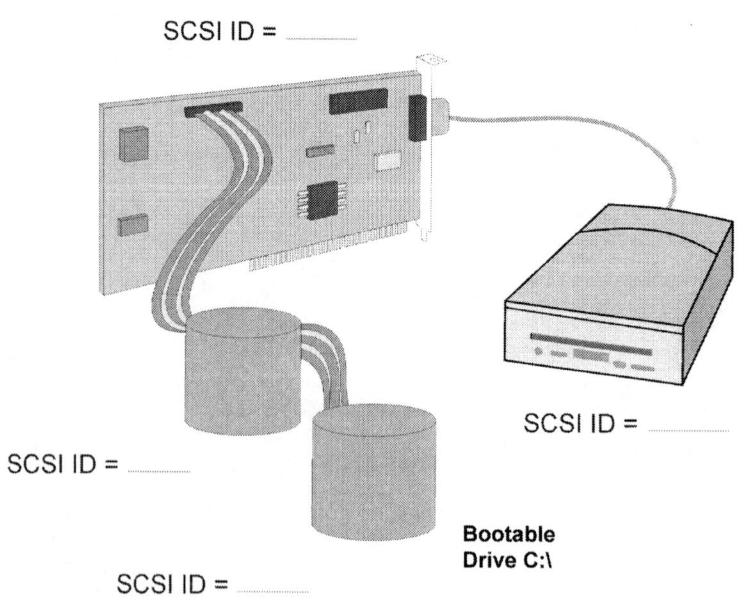

SCSI Termination

Another important configuration issue when using SCSI devices is termination. The host adapter or controller, as well as the last SCSI device in the chain, must be terminated. For both hard disk and host adapters, this termination is accomplished through a device called a ***resistor pack***. Usually hard drives are shipped with this resistor pack already installed. But the resistor pack can be removed if termination is not necessary or required. In the case of an external SCSI device, switches, or perhaps a dummy SCSI connector, provide the necessary termination. It is imperative for SCSI configuration that there never be more than two terminators in a SCSI chain. The basic rule for SCSI termination could be stated as the following:

The **first** and **last** device in a SCSI chain **must be terminated!**

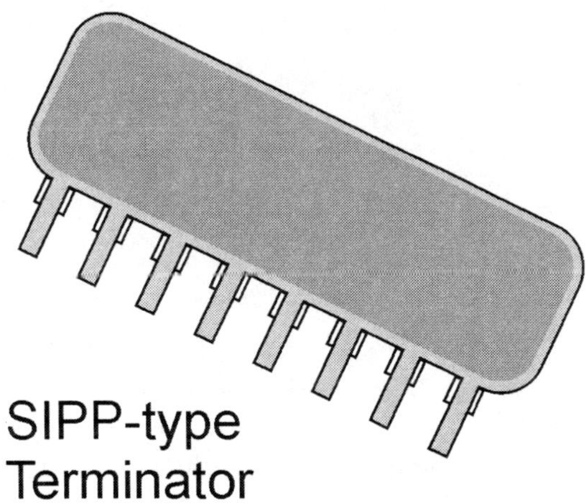

Based on the example shown below, which devices will be terminated?

Which device will have the termination removed?

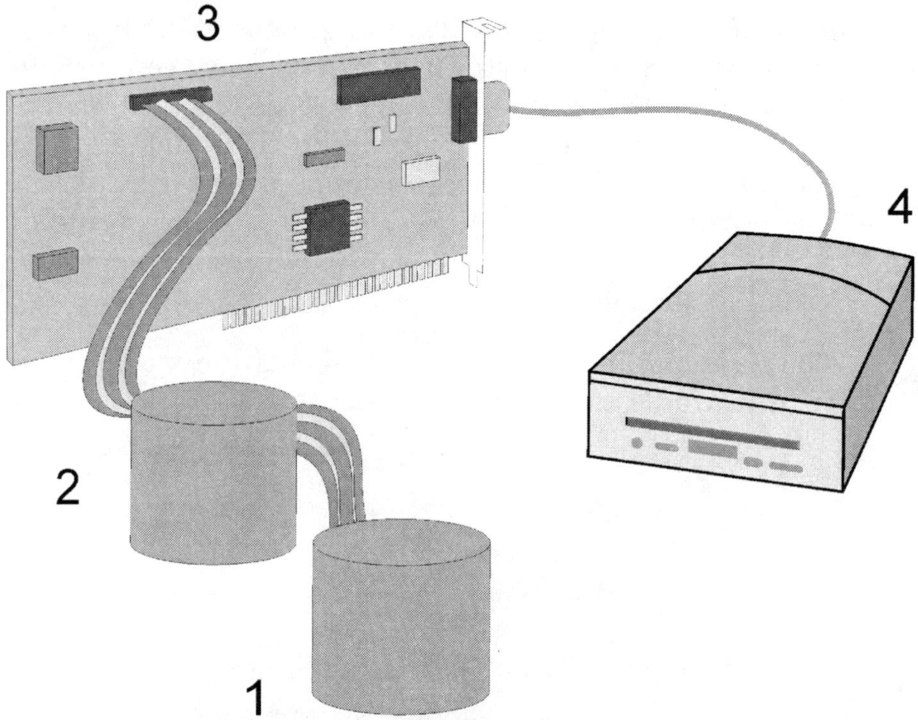

*Devices **1** and **4** would be terminated, as they are the first and last devices in the SCSI chain. Device 2 (hard disk) and device 3 (SCSI host adapter) would have termination removed. **Remember**, only two terminating points should be made: the **first** and the **last**!*

Installing a SCSI Hard Drive

You will find that installing a SCSI hard drive is actually quite similar to the IDE installation. The major difference is in the setup and the need to install a separate SCSI host adaptor card (usually). Remember, we said that IDE support is built into most motherboards today. On the other hand, there are few motherboards that have built in support for SCSI.

To install a SCSI disk and card you need to complete the following steps:

- Configure the drive's SCSI ID.
- Mount the drive in the intended bay.
- Install and configure the SCSI Host Adaptor.
- Attach the Cable(s).
- Terminate the SCSI Chain.
- Configure the computer's CMOS.
- Load the Operating System.

Configure the Drive's SCSI ID

Remember, if this disk is going to be the only drive or the bootable drive in the system you will configure the SCSI ID for 0. If the drive is being added as a second device (non-bootable), then you would choose any other available SCSI ID. This configuration will typically be made using a series of jumpers located on the drive itself.

Mount the Drive

Once the disk has been configured, you can physically mount the drive in any available drive bay. Ensure that the location allows for easy access for the routing of the SCSI cable and access to a power supply connector.

Install SCSI Host Adaptor

Configure the SCSI adaptor card for an ID that matches your installation plan. Usually the SCSI Host Adaptor will be set to use SCSI ID 7 (the default of most cards). Install the card into an available open slot. Make sure that the card is fully seated and secure. You should also make sure that it has been installed in a slot that will permit easy routing of the SCSI cable.

Attach the Cable(s)

Now that your drive and interface card have been installed you can attach the SCSI cable between the drive and the controller. Make sure that the cable is properly oriented, pin 1 to pin 1, paying attention to the red stripe. In the SCSI environment this is normally simplified because the ribbon connector is typically "keyed" so that it can only be attached one way. This helps prevent any potential mishaps. You will also have to connect the power connector (Molex connector) to the drive.

Terminate the SCSI Chain

Remove or add terminators as required. If you are installing a single SCSI drive, the drive should be terminated as well as the SCSI Host adaptor since they are the only two devices in the chain. Remember, the first and the last device should always be terminated.

Configure the Computer's CMOS

Before the system can recognize your disk you will need to configure the computer's CMOS. Typically you will configure the CMOS in one of three ways: either set the disk type to **0** (zero) or depending on the type of CMOS it may be set to **Not Installed**, or **SCSI** if listed.

Load the Operating System

The final step of any drive installation is to prepare and load an operating system. This may or may not include creating partitions and pre-formatting the disk. These steps will depend upon the type and version of the operating system installed.

Troubleshooting the SCSI Drive Installation

Now that you have configured the Host Adaptor and the SCSI IDs, installed the devices, attached the cables and configured the CMOS and nothing works... then what? Well the steps involved in troubleshooting the SCSI installation are very similar to the IDE troubleshooting model. You should always re-check the following items:

- Have the drive and controller been set with valid SCSI IDs?
- Are the cables all connected and securely seated?
- Are the cables properly oriented, pin 1 to pin 1, on the connector? Remember, the red stripe should always go to pin 1 on the connector.
- Have you attached the DC power connector?
- Has the SCSI chain been properly terminated?
- Is the CMOS configured for the proper drive type? For a SCSI device this could be drive type 0 or set for Not Installed or for SCSI if the option is available.

As mentioned previously, the list could go on and on. However, this list includes the most common types of problems that occur with a new installation.

Hard Disk Characteristics

Capacity

The basic unit of storage on the hard drive is a sector. Each sector holds 512 bytes of data. By multiplying the number of tracks the drive contains by the amount of data each track can hold, you will have the approximate capacity of the hard disk.

The amount of data capacity is not the only factor to consider when evaluating a hard disk. Performance is also a very important issue. A hard disk may be able to store vast amounts of information, but if you are unable to access the data efficiently, the increased amount of data will cause performance to suffer.

Access Time

An important performance criteria for hard drives is the Drive Access Time. This access time is the actual time it takes to find data on the hard disk. Access time is usually measured in milliseconds — the lower the better. Hard drives manufactured just a few years ago were considered fast at access times around 85 milliseconds. A typical hard drive manufactured today will have an access time of less than 10 milliseconds.

Data Transfer Rate

Another performance benchmark is the Data Transfer Rate. Access speed measures how fast data can be located on the disk. The data transfer rate measures how fast that data can then move between the hard disk and the CPU itself. The data transfer rate of a hard disk is usually expressed in megahertz or megabytes per second.

Sector Interleaves

The hard drives of modern PCs no longer use sector interleaves, although they're still used by CD-ROMs. There was a time when the speed of the microprocessor was actually slower than the speed of the hard disk. This meant that the data transfer speed of the drive needed to be slowed to match the data handling ability of the CPU. Sector interleaves allowed the CPU to process data in pieces, allowing the CPU to finish with a piece of data before reading further. This was accomplished by forcing the disk drive to skip a given number of sectors. The time lapse created by skipping sectors would give the CPU a chance to catch up with the disk. Interleaves were measured in terms of ratios. For example, a one-to-one ratio meant that no sectors were skipped. A one-to-four ratio meant that four sectors were skipped before any more data was read from the drive.

Caching

Hard drive performance will always be limited by the sheer mechanical operation of the disk itself. There will always be limits to how fast a hard drive can spin due to centrifugal force. One method used to overcome this limitation of mechanical hard drives is something called *caching*. A cache is an area of Random Access Memory (RAM) where the most frequently used files are stored. Access to the data and files located in cache is theoretically one hundred times faster than access to that same information on the hard disk.

Preparing the Hard Disk

The three basic steps to prepare a hard disk to accept data are:

- Low-level formatting
- Partitioning
- High-level formatting

Low-Level Formatting

A hard drive is a lot like a new file cabinet. When you first buy it, it is essentially empty. Just like an empty file cabinet, the hard drive must be organized. Organization, as it pertains to the hard drive, is the process of defining the hard drive's tracks and sectors. This process of creating tracks and sectors on the new hard disk is called low-level formatting.

The process of low-level formatting will also detect areas on the hard disk that may be defective and prevents data from being stored there. Low-level formatting software comes in a variety of flavors. Some low-level software routines are included with the purchase of a new hard disk. Some computer systems also include in their CMOS and BIOS settings a low-level software routine. For the most part, this low-level software formatting routine is for older models of hard disks. Most newer drives, especially IDE drives, rarely use low-level software formatting.

Partitioning

Partitioning is the first step in configuring the hard drive on your system. In order to accommodate multiple operating systems on a hard disk, DOS allows you to create multiple partitions with a program called **FDISK** found in the DOS directory. Another reason to create partitions on a hard disk is that, prior to DOS Version 4.0, DOS only recognized a 32MB partition or smaller. The newer versions of DOS allow for partitions as large as 512 megabytes.

When creating multiple partitions on a hard disk, one partition will be set aside to contain the information necessary to "boot" or start-up the system. The partition that contains the boot information is called the bootable partition. The DOS **FDISK** program is the software that tells the computer which partition will be bootable. The **FDISK** program will ask which partition to make active. The primary or bootable DOS partition should be partition number one. After selecting number one from the **FDISK** menu, you can escape once to get back to the main menu and then exit the **FDISK**program. The computer will now reboot to the partition set as active.

When you partition your hard drives it is important to understand that each logical disk in the system will be identified with a different letter of the alphabet. A and B are reserved for the system's floppy drives. The C drive is designated for the first primary partition, and the D drive is reserved for the first extended partition, etc. If a disk is present in either the A or B drives when you start up the system, it will check there first for the information necessary to boot up your system. If the disk present is not a system disk, you will get a "non-system disk" error. Simply remove the disk and continue with the boot process. Your system will automatically search the C drive for boot up information if the A and B drives are empty.

High-Level Formatting

Finally, the last step for DOS-based systems is to run the DOS **FORMAT** program. The **FORMAT** command creates a DOS boot record, a File Allocation Table (sometimes called FAT) and DOS root directory. The **FORMAT** program allows a hard disk to be formatted with or without system files.

Hard Disk Maintenance

Hard disk preventive maintenance is performed to protect the data on the drive. The hard disk itself is fairly fragile, so careful handling procedures can minimize the chances of damage. One of the best methods to reduce harm or loss of data is to park the heads outside the data area and power down. This process of moving the heads to an area on the hard drive that does not contain data is called "parking and locking." On some of the very early hard disks this required a separate software program. Newer equipment now includes automatic head parking.

Disk Fragmentation

Normally new files are all contiguous, meaning that they are written to sequential sectors. As files are deleted they create holes in the usable disk space. When DOS is requested to write a new file and find new sectors, it responds by taking the first sector available. This can easily lead to a new file being spread out over several separate areas or sectors. These files are then called "noncontiguous files" and are inefficient for a number of reasons.

The disadvantage of noncontiguous files is that they take longer to read. The drive must search all over the disk platter to read the information, slowing down the disk access time.

Another disadvantage of noncontiguous files is that they are more difficult to recover if erased. In the event a file is erased and then needs to be accessed again, certain steps can be taken to recover the file. If you have kept your disk de-fragmented, you increase your odds for successful recovery of the erased file.

There are many programs that will rearrange the data on your disk so that all files are contiguous. DOS itself is bundled with programs like **CHKDSK** and **SCANDISK**. There is also a wide variety of third party programs that will defragment a disk, such as Disk Optimizer from *Soft Logic Solutions* and *Norton*'s Speed Disk program.

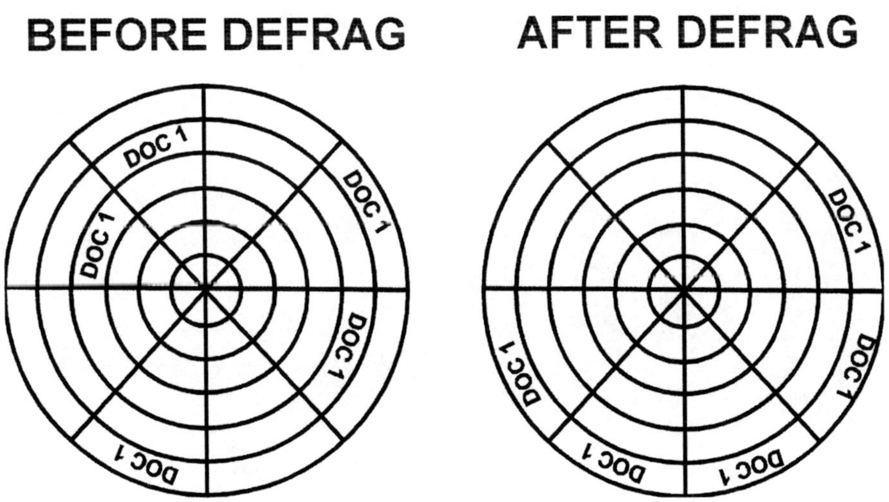

Before and After Disk Fragmentation

Floppy Disks

Before the creation of the hard disk, the floppy disk was the primary method of storage. It is still used widely today as a convenient method of transporting and moving data between PCs. Virtually all PCs purchased today come with at least one floppy disk drive as standard equipment. Floppy disk drives come in different sizes and capacities, but all work essentially the same way.

The two most common types of floppy diskettes are the 5¼" diskette, introduced in 1976 by IBM for use in the original IBM PC, and the 3½" floppy. The most common type of floppy diskette used today in personal computers is the 3.5-inch, 1.44MB disk. However, newer technologies that facilitate higher capacity drives are emerging everyday. A simple way to determine approximate capacity is to multiply the number of tracks times the number of sectors per track. 80 tracks x 18 sectors would yield about 1.44MB, which is a high density diskette. A low density, 3.5-inch disk that has 80 tracks and only 9 sectors per track, would yield about 720KB. The shell surrounding the 3½" floppy is more rigid than the shell for the 5¼," with a metal shield covering the head access area. This makes for a safer storage medium than the older 5¼" floppies.

Floppy disk drives work in a similar fashion to hard drives by using heads that read and write to the disk. Drives use a spindle motor to rotate the disk and stepper motor to move the read/write heads to appropriate position.

Floppy disks are connected to the system board via the floppy disk controller. The floppy disk controller not only acts as a pathway or means of connecting the disk drive to the system board, but it also translates the logical signals of the computer into electrical pulses the disk drive can understand.

A ribbon cable with connectors for two floppy drives is used to connect the floppy disk controller and drives. This cable is usually a 34-pin cable with a twist at one end. The floppy cable will determine whether a drive will be identified as the 'A' drive or 'B' drive. Drive A uses the connector with a twist, while Drive B uses the connector without it.

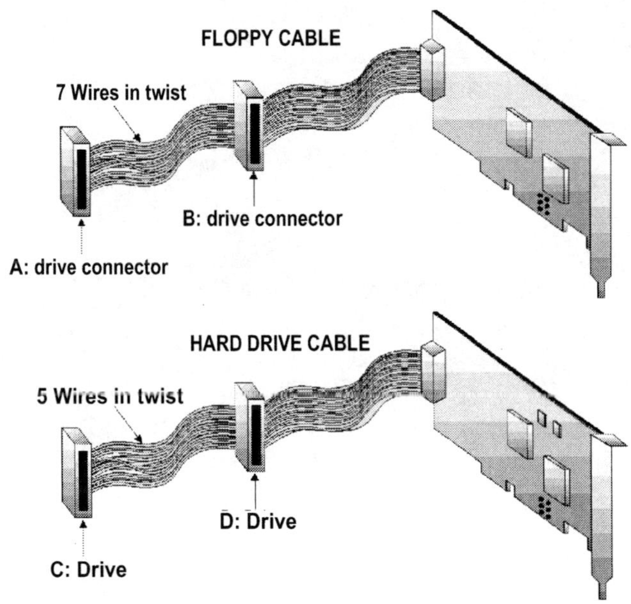

FLOPPY DRIVE CONNECTORS

Removable Disk Storage

Floppy diskettes offer a very convenient way to store and transport small files but do little to address the needs of working with the larger graphic and database files that we typically work with today. New and larger capacity removable media like the Zip and Jaz disks from the Iomega Company help fill this need. Another high capacity solution comes from the SyQuest Company in the form of their removable hard drive. Using a SCSI interface, SyQuest's 5.25" drive supports up to 200 MB cartridges, while their 3.5" drive provides support for 105 and 270 MB cartridges.

ZIP DISK

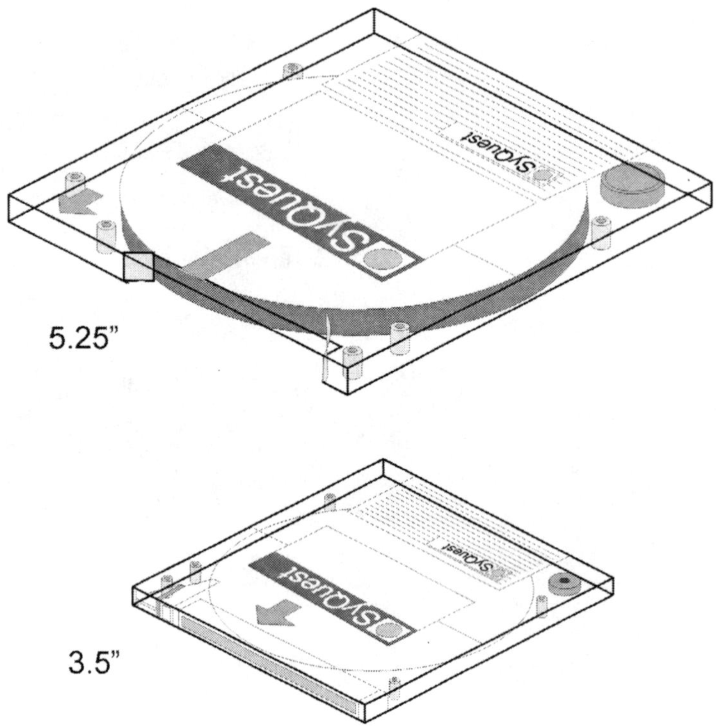

SYQUEST REMOVABLE DISK

Complementary Metal Oxide Semiconductor (CMOS)

The CMOS holds system information, like time, date, installed memory and type drives installed in the machine. The CMOS is a special type of chip that combines a Real Time Clock (RTC) with at least 64KB of Non-Volatile RAM (NVRAM).

The clock's function is to provide date and time information to all the software applications that need it. The NVRAM's function is to store system configuration information. Every time the computer is turned on it needs to be told what type of hardware it contains so that it can control it. The NVRAM provides that information.

A battery provides the CMOS with the power it requires to preserve stored information and run the clock while the computer is turned off or unplugged. Due to very low power consumption, the CMOS can run on a battery for several years.

Information or software programs stored on a non-volatile chip (such as CMOS) is called **firmware**. The non-volatile nature of the chip insures that the information stored within the chip will not be lost after power is removed.

A word of caution: If you are performing maintenance that requires the removal of the battery, make sure to record all setup information prior to disconnecting the battery. Once power is removed, all the information contained on the chip is lost.

Communication Ports and Devices

Computers communicate with devices through communication ports. Each computer is outfitted with two basic types of ports: serial and parallel.

Serial Ports

Generally used by devices that require bi-directional communication with the computer, serial ports are also known as Asynchronous Serial Interfaces and are used by devices such as mice, scanners and digitizers. Asynchronous means that no synchronization or clocking is taking place. This allows data to be entered at irregular time intervals. For example, data coming from the keyboard is fed to the computer in irregular patterns by the computer user. Serial ports channel data one bit at a time.

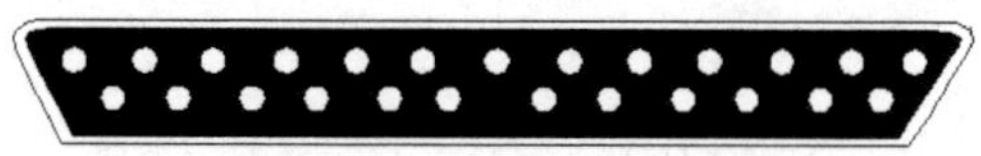

25-PIN MALE CONNECTOR

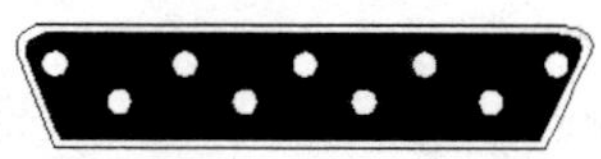

9-PIN MALE CONNECTOR

Parallel Ports

Parallel ports operate normally as one-way ports but they may also be used for bidirectional communications. They are also known as Centronics Interfaces and their most common use is to support printers. PCs can support three parallel ports. They are referred to as LPT1, LPT2 and LPT3 (**L**ine **P**rin**T**er one, etc.). Parallel ports are much faster than serial ports. They move data in 8-bit clumps along parallel lines.

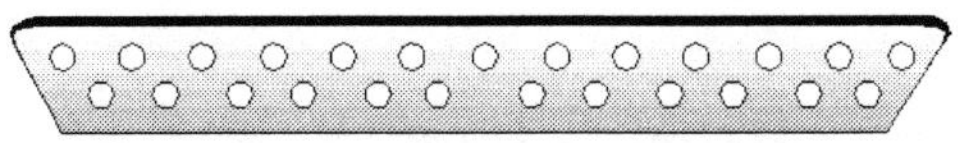

25-PIN FEMALE CONNECTOR

NOTE: **GENERALLY, THE ABOVE CONENCTORS ARE ALSO CALLED D-SHELL CONNECTORS.**

The Extended Capabilities Port (ECP)

Parallel ports have been in constant change over the years. Standard Parallel Ports (SPP) are the earliest and slowest versions of the family. SPP interfaces are unidirectional.

The Enhanced Parallel Port (EPP) the **IEEE specifications 1284**, increased throughput by enabling bi-directional communication. The Extended Capabilities Port (ECP) boasts the fastest parallel throughput, by combining DMA channel technology and bi-directional communication. The 1284 specification also defined the required cable type that increased distances up to 32 feet.

Boards and Connectors

Circuit boards are used to handle the communications between the computer and the peripherals they support. Each one of them has a built-in connector that is used by the peripheral to attach to the computer. A good way to identify individual boards is by the type of connector they have. This section outlines the different types of connectors available and their various applications.

BNC Connector

Named after its inventor (Naur), the Bayonet Naur Connector, is used mostly for network applications.

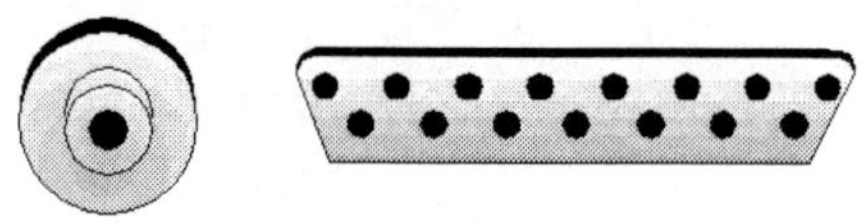

ETHERNET LAN BOARD
BNC & AUI PORTS

The Centronics Connector

Not to be confused with the Centronics interface, this connector takes its name from the company that made it popular. This type of connector is used on SCSI interfaces and also on printers.

DIN Connector

DIN is a German name that stands for "German Industry Standard." The DIN Connector is about one inch across and is round in shape. This type of connector is commonly used to fasten the keyboard to the motherboard and may have anywhere from three to seven pins.

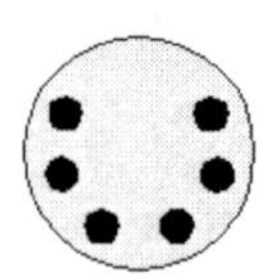

DIN CONNECTOR

Miniature DIN Connector

This smaller version of the DIN connector is used for some Bus mouse interfaces, some keyboard interfaces, and serial port applications.

RJ45 or RJ11 Connector

Registered Jack type 45 or 11 connectors are modular jacks. The RJ45 has eight wires and is used for Ethernet and LocalTalk (Macintosh Network) connections. The RJ11 is a regular phone line jack and is used on fax/modem boards. The RJ45 is a somewhat larger version of the RJ11 telephone connector, except the RJ11 only uses two pair of wires.

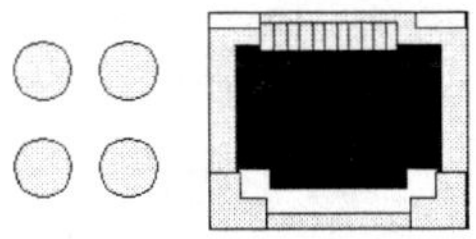

A 10BASE T ETHERNET CARD WITH RJ45 CONNECTOR AND A FEW LEDS

Mini-plug

Mini-plugs are found in the back of sound cards or CD-ROM players. They are used to connect a set of speakers, a microphone or headsets to the computer.

RCA Plug

RCA plugs are used on video capture boards for video inputs or on sound cards for sound inputs and outputs.

Portable Systems

As the world of computers grows beyond the traditional office setting, more users are relying on portable computing systems such as laptops to conduct business away from the office. Whether working from home, on an airplane, in a foreign country, or at a remote job site, portable systems are a vital link in the communication highway.

Components

Most laptop computers contain the following components:

Battery Power Supply

Three different types of batteries can power laptop systems. Whichever type is used, a good rule of thumb is to always carry an extra battery for your laptop so that you won't risk losing valuable data when your laptop runs out of juice.

The most common types of laptop batteries would include the following:

- **Nickel Cadmium (NiCd)** - The nickel cadmium battery is a rechargeable technology also used in camcorders, portable shavers and mobile phones. It provides more charge per weight than lead-based batteries. A major drawback if this type of battery is the so called "memory effect." These batteries tend to remember how full the charge was the last time they were on the charger, and refuse to go beyond that point the next time you charge them. The nickel cadmium battery should be completely discharged before it can be recharged.
- **Nickel Metal Hydride (NiMH)** - Another type of battery is the nickel metal hydride battery, which was designed to hold 50 to 80% more charge than the nickel cadmium battery. It does not suffer from the "memory effect." However, the nickel metal hydride battery does take longer to charge than the nickel cadmium.

- **Lithium Ion** - Lithium ion is a rechargeable battery technology that provides a 10 to 15% improvement in charge capacity over a similar size Nickel metal hydride battery. Toshiba introduced this type of battery in their notebooks and since then they have become very popular in many other devices as well.
- **Lithium Polymer** - Introduced in 1998, lithium polymer is very similar to the lithium ion battery in terms of power ratings. The major difference between the two is the lithium polymer battery uses a gelatinous electrolyte rather than a liquid. This enables the lithium polymer battery to be manufactured in many different sizes and shapes, suited for custom applications.
- **Zinc Air** - Zinc air technology dates from the 1920s when large batteries were used for remote devices. It provides more charge per physical size than does either the nickel cadmium or the nickel metal hydride. Another advantage of zinc air technology is that it does not suffer from memory effects. This type of battery is typically used in situations where continuous power is required. Air causes a chemical reaction and must be present when power is required and denied when not required.

Tips To Conserve Battery Life

- Lower the LCD screen's light output.
- Use **Disk Cache** to make the hard and floppy drives work less. Use **SmartDrive** if you're running *Windows* on your laptop, or *PC Tools* **Cache** utility if you're running *DOS*.

When you're selecting a laptop, buy one that allows you to replace a low battery in the middle of a session without losing data, ending your current session or blowing a fuse.

LCD

A portable computer uses a **Liquid Crystal Display** (LCD), a flat-screen display using several hundred "tanks" of liquid crystal, each connected to its own capacitor. Earlier laptops used a monochrome LCD but most of today's laptops have color displays. To prolong the life of the LCD (and prolong the laptop's battery life), it's a good idea to lower the screen's light output. To adjust the settings for your LCD screen, click on the **Color** icon within **Control Panel** and select colors that give off less light but are still readable. Don't sacrifice readability, however, just to conserve battery power.

AC Power Supply

Most laptop manufacturers provide a grounded AC adapter to use when a power outlet is available. Check your laptop's transformer (converts AC to DC) if you plan to use your laptop overseas where foreign voltages and currents vary greatly. Consult a computer retailer to see if your adapter will function properly in the country you will be visiting.

PCMCIA Card (Types I, II and III)

Most laptops have at least one, if not two, PC card slots to link to devices like modems and printers. These are the Personal Computer Memory and International Association (PCMIA) cards. Usually the size of a credit card, these peripheral cards for memory, network interfaces and modems, plug into the laptop's slots. There are three types of PCMCIA card slots: I, II and III, which can be identified by their thickness. Type I cards can also fit in Type II slots.

- **Type I slot (3.3MM thick)**
  Either normal RAM or flash memory card interface
- **Type II slot (5MM thick)**
  Internal modem
- **Type III slot (10.5MM thick)**
  Removable hard disks

Network Cards

If you have the need to connect your laptop to a network, purchase a Network Interface Card (NIC) — either an Ethernet or ARCNet card — and the necessary device drivers and networking software to make your laptop compatible with the network.

Memory

Today's laptops are comparable to a desktop PC in RAM. There is normally an expansion slot, but you might want to save the expansion slot for a peripheral such as a fax-modem, network interface card, etc.

Docking Stations

There can be no argument that laptop computers are great platforms for enabling mobile computing. However, they don't come without some disadvantages. The keyboards are smaller especially for those people with larger hands and the monitors are constantly improving but still lacking as compared to a desktop. A **docking station** is a platform designed to overcome these drawbacks in a home or office environment. Essentially, the docking station is a platform that turns the portable laptop computer into a true desktop solution, including a full size monitor and keyboard. It uses a large connector and socket to quickly connect the laptop. This station duplicates all the cables and connections for a full size monitor, keyboard and mouse. The docking stations may also have openings available for expansion boards and could also include built-in features for speakers or external CD drives.

The following is an example of a typical laptop and docking station configuration:

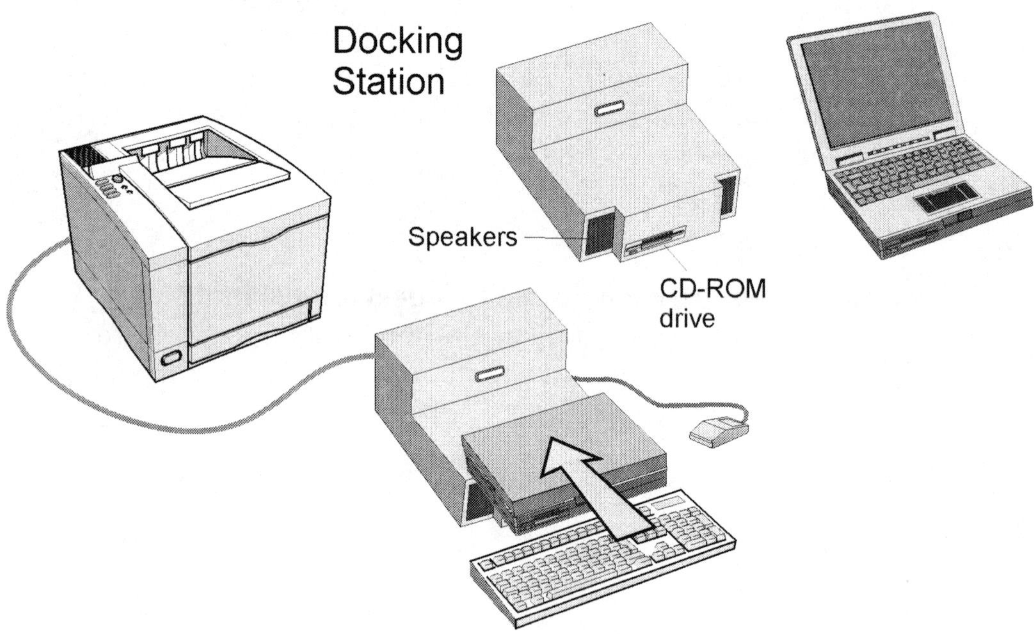

Port Replicator

A port replicator is a device very similar to a docking station in that it allows you to connect a laptop computer to desktop devices that are permanently plugged into it. The major difference between the port replicator and a docking station is that the port replicator does not usually include any slots for expansion boards or extra peripherals such as speakers.

Summary

In this section, the various components integral to a personal computer were discussed.

- The **CPU,** or processor, is the heart and soul of the computer and processes all communication among the various components of the PC.
- The **system board**, with its Bus design and expansion slots, provides the connections and means for communicating among the components; the processor, RAM, hard and floppy drives and input/output devices are all connected together through their attachment to the system board.
- **Memory**, or RAM, temporarily stores information for quick access by the processor.
- The **power supply** converts the standard 110V AC electricity from a wall outlet to the 5 and 12 volt DC currents required by the computer.
- **Hard and floppy drives** provide more static, permanent memory storage. Most programs are installed on the hard drives and this is also where files are most frequently stored. Floppy drives are used most often for transporting files from one computer to another and installing new programs.
- **Input/output devices,** such as the keyboard, monitor and printers, make it possible for the computer user to communicate with the computer and vice-versa.
- **Portable systems**, such as laptops, give users the flexibility to conduct business away from the office.

Review Questions

1. A system board is sometimes called a planar board.

   A. True
   B. False

2. The AT computer is usually equated with what type of Intel processor?

   A. The 80486
   B. The 80386
   C. The 8088
   D. The 80286

3. The EISA took the most popular features from the other Buses and enhanced them.

   A. True
   B. False

4. The MCA Bus architecture was developed by:

   A. Intel
   B. IBM
   C. Compaq
   D. Olivetti

5. What are the three steps in preparing a hard disk?

6. When connecting two floppy disk drives, Drive A should be attached to the connector with a____________.

7. The MCA architecture comes in both ___________ data paths.

    A. 8- and 16-bit
    B. 16- and 32-bit
    C. 32- and 64-bit
    D. 8- and 24-bit

8. A 25-pin female connector located on the back of the PC would be typical of what type of port?

    A. Parallel
    B. Serial
    C. Bus
    D. SCSI

9. What are the typical output voltages on a PC power supply?

    A. 120 V AC
    B. 120 V DC
    C. 5 V and 12 V DC
    D. 5 V and 12 V AC

10. A computer's digital logic circuitry uses which of the following voltages?

    A. 12 V DS
    B. 5 V DC
    C. 5 AC
    D. 15 DC

Section 5

PC Configuration

Section 5: PC Configuration

Introduction

Installing new hardware involves more than just attaching the pieces together. New components need to be told how to communicate with other hardware. This is what configuration is all about. When a manufacturer ships new equipment with a preset configuration, but it doesn't always match the configuration of your system.

In order for a personal computer to function, each of its components must be configured properly. Much like communication by mail, the communication between the different PC components relies on addresses. Input and output devices are assigned addresses and given unique settings so that information is sent to and from the appropriate component, and so conflicts do not arise. If components share the same settings, they will not be able to communicate. This kind of conflict is similar to what happens when two people try to talk at the same time: they cancel each other out and neither can communicate.

In this section, we will discuss the various addresses and settings that a PC uses to communicate with itself and we will learn how to resolve conflicts between components.

Objectives

When you've competed this section, you will be able to:

- Understand and know how to work with I/O addresses, DMA, and IRQ settings
- Configure new circuit boards for an installation
- Resolve device conflicts

Understanding I/O Addresses, DMA Channels and IRQ Lines

Part of the hardware configuration process requires you to select the paths or channels the CPU utilizes to communicate with the devices it serves. The CPU recognizes a device by the path it uses to communicate. When a path is assigned to more than one device, the CPU cannot talk to the devices and they will likely fail. Most computer manufacturers reserve addresses for specific uses. There are only a few channels that remain available for additional peripheral installations. Manufacturers provide their boards with a preset address, but since they do not know what channels may already be taken, it is up to you to determine the correct settings. In order to solve device conflicts, you must understand how devices communicate. The descriptions and tables in this section outline the rules that govern communication between devices.

Input / Output (I/O) Addresses

These addresses are the paths that a circuit board uses to communicate with the CPU. Each peripheral must have an exclusive I/O address. These addresses are actually locations set aside in the PC's RAM (Random Access Memory). Think of these locations as a mail drop or box. When the circuit board wants to communicate with the CPU, it drops off a request in this "box." The CPU then retrieves the information and replies with a message in this same "box." The CPU and circuit board use this address as a pipeline for communication between the two of them. The following chart gives you a list of commonly used I/O addresses in PCs.

PC Component	I/O Address (Hex Address Range)
CD-ROM	230-233
Bus Mouse	238-23B
PnP (ISA) I/O slot	274-277
LPT2	278-27F
EGA graphic (legacy item)	2B0-2DF
COM4 serial port	2E8-2EF
COM2 serial port	2F8-2FF
NIC (typical defacto Ethernet location)	300-30F
XT Hard disk controller (legacy item)	320-32F
MIDI port	330-33F
Secondary floppy controller	370-377
Standard LPT1 printer port	378-37F
Monochrome adapter	3B0-3BF
LPT3 secondary printer port	3BC-3BF
Color graphics adapter	3D0-3DF
COM3 serial port	3E8-3EF
Primary floppy disk controller	3F0-3F7
COM1 serial port	3F8-3FF
LPT1 I/O port	778-77F

Common I/O Address Listings

DMA (Direct Memory Access) Channels

When a peripheral device needs to access or write to a location in memory, it will normally have to go through the CPU for the request. This process can at times be very slow. DMA (Direct Memory Access) attempts to speed up this process. When a device uses a DMA channel, the CPU is bypassed. One way to understand DMA channels is to think of them as a trust relationship between the CPU and device. The CPU trusts that the device will use only the memory allocated to it and thus does not have to intervene with each request to use memory.

There are eight DMA channels on today's PCs, which are numbered 0-7. The following table lists the DMA channels and their availability.

DMA CHANNEL	USE
0	(Available by most machines) used by XT class machines
1	Used by XT class for hard disk. Controller available for others
2	Used by Floppy controller
3	Available
4-7	Available

DMA Channels

IRQ (Interrupt Request) Levels

IRQs make a physical connection between a device and the interrupt controllers inside a computer. When a device requires service from the CPU, an IRQ line is used to get the CPU's attention. When the interrupt signal arrives, the CPU puts its current task on hold and executes an "interrupt service routine." Then it goes back to the original task. Motherboards have up to 16 different interrupt levels built in, numbered from 0 through 15. Lower interrupt numbers get higher service priority.

Just as with DMA channels, it is very important that no two devices use the same interrupt. Avoiding these conflicts is one of the major challenges when installing new equipment.

The following table lists the 16 different interrupt levels and their typical assignments:

IRQ	DEVICE
0	TIMER
1	KEYBOARD
2	CASCADE
3	COM2
4	COM1
5	LPT2
6	FLOPPY
7	LPT1
8	CLOCK
9	IRQ2 REDIRECTED
10 - 12	USUALLY AVAILABLE
13	COPROCESSOR
14	HARD DISK
15	USUALLY AVAILABLE

Interrupt Levels

Installing Circuit Boards

When you buy a new peripheral for your system, such as a new sound card, most likely it will come configured with default settings. This is no guarantee that the card will work with your system. Configuring the board is not a difficult task, but complications may arise if you lack proper board documentation or information about the computer you are installing the board into. A successful board installation involves three steps: **configuration**, **installation**, and **testing**.

Configuration

Configuration consists of identifying and resolving any device conflicts and providing software support for the board in the form of BIOS or device drivers. In essence, the configuration tells the board how to communicate with the rest of the system. Configuration may also involve selecting specific combinations of jumper or DIP switch settings that tell the board which services to provide. Information about jumper or DIP switch settings should be included in the board's installation documents.

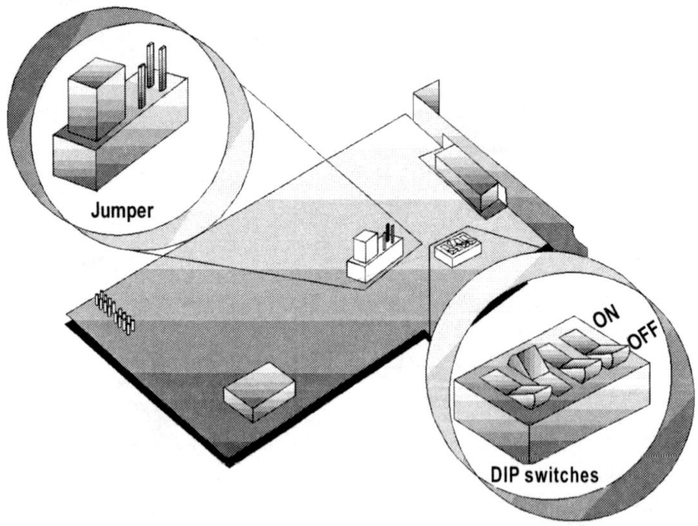

Jumper and DIP Switch Configurations

Even with the proper documentation supplied by the vendor, sometimes configuring jumper settings can be tricky. Let's take a more detailed look at **jumper blocks** and how to configure them. A **jumper block** is nothing more than a set of two or more metal pins in a plastic base attached to a system board, hard drive or expansion card. A plastic **jumper cap** with a metal strip inside fits over two pins to create electrical contact between them. This electrical contact establishes a specific hardware setting on that device.

Some jumper blocks have only two pins, while others will have three or more depending on how many different settings and configurations are required by the device.

The following are examples of a jumper cap and various block configurations:

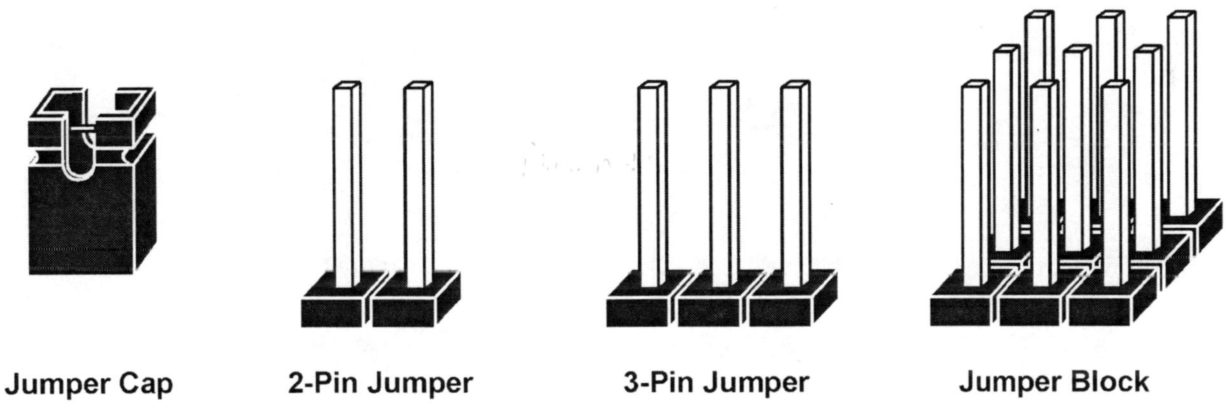

JUMPER CAP AND BLOCK

Typically jumper settings are stenciled or printed on the board. These settings will also coincide with the diagrams printed in the user manual. They are usually marked by a line or bar connecting two pins together. If a jumper block is composed of three pins, then connecting the first and the second pin would establish one setting while connecting the second (middle) and third pin would create yet another configuration. This process of connecting two pins may also be referred to as **jumpering**, **shorting** or **closing** the pins. If no jumper cap is required or used, the condition is referred to as **open**. The names will change depending on who is writing the configuration instructions. Whatever the name they use, the process itself is still the same.

The following diagram shows how this might look:

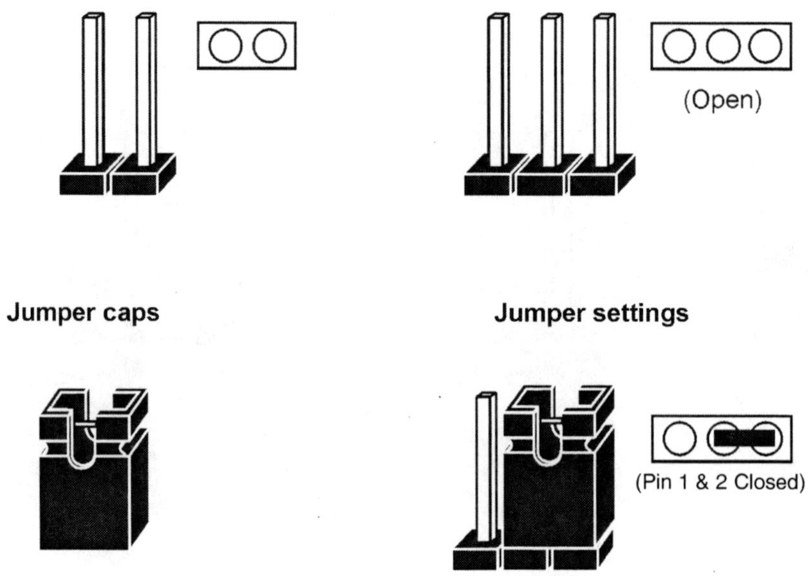

Handy Tip: If a particular configuration does not require you to use a jumper cap **DO NOT** discard it. Instead, simply hang the jumper cap off a single pin. This will not make contact. However, it will be there in the event the configuration changes in the future and you find yourself needing a jumper cap.

Installation

The board needs to be installed to an open expansion slot in the computer and all required cables should be appropriately connected. Again, the board should come with documentation to demonstrate correct installation.

Testing

After configuration and installation, test the board to see if it actually works. Testing is a necessary step and will tell you if the board is functioning. However, configuration problems are varied and may or may not directly affect the new board's operation. Here are some examples of problems that may arise before and after testing a new board:

1. You just installed a new sound card and it seems to be working properly, but your system crashes every time you try to print from Windows.
2. A newly installed internal modem refuses to work. In addition, the computer's mouse also refuses to respond.
3. You installed a new network card on a system and it did not work, so you replaced it a second and even a third time with an identical card. None of the cards function.

These types of problems can be directly attributed to device conflicts. In the case of the sound card, it is likely that both the printer and the card are using the same interrupt address. In the second example, the modem is most likely using the same COM port as the mouse. In the third example, the network card is probably trying to utilize a memory address reserved to another device. (This is a software-related problem.)

A Typical Configuration

A typical configuration requires:

- Telling a serial port whether it is COM1 or COM2.
- Telling a printer port whether it is LPT1, LPT2, or LPT3.
- Selecting DMA channels on a board.
- Selecting IRQ lines on a board.
- Selecting I/O addresses on a board.

There are many software programs that will aid in avoiding potential address and IRQ conflicts. **MSD**, Microsoft Diagnostics Program, ships with DOS version 6.0. **MSD** will list devices, the address and interrupts used by that device. However, these programs are not perfect. They will sometimes provide misinformation. As a last resort, you may have to physically examine each device, modem, printer port, etc. in order to determine what I/O address and IRQ it uses.

Exercise 5.1: Avoiding Conflicts

OBJECTIVE

Configuring a network interface card for non-conflicting IRQ and I/O address.

PREPARATION

You are installing a 3COM 509 network board in your PC which has the following equipment:

- Standard disk controller
- Serial ports COM1 and COM2
- Parallel port LPT1
- Standard VGA monitor

Using the charts from the previous pages, determine what IRQs and I/O Addresses are currently in use.

	IRQ	I/O Address
Standard Disk Controller		
COM1		
COM2		
Parallel Port LPT1		
Standard VGA Monitor		

Available IRQs______________________________

Available I/O addresses__________________________

Exercise 5.2: Installing and Configuring Peripheral Cards

OBJECTIVE

Configure and install one of the following: modem, network interface card or sound card into your PC.

PREPARATION

Obtain a peripheral device as listed above with the required software and documentation necessary to complete the exercise.

Step 1: Determine what IRQs and I/O addresses are currently in use and which ones are available.

- Boot your PC to DOS.
- Change to the MS DOS directory by typing **cd\dos**
- Locate and run the **MSD** program (Microsoft Diagnostic Program).
- Determine what IRQs and memory I/O addresses are currently available.

Step 2: Using the board and documentation provided, configure the board with nonconflicting settings.

Step 3: Install the board into any open Bus slot.

Step 4: Test the board by using the diagnostics that came with it.

Step 5 (Optional): Set the board for a conflict.

(*For example*, you might configure the board for IRQ 7, which is the printer port.) Run the diagnostics again and review the resulting message.

Summary

The various components that comprise a personal computer need to communicate with each other. In order for this to happen, these components are designed with unique addresses and settings.

- **Input/Output addresses** are locations in RAM that act as "mailboxes" for input and output devices to trade messages with the CPU.
- **Interrupt levels (IRQs)** make a physical connection with the interrupt controllers that demand the immediate attention of the CPU with an interrupt service routine. This action causes the CPU to pause its current operation and perform the process that the interrupting device requests.
- **DMA channels** allow a device to circumvent the CPU and communicate directly with RAM.

Through these configuration addresses and settings, the PC components are able to communicate with the CPU and each other. **The key to configuring a PC is to make sure that each device has its own unique address and settings.** If multiple devices share an I/O address or are configured to the same DMA or IRQ settings, conflicts will arise and the computer will not function properly.

Review Questions

1. The floppy drive uses which IRQ?

   A. 1
   B. 6
   C. 7
   D. 5

2. Two devices can share a common IRQ.

   A. True
   B. False

3. IRQ 4 is used by what device?

   A. Floppy
   B. Com1
   C. Com2
   D. Hard Disk

4. DMA stands for which of the following?

   A. Direct Memory Address
   B. Diverted Memory Access
   C. Direct Memory Access
   D. DRAM Memory Address

5. What MS-DOS version 6.0 program aids in troubleshooting potential IRQ conflicts?

   A. FDISK
   B. MEM
   C. MSD
   D. SCANDISK

6. How many DMA channels are available on today's PC?

   A. 8
   B. 4
   C. 2
   D. 6

7. Jumper blocks will typically be composed of only two pins.

   True
   False

8. The standard LPT1 printer port will typically use which I/O address range?

   A. 3BC-3BF
   B. 378-37F
   C. 2B0-2DF
   D. 3BC-3AD

9. If an expansion card vendor instructs you to short jumper pins 1 and 2 together, which of the following would you use?

   A. Clip
   B. Jumper cap
   C. Screw
   D. Bridge

10. A bus mouse will typically use which of the following I/O address ranges?

   A. 238-23B
   B. 2B0-2B4
   C. 370-377
   D. Does not usc onc

Section 6

Peripheral Hardware Devices

Section 6: Peripheral Hardware Devices

Introduction

In Section 5, we discussed internal PC components such as the system board, Buses, microprocessors, memory, disk drives, and power supplies. In this section, we'll discuss external hardware components such as the keyboard, monitors and the various peripheral devices that can be attached to the PC.

Objectives

When you've completed this section, you will be able to:

- Describe the different types of monitors used with microcomputers
- Discuss the different types of PC input devices such as keyboards, scanners and digitizers
- Discuss Multimedia Devices
- Discuss a modem and its functions

Monitors

The monitor, or video display unit, is the television-like screen the computer uses to display information to the user. Some of the earliest PCs could only display text and certain fixed graphic items that took up the full space of a single character. Most modern PCs, however, display high resolution and full graphics in a full color environment.

Monitors today still use a rather old technology invented around the turn of the century, called cathode ray technology. The monitor, or CRT (Cathode Ray Tube), is a vacuum tube that houses a flat phosphor-covered screen at one end and an electron gun at the other end. The video image on your monitor is created by projecting a narrow beam of electrons onto the phosphor-covered screen. The area where the beam hits the phosphor will glow for a brief period of time and then fade out.

Because the glow created by the electron beam fades very quickly (actually in hundredths of a second), it must retrace its path constantly to keep the image on the screen. The electron beam in the video monitor must repaint the screen at least 60 times per second or your eye will perceive flicker. This retracing is referred to as the monitor's refresh rate. The higher the refresh rate the less flicker and eye strain. Monitors that utilize a very low refresh rate are termed "interlaced monitors." Non-interlaced monitors use a higher refresh rate and thus reduce or eliminate the effects of flicker altogether. Most monitors today are non-interlaced.

Video Resolution

A monitor's resolution is determined by how dots (sometimes called pixels) can be displayed both across and down the screen. For example, a resolution of 800 by 600 means that 800 dots can be displayed horizontally and 600 dots vertically. The more dots, the higher the resolution and the sharper the image.

For performance reasons, sometimes a lower resolution might be the preferred choice. When displaying full-color graphics, especially with today's multimedia systems, lower resolution settings will increase the speed of the system.

The following table lists the different types of monitors used with PCs and their corresponding maximum resolutions. Most monitors sold today are SVGA monitors.

Standard	Maximum Resolution	Colors Supported
Mono	720 x 350	Mono
CGA (Color Graphics Adapter)	640 x 200	2
EGA (Enhanced Graphics)	640 x 350	64
HGC (Hercules)	720 x 350	3
MCGA (Multi Color Graphics Array)	640 x 480	2
VGA (Video Graphics Array)	640 x 480	256
SVGA Super VGA	800 x 600	256

COMMON TYPES OF MONITORS

The following graphic shows some common screen resolutions. Typically higher resolutions are used for graphic intensive applications. The higher the resolution, the more information (pixels) can be displayed on screen at one time.

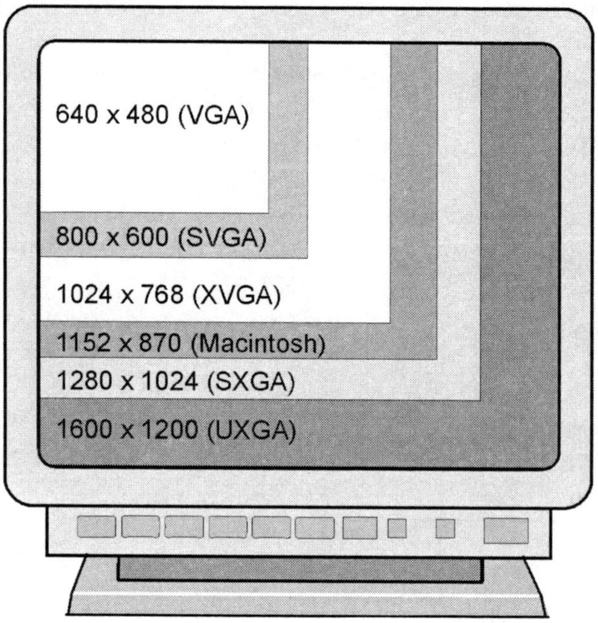

On Windows-based computers, you can change the resolution settings under the **Settings** tab in the **Display Properties** dialog box. To do this you would:

- Right-click on any open area on your desktop
- Click the **Properties** button
- Then select the **Settings** tab

The following is an example of the **Display Properties** dialog box:

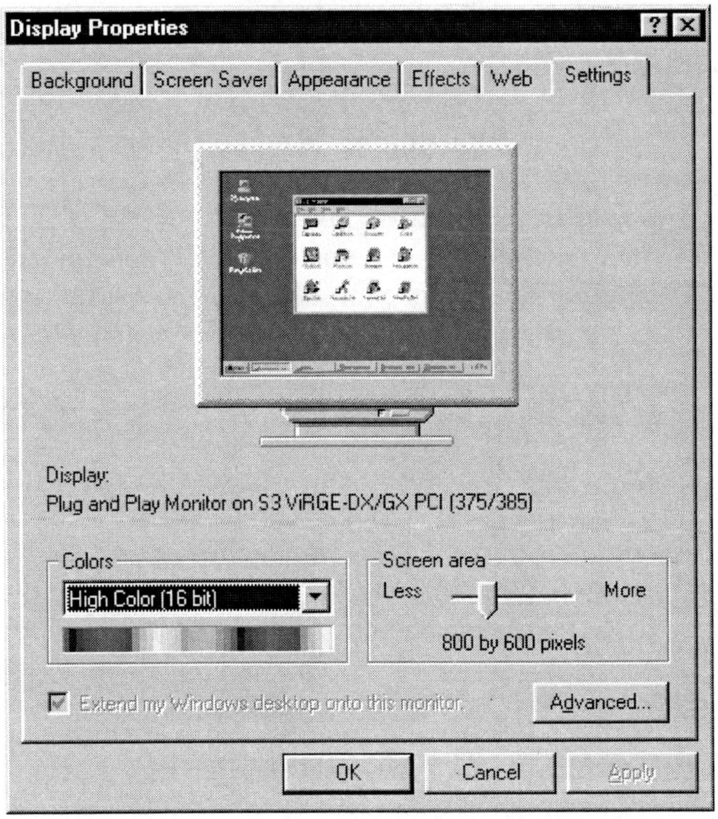

New Display Technologies

Flat Panel Display

The Flat Panel Display is a very thin display screen that has been used in laptop computers for many years now. This flat panel technology (design) is also gaining momentum in replacing traditional desktop CRTs as well. They are an ideal solution in today's energy aware market place, with their low power consumption and space saving design. It would be very safe to assume that this technology will soon become the standard for most users desktops. The flat panel displays rely upon the following technologies:

- **LCD** (Liquid Crystal Display) is a display technology that uses molecules (liquid crystals) that flow like liquid and have the ability to bend light waves. It takes much less power to stimulate (move) molecules than it does to turn on a light-emitting device. For this reason, LCD technology is ideal for mobile computing devices (laptops) that require low power consumption.
- **FED** (Field Emission Display) is a display technology that is very similar to a thin CRT, using a vacuum-filled cavity and phosphor-coated glass. However, instead of illuminating phosphors with electron guns that scan the entire screen, FED technology uses millions of stationary cone-shaped emitters. FED technology creates an image that is equal to or better than a standard CRT based monitor.

Note: A **flat screen** monitor should not be confused with **flat panel** monitors. Flat screen monitors are actually CRTs in which the viewing surface has a flatter appearance than older CRTs, which are slightly rounded at the corners. The flat screen provides less distortion at the edges.

Keyboards

While the monitor is probably the most common type of **output** device for the PC, the keyboard is probably the most frequently used **input** device. To the user, the keyboard may seem a simple device on the exterior. Inside the keyboard, however, there are many complex operations taking place both mechanically and electronically.

The original PC keyboard had a full typewriter key set plus a numeric keypad. The keyboard also incorporated ten function keys that programs use for their own special purposes. The most common keyboard today is the 101 Enhanced keyboard. This keyboard has all of the original keys plus two more function keys, a group of cursor keys, and nine additional keys dedicated to special functions. Recently, special compact and ergonomic keyboards have been developed, as well, as a special keyboard designed for use with the latest version of the Microsoft Windows software.

These different designs all function in the same way. Every key on the keyboard is linked to a switch on the circuit board inside the keyboard. A chip on this board constantly scans every circuit and, if the switch opens or closes, the chip passes that information along to the computer. The keyboard sends a message every time a key is pressed and another one when you take your finger off the key and it springs back up. The PC can tell when you are holding a key down.

There are two types of technologies used in today's keyboards: **capacitive** and **mechanical** switches. Capacitive technology is generally used in more expensive keyboards, while mechanical switches are found in less expensive keyboards. There are far fewer moving parts in a capacitive keyboard. This makes them less prone to failure.

Compatibility problems do exist between PC keyboards. However, most keyboards will work on the majority of desktop PCs. Some of the very old keyboards may still have a manual switch that changes internal electronics from the first type of PC keyboard compatible with the original IBM XTs to the later AT style keyboards. Keyboards plug into either a 5-pin DIN or a 6-pin mini-DIN socket on the motherboard. Adapters connect a 5-pin plug to a 6-pin socket.

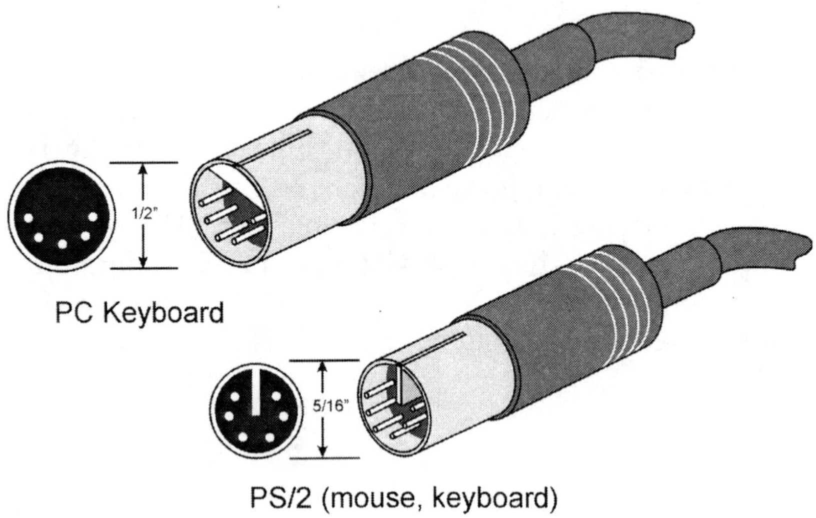

New Keyboard Technologies

Cordless Keyboards

Many manufacturers are now making cordless keyboards. These are very similar to regular keyboards, except instead of having a keyboard cable that runs from the keyboard to the computer, they have no cord. There are actually two types of cordless keyboard technology used today:

- **Radio Frequency (RF) -** The cord between the keyboard and the computer is replaced with a wireless connection. Two transceivers communicate to each other over a radio link; one is embedded within the keyboard and wired to the keyboard's internal controller, and the other is a separate unit that is composed of a length of standard keyboard cable and a conventional keyboard connector to attach to the PC. It is somewhat like the two devices are communicating like two people would using a pair of walkie-talkies.

- **Infrared Technology -** Infrared keyboards are very similar to RF keyboards, in that they don't require any physical cabling between the keyboard and the computer. However, the major difference is that unlike RF keyboards, infrared keyboards require an unobstructed line of site between the keyboard and the receiving unit. Many users find this inconvenient and prefer the RF technology to the infrared keyboards.

Typically cordless keyboards are a bit more expensive than comparable corded models. Since cordless is looked upon as a high-end feature, they are usually found bundled only with higher-end models of computers.

Keyboard Interface

The first interface between the keyboard cable and the PC is the DIN plug, which has five pins. The voltages between the pins 1, 2, and 3, or between pins 5 and 4 should be in the range of 2 - 5.5 volts DC. When troubleshooting a keyboard, check these voltages. If the voltages do not fall within the acceptable range, the problem probably lies in the computer itself, most likely in the system board. If all the voltages are present and within the required ranges, the problem is probably in the keyboard.

Perhaps one of the major problems with keyboards is not caused by system board malfunctions or cables, but rather from spills. Disassembling a keyboard for repair or cleaning is not hard in-and-of itself, but reassembling the keyboard is not recommended for the faint-hearted. As with other PC components, you might want to view the keyboard as a disposable unit.

Multimedia Components

Before we look at the actual components of a multimedia system let's take a few minutes to define it. Multimedia is technically the process of transmitting information in more than one format. It can include the use of text, audio, graphics and in some cases full-motion video. Today, multimedia programs are used extensively in the PC gaming environment and are incorporated into CBTs (**C**omputer **B**ased **T**raining) and CD-based encyclopedias.

Multimedia PC

A multimedia PC could be defined as a computer that includes stereo sound (speakers) and a CD drive. PCs that are sold with the **MPC** label meet the stringent requirements of the Multimedia PC Marketing Council.

Older computer systems can be upgraded to meet multimedia specifications by installing a CD drive, a sound card and shielded speakers, which could be purchased separately or together in a multimedia upgrade kit.

The advantage of purchasing the kit over buying the components individually is that, the CD controller card and sound card have been configured and tested to avoid potential conflicts with each other, and the correct cables are included.

Sound Boards

From the very first PC, sound was possible although very limited by the small speaker embedded in the PC's case. There were even early programs that attempted to make our computers speak, but for the most part, they just beeped. Thanks to the new sound boards (adaptors), a whole new world of sounds and music are available to us. A sound card is an expansion board that will allow you to record and play back bits of sound. The de facto standard for sound card compatibility in PCs is Creative Labs' Sound Blaster. The sounds are saved to files, usually with multimedia extensions like: **WAV** (Windows sound files) or a **MIDI** (Music Instrument Digital Interface) extension. An example of this type of file would be: **chime.wav**. Digital audio files like Windows WAV files contain the actual sound waves that have been converted into a digital format. In their native uncompressed format these files can take up considerable storage space.

Examples of other proprietary sound files would include MAC **AIFF** files and Sun's **AU** format.

Multimedia Speakers

While the sound card generates the sounds, it's the speaker that allows us to hear the sound. The types of speakers available for today's PCs are unlimited. Most PC speakers will be stereo, some powered by the sound card itself, while other speakers require an external power supply. Whatever your choice, it's important the speaker is properly shielded to avoid interfering with other components such as your monitor.

Digital Cameras

Unlike traditional cameras that record images on film, digital cameras capture still and video images in an electronic format, which they store on flash memory cards, floppy disk or on the computer's hard drive. As with all digital devices, there is a maximum resolution and number of colors that can be represented. The images are typically transferred to the computer via a serial or USB cable. Many of the newer cameras also include features like built in microphones.

Digital PC cameras are becoming increasingly more popular and are now included as standard equipment on many PCs.

The basic criteria that you will want to look for when selecting a digital PC camera is:

- Does it support up to 16 million colors?
- Does it support resolution of at least 352x228?
- Does it support between 25fps and 30fps (frames per second)?
- Does it come with a good software package?
- Does it come with a stable base that enables you to pivot and move the camera easily
- Does it come with easy-to-understand installation instructions?

DVD

In an effort to meet the needs for higher capacity storage media a new type of optical disc technology (DVDs) was created. The DVD has the same overall dimensions of a CD, but has significantly higher capacities. DVDs are also double sided, whereas CDs are single sided. At minimum, the capacity of a DVD is between 700 to 800% that of a CD-ROM because it uses a much shorter wavelength and the tracks and pits are more than twice as dense.

If you are considering installing or upgrading a PC to include a DVD, you should be aware of the following system requirements. The PC should be based on a Pentium II 400 processor or equivalent at a minimum. The system should also have ample RAM installed: at least 32 MB, and more would be better! The system should also be equipped with a good high-end sound card as well. Installing a DVD into a system with anything less will either not work at all or at best yield a very undesirable level of quality.

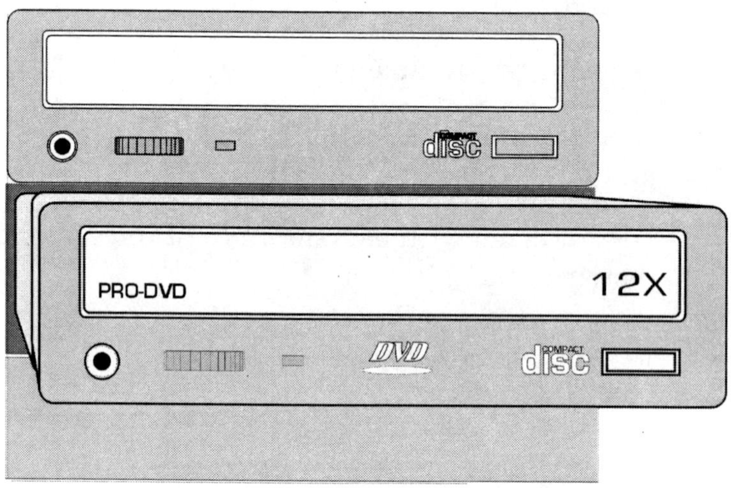

Pointing Devices

Mouse

The mouse is a device used to position the cursor or pointer on screen. Using a mouse is relatively easy. When you slide the mouse left across the table or mouse pad the pointer moves to the left hand side of the screen. Slide it to the right, and the mouse moves to the right. Pushing the mouse forward or back causes the pointer to move up and down.

Seeing the cursor move in the same direction as the mouse makes the mouse much more instinctive and precise than the cursor keys. When using the cursor keys, you tell the computer what direction to move with the cursor. When using a mouse, you are not giving the computer a direction you're giving it an exact position to place the cursor or pointer.

Depending on the type of mouse, it will also have a number of buttons on the top, which are used in different ways. For example, in the Paint Program, the left button might be for drawing and the right button would be for erasing.

There are generally two different types of mice. The mechanical mouse has a ball on the bottom. When you slide the mouse, the ball rolls against a set of rollers inside the mouse. One roller will pick up the side-to-side movement. The other will sense the up-and-down movement. The rollers are both connected to axles. Each axle is then connected to an encoder wheel. By telling how fast and how far those wheels are turning, the system can then determine how fast and far you have moved the mouse.

The second type of mouse is the optical mouse. It does not have a ball on the bottom. Instead, an optical mouse shoots a beam of infrared light. This type of mouse requires a special reflective pad with a grid painted on it

Joy Stick

A joystick is a simple, limited controller used mainly for playing games. The basic joystick design is a moveable rod sticking out of a pad, with a couple of buttons attached to it.

Light Pens

Light pens are pointing devices that look like a pen. They are attached to the computer via a long cord. Light pens allow you to touch and interact directly with the screen. These pointing devices take advantage of the fact that the computer always knows precisely where the scanning electron beam is on the screen.

The pen itself has a photo detector in the tip. This photo detector is designed to be fast enough to detect when the electron beam sweeps past it. The computer can then calculate the X and the Y position of the light pen. When the light pen is pressed against the screen, it activates a switch in the very tip of the pen. This switch is roughly analogous to the function of a mouse button. Depending on the type of pen, it may have at least one or two additional switches that can be programmed like the mouse button and utilized for different purposes depending on the program or software.

Scanners

A scanner is a device that transfers paper images and text into the computer. The scanner does this by converting the images and text into digital information. Scanners are rated by two factors: the size of the grid they break the image into and how many different shades those dots can be. The actual grid size is measured in dots per inch. Usually, a single number refers to both the horizontal and the vertical measurements. The number of shades on a non-color scanner is referred to as the "gray scale." In the case of a color scanner, color resolution is referred to by the number of bits or the total number of colors those bits can represent. For example, an 8-bit color scanner is the same as a 256-color scanner.

There are generally three types of scanners: hand held, flatbed, and drum scanners.

Hand-held Scanners

By far the most affordable scanners are hand-held scanners. These are simple, hand-held devices, which are dragged across the page you wish to scan.

Flatbed Scanners

Flatbed scanners are very similar to office photocopiers, having a large glass surface on which the original can be placed face down. The document is not moved. Instead, the scanning head is moved past the document at a precise speed. This ensures a smoother scan. The cost of a flatbed scanner is considerably more than that of the hand-held scanner. Flatbed scanners were designed for more than casual scanning needs and are generally worth the additional cost.

Drum Scanners

Drum scanners are similar to a laser printer running in reverse order. Drum scanners keep the scanning head stationary and use a transport mechanism to move the document past the scanning head.

Modems

A modem is the most common type of hardware to interface with a serial port. It enables computers to communicate over standard telephone lines. Modems take the incoming analog data signal from the telephone lines and convert it to a digital format that the computer understands.

A modem allows you to access other computers attached to modems at remote locations. Anywhere you can reach by a phone, your computer may now also be able to reach. The modem gives you the ability to transfer files between distant computers. It also allows you to have access to a wide range and variety of computer networks, bulletin boards, and other specially-designed services.

The word "modem" is actually derived from two words. The first, "**Mo**dulate," means to adapt and to vary the pitch of a sound. A modem adapts data from the cable to a telephone line by creating a tone of varying pitch. "**Dem**odulate," the second word, means to interpret this tone back into data. A modem does both, modulating data going out and interpreting the modulated data that comes in.

Just like all other peripheral PC devices, modems have evolved over the years, getting faster, cheaper and sometimes smaller. However, they still serve the same basic purpose: connecting computers over long distances as if they were hooked up locally via their serial ports.

PC Modems

PC modems are divided into three basic types: external, internal, and acoustic. Most PC modems, regardless of whether they are internal or external, are usually serial devices. External modems can be attached to any serial port. However, you must configure your software for that port. For example, you must set the software for COM1 or COM2. Serial ports are often referred to as RS 232 ports.

- **External Modems** - As the name implies, external modems are peripheral devices that are attached to the serial port of the computer. These are very popular because they can be hooked up to any type of computer with a serial port. They also have a series of LEDs that display status information, such as the modem speed or whether the modem is set to answer the phone or the state of incoming signals.

- **Internal modems** - Internal modems contain the same circuitry as external modems. The difference is that while an external modem is housed in its own casing and attached to the system's serial port, an internal modem is a board that fits into any open expansion slot on the motherboard. Internal modems are generally cheaper than external modems and don't tie up any serial ports.

- **Acoustic Modems** - Acoustic modems are all but obsolete. Unlike today's modems, acoustic modems did not plug directly into a phone jack but were built with a "cradle" for the phone headset. The computer user would dial the phone number manually, as if placing a normal call, then place the headset in the modem's cradle. The modem would then communicate with tones through the headset.

Modem Speed

Today's modems are rated for performance according to their **baud rate**. The term baud rate is a bit confusing. Early modems could only send out one bit per second, so the baud rate and bits per second measurement were the same. Baud rate became the general term for referring to modem speed. This is misleading because today's baud rates actually refer to the number of bits per second a modem can transmit.

Since the modem was introduced in early 80s, the speed of the data transmission has constantly been improved. Gone are the days of the 300, 1200 and 2400 baud modems. These have all become, for the most part, obsolete. Today's modems run at baud rates greater than 14.4, which translates to greater than 14,000 bits per second. Modem speed can also be improved beyond the rated speeds through the use of data compression techniques.

Another important factor that affects the speed of modems is the version of the UART chip that is installed on the serial card. UART is short for Universal Asynchronous Receiver/ Transmitter. There are three main UART chips: **8250**, **16450** and **16550**.

If you find yourself troubleshooting a modem that is not transferring data at the full rated speed, check the version of the UART chip and replace it with the newest and fastest. In most cases, this would be the 16550 chip.

There are also two other chips that you will find installed on most serial cards, the 1488 and 1489. Both the 1488 and 1489 chips are very sensitive to power surges caused by electric spikes and lightning storms. These chips are very inexpensive, about a dollar a piece, but they are usually soldered in and not easily replaced.

AT Command Set

When modems were first introduced for PCs in the early 80s, they were programmed with a set of commands written to control the various functions and settings of the modem. Originally this set of commands was developed by the Hayes Company and became known as the AT Command Set.

As other companies started manufacturing PC modems, they used the same AT command set and soon the AT command set became the *de facto* industry standard. However, the AT command set can vary between different manufacturers and is specific to each modem type. The AT in the AT command set actually stands for Attention Code. Listed below are two of the more common AT commands:

AT Z sets a modem back to its default.

AT D tells the modem to dial a specified number.

The standard Hayes compatible code to dial is **ATDxxxxxxx.** A **T** is sometimes added to signify tone dial. The following is a list of the more common AT commands.

AT Commands	
A	Answer the phone immediately.
D	Dial a phone number and then wait for connection.
E	Set command echoing (0=off, 1=on)
H	Hang up phone line = (HO), Pick up phone line = (H1)
L	Set speaker volume (both 0 and 1 = low, 2 = medium, 3 = high)
M	Speaker control (0 = off, 1 = on while connecting, 2 = always on, 3 = on until a carrier is detected).
V	Set type of return codes (0 = numeric, 1 = verbose/words)
Z	Reset parameters and register settings.
&C	Data Carrier Detect Control (0 = always on, 1 = only when a carrier is detected.)
&F	Reset parameters and settings to factory defaults.
&W	Write current parameter values and settings.
+++	Break signal, change from data mode to command mode.

Modem Status Signals

The following list of acronyms are used in conjunction with the display lights (LEDs) on the modem to identify operational status conditions:

Acronym Descriptions	
AA	Auto answer mode
CA	Compression active
CD	Carrier detect
CTR	Clear to send
DTR	Data terminal ready
EC	Error control active
HS	High speed (greater than > 4,800 bps)
LB	Low battery
MR	Modem ready
OH	Off hook
PWR	Power on
RI	Ringing
RNG	Ringing
RTS	Request to send
RXD	Receiving data
SD	Transmitting (sending) data
TM	Test mode
TD	Transmitting (sending) data
TR	Terminal ready
TXD	Transmitting (sending) data

Summary

In this section we discussed some of the most common peripheral devices, such as monitors, keyboards, modems, and multimedia hardware.

We mentioned that today's monitors are still built around old technology called cathode ray technology (CRT). Most of the monitors in the marketplace today are non-interlaced, meaning that they incorporate a very high refresh rate to eliminate flicker.

Modems are devices that act as an interface between your computer and standard telephone lines. They convert digital data from your computer into analog data suitable for transmission over telephone lines.

Some of the newest peripheral hardware today falls under the broad category of multimedia, which includes CD and DVD drives, sound boards, external speakers and digital cameras.

Review Questions

1. What is the resolution of the typical VGA monitor?

   A. 800x600
   B. 720x480
   C. 640x480
   D. 640x200

2. Which type of display will yield the best performance?

   A. XGA
   B. SVGA
   C. VGA
   D. CGA

3. What is another term for monitor?

   A. TV
   B. CBT
   C. Tube
   D. CRT

4. What modem AT command will set a modem to default settings?

   A. AT D
   B. AT Z
   C. AT DD
   D. AT S

5. Which of the following is the newest version of the UART chip?

   A. 16450
   B. 16550
   C. 16850
   D. 14850

6. What are the two types of switches used on most keyboards?

   A. Mechanical and infrared
   B. Mechanical and capacitive
   C. Click and non-click
   D. Magnet and wireless

7. A 14.4 modem should transmit how many bits per second?

   A. 14,000-15,000
   B. 140-150
   C. 1400-1500
   D. 140,000-150,000

8. The modem acronym **RTS** represents which of the following?

   A. Request for Information
   B. Request Transmit Signal
   C. Request to Send
   D. Request to Save

9. A **.WAV** file extension is associated with which of the following vendors?

   A. Sun Systems
   B. Apple
   C. Microsoft
   D. Waffle

10. LCD refers to which of the following technologies?

    A. Liquid Cryro Display
    B. Liquid Crystal Display
    C. Long Computer Division
    D. Lapse Critical Design

DISASSEMBLY / REASSEMBLY

Section 7

Disassembly and Reassembly

Section 7: Disassembly and Reassembly

Introduction

Proper computer disassembly requires organization and attention to detail. It is not difficult to take apart a computer, but, if you do not take careful steps as you disassemble, you may damage components and reassembly will be complicated. No matter how many times you have disassembled a computer, you are liable to create problems for yourself if your work is not organized. Simple steps will help you to properly organize your work as you disassemble. These steps will make the reassembly process much easier.

Objectives

When you've completed this section, you will be able to:

- List procedures that will optimize PC disassembly and reassembly
- Properly disassemble a personal computer
- Properly reassemble a personal computer
- Test for proper operation

Before You Begin

Attention to detail is crucial as you prepare for disassembly of a PC. There are several steps you need to take before you begin to prevent you from making some common mistakes:

- First, always have a **complete back-up** of your system software and files before you remove the first screw from the case.
- Secure the **proper tools** for disassembly. Using the right tools not only saves time, but also prevents damage to the equipment.
- **Record all information for your system's CMOS program.** This may be one of the most important steps you take before disassembly. If the CMOS loses its memory, you'll need that information to reconfigure it.
- Write down information about any peripheral boards, noting the location and positions of any switches and jumper settings. It may be helpful to draw diagrams and pictures.

Disassembly

Now that you have taken the proper steps to prepare for disassembly, you may begin:

- Turn the computer and all peripherals off. Do not disconnect the power supply until you are ready to remove it from the case. The power supply connection is a good, reliable connection to ground.
- Wear your anti-static wrist strap. If you do not have an anti-static wrist strap, touch the power supply metal case. If it is still plugged into an outlet, it will help reduce your electrostatic potential.
- If you need to remove the monitor, do it carefully and place it in a safe spot.
- Locate, remove, and store the screws that hold the cover in place. On most units you will find some retaining screws in the back. Be careful not to confuse them with the screws that secure the power supply.
- Remove the cover gently. Most covers may be removed by applying a gentle lifting action at the back of the PC. Be careful not to damage any of the components inside.
- Start taking notes. Draw diagrams and label wires.

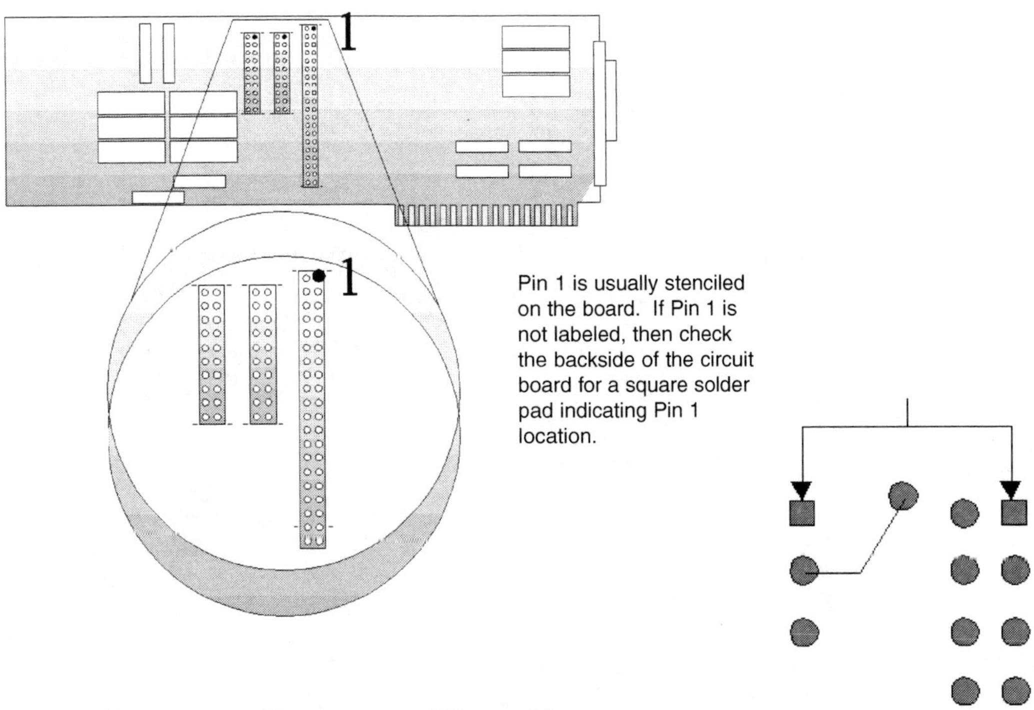

Example of Disassembly Wiring Notes

Remove Boards

Removing the expansion boards is a simple and straight-forward procedure as long as you follow these steps:

- Gently remove all cables attached to the boards. Make a note about the orientation of the colored stripe.
- Remove the retaining screw.
- Grasp the top edge of the board, front and back with both hands, then pull the board gently UPWARDS with a rocking motion. Do NOT rock the board from side to side.

Disconnect Cables

Before you start disconnecting cables, remember to diagram carefully how they are laid out. An improperly connected power cable may cause a short.

There are two different types of cables connected to a drive:

- A *power* cable, which brings energy to the drive from the power supply.
- A *data* cable (the flat ribbon type) connected to a controller.

None of these cables require a great deal of force to pull out, but some of the connectors may have a plastic latch that secures them in place. If your connector has a latch, gently pick the latch with a small screw driver and pull it out with a gentle rocking action.

Remove Drives

There are four different types of drives that may be installed in your PC:

- Floppy drives
- Hard drive
- Tape back up
- CD

All drives will be connected to the computer in much the same way. Locate and remove the screws that secure each drive to the chassis. Generally there are four of them: two on either side of the drive. Gently pull the drive out of the metal frame.

Remove the Power Supply

In addition to the power cables that you already removed from the drives, the power supply has two other cables that connect to the motherboard. These cables need to be removed next. Be very careful to label them properly since improper reassembly will damage the motherboard. These two cables may already be labeled **P8** and **P9**. Tower-type cases may have an additional cable going to the back of the computer's power switch. Once the cables are disconnected, locate and remove the screws which secure the power supply to the frame, and remove it from the case. If you are working on an ATX power supply, you will remove the single P1 connector. This new, single connector eliminates the possibility of confusing the two cables.

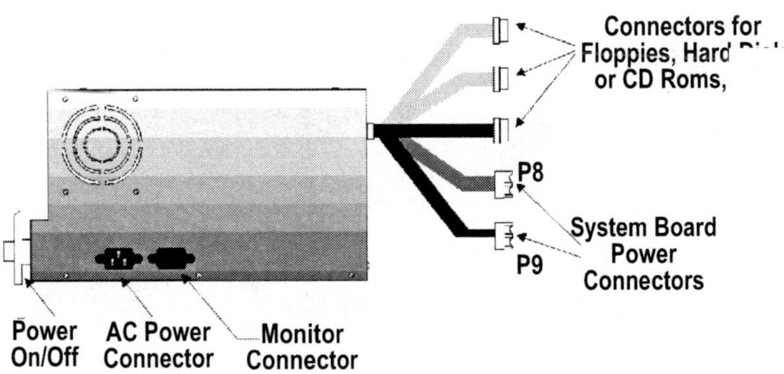

AT Power Supply

Remove the Motherboard

There may be several small, colored cables still attached to the motherboard. These are used to power the LED lights in the front of the case, the speaker, and the keylock, for example. Not all motherboards have batteries, but if it does and you have to remove it, remember that you will need to rewrite the CMOS data when you restart the computer. There may be a combination of screws and plastic spacers securing the motherboard. Once you remove the screws it should slide over with ease. If no spacers are visible, the board should lift out of the case as soon as all screws are removed.

Reassembly

Reassembly may seem like an uncomplicated process: simply put the pieces back together in the reverse order that you disassembled them. But as easy and straightforward as it may seem, it is during reassembly that mistakes are most often made. If you are replacing components, switches and jumpers may need to be configured before installation. This increases the odds that you will make mistakes. One very good piece of advice is to take your time. If you rush, you are more likely to make mistakes. The following is a list of common oversights:

Improper Cable Connections

Computer components are very unforgiving when it comes to mistakes in attaching cables between them. Make sure that you link the right objects and the cable itself is attached correctly and seated properly. Data cables carry a different color lead in one of the extreme edges. This lead attaches to pin # 1 on the connector ONLY. Most board connectors have numbers stenciled on them for easy identification.

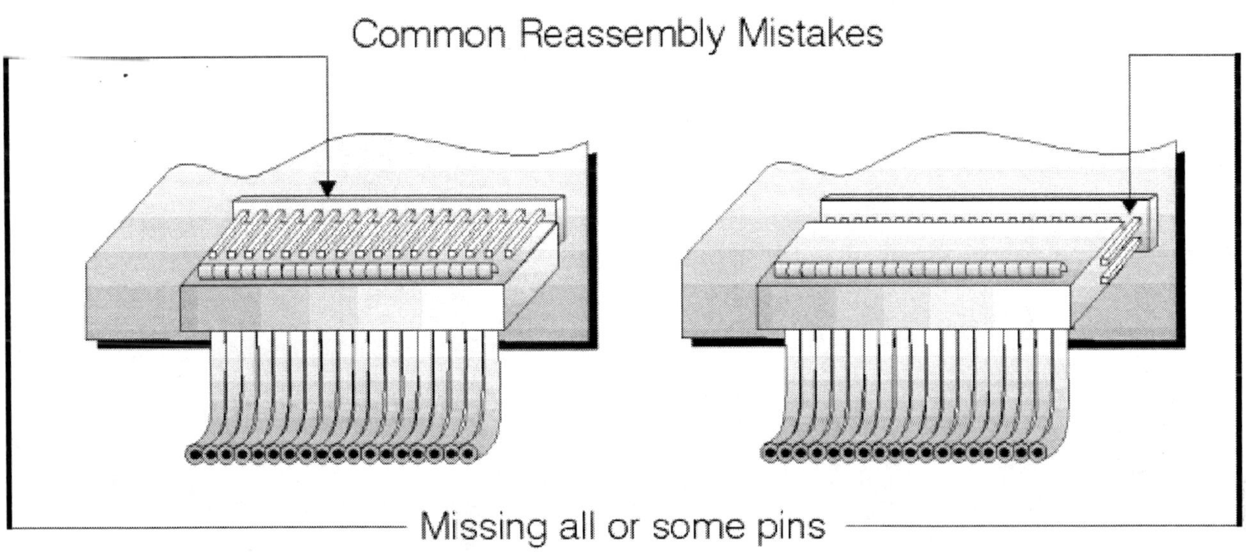

Common Reassembly Mistakes

Power Supply Not Connected to Motherboard

This could potentially be a dangerous mistake. There are two small cables labeled **P8** and **P9** that carry power to the motherboard.

This problem will not occur with ATX power supplies since they use the simple P1 connector.

Power Supply Not Connected to Hard Drive

The screen will display a Disk Boot failure message. This is an easily corrected error.

Improper Motherboard Seating

Anytime that you insert the motherboard back into the case, make sure that it is not touching the frame. This could cause it to short circuit. Also, check to be sure the motherboard is properly positioned on the spacers.

Forgot to Connect the Battery

This oversight will prevent you from saving the configuration of the system.

Proper Seating of ICs (chips) *Note the graphic below.

When replacing one chip with an identical chip, the most important thing to remember is the orientation of the chip as it applies to the socket. Most CPUs have a notched corner that must be aligned with a corresponding notch in the socket.

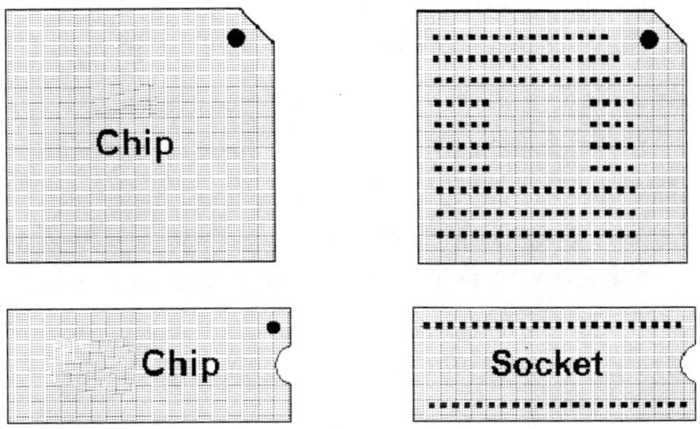

PROPER SEATING OF ICS (CHIPS)

* The notch of the IC must match the corresponding notch on the socket.

Final Check List

The following is a list of commonly overlooked check points:

- Connect the ribbon cable to the floppy drive(s).Remember, the floppy cable will determine whether a drive will be identified as the 'A' drive or 'B' drive.
- Connect the ribbon cable to the controller card.
- Connect the power cable to the floppy drive.
- Connect all cables and power to the hard drive.
- Replace all slot covers. Computer manufacturers spend large amounts of time and money engineering case design to create optimal air flow. If empty slots are not covered, the air flow may change enough to cause heat related problems.
- Check all connections for the reset button, power LEDs, etc.
- Plug in the keyboard.
- Plug in the monitor.

These steps may seem basic, but because they are basic, they are very often overlooked. Remember to always take a systematic, step-by-step approach to reassembly and you will not forget to take each necessary step

Testing the System

Once you have completed reassembly and reviewed the final check list to make sure all of the system components are properly connected, you may power on the system. Allow the system to boot up and begin the operating system. Test the different system components to make sure they are functioning correctly. Is the keyboard working? Is the system responding to the mouse? Are you able to open software programs and files?

If each system component is functioning properly, you have successfully disassembled and reassembled a personal computer!

Summary

In this section we discussed the procedures you should follow before, during and after the disassembly and reassembly of a personal computer. Always ensure that you have a complete system back-up before disassembling a PC.

Record the system CMOS settings. Choose proper tools and create a clean and static-free work environment. Document and note configuration settings of boards before removing. Follow careful steps as you disassemble and reassemble the PC.

By taking a systematic approach, you will make the process much easier and reduce the possibility for error. After reassembly, test your system to ensure that all components are functioning properly.

Review Questions

1. What connectors attach to the AT system board in most internal PC power supplies?

   A. P1 and P2
   B. F5 and F8
   C. P8 and P9
   D. Positive and Negative

2. How is Pin number 1 on a peripheral circuit board usually designated?

   A. Round solder joint
   B. Red arrow
   C. Square solder pad
   D. Triangle

3. It is very important to record all the information from your system _______ before disassembly?

   A. Floppy disk
   B. CMOS
   C. RAM
   D. DRAM

4. When inserting a chip (IC) into a socket, the notch may go in either direction.

   A. True
   B. False

5. The colored strip on a ribbon cable indicates which of the following?

   A. Pin 0
   B. Pin 1
   C. Negative
   D. Positive

6. When removing a battery from the system board, what must be done first?

   A. Secure a new battery.
   B. Record CMOS settings.
   C. Short the battery in the case.
   D. Remove the ground wire.

7. Recording jumper settings is not crucial because they are usually set for defaults.

   A. True
   B. False

8. After assembling a PC, you are asked to enter system configuration each time you boot. What could be the problem?

   A. No serial port.
   B. Reversed hard disk cable.
   C. Forgot to connect battery.
   D. Forgot to connect P8 and P9.

Section 8

DOS

Section 8: DOS

Introduction

Since its introduction in the early 1980s, DOS (Disk Operating System) has fast become the most widely-used operating system in the world. Literally hundreds of thousands of programs have been written for the DOS environment. With millions of users worldwide, DOS affects more people than any other software product ever developed. There have been volumes and volumes written about DOS. The following section will focus on the key concepts and functions of DOS.

Objectives

When you've completed this section, you will be able to:

- Understand DOS file and directory naming conventions
- Use basic DOS commands
- Discuss the use and contents of the **CONFIG.SYS** and **AUTOEXEC.BAT** configuration files
- Understand and create DOS batch file programs

IMPORTANT NOTE

This section is OPTIONAL. DOS is NOT covered in the A+ Certification Exams. While DOS is not explicitly covered in the A+ Exams, knowledge of DOS commands is still extremely helpful for PC technicians and support staff. For example, when a Windows-based system does not boot correctly, a basic understanding of DOS commands will allow you to troubleshoot and recover the system.

What is an Operating System?

Now that we have talked about all the different individual hardware components that make up a personal computer, it's time to talk about how we bring them to "life". Perhaps the best way to describe an operating system is to discuss life without one. We said in the previous section that a PC was made up of various components like the system board, processor, power supply, hard disk and floppies. Well, once all these components have been assembled, just what can we do? The answer is: not much. At this point the system is just a bunch of hardware without any functionality, except maybe as a good boat anchor or a very large paperweight! Before any work can be done on the microcomputer, the operating system must be present. It is the job of the operating system, the (OS) to bring the hardware to life. The operating system is a computer program that, after being loaded into the PC, manages all other programs. These other programs are called applications. An example of these applications would be word processors, spreadsheets, games, etc. In addition to managing the applications on the computer the OS also provides us with an interface so that we can interact with the operating system itself. This is usually done via a command language or a graphical interface.

Another primary function of the operating system is to organize the way in which information is processed and stored on the computer. A disk operating system allows users to perform certain functions such as naming files, copying files, formatting disks, creating folders and subdirectories and deleting files.

DOS: A Brief History

DOS (Disk Operating System) was the first widely installed and accepted operating system in the personal computer arena. Actually, it was referred to as PC-DOS. It was co-developed by Paul Allen and Bill Gates and their then up start company Microsoft. The operating system was selected by IBM for use in its first line of personal computers. Fortunately for Microsoft, the IBM agreement did not preclude them from marketing an almost identical version called MS- DOS to the rest of the world.

Both PC-DOS and MS-DOS were non-graphical command line based operating systems. This means that all interaction is done from a blank screen through a series of "not-so-user-friendly" commands. In the early days other programs called menus were written in attempt to simplify this process. It wasn't until the first release of Microsoft Windows, that PCs had a true graphical interface. The first several versions of Windows were really just another application that ran on top of the DOS operating system.

Starting DOS

When you turn the power on, the computer runs a series of self-diagnostic tests that check for hardware configuration problems. Once the tests are completed, the computer is ready for use. This process is commonly known as ***booting***.

The first step involves the activation of the **Power On Self-Test** or **POST**. **POST** is a program recorded on a ROM chip (BIOS), which instructs the computer to diagnose the hardware. **POST** needs RAM to work, so one of the first things **POST** will check is the lower contiguous portion of RAM. The numeric count that you see on screen at the beginning of the boot process is the computer testing the installed memory (RAM) chips.

Next, **POST** analyzes the computer's setup information, which is stored in a special kind of chip called the CMOS (Complementary Metal Oxide Semiconductor). The CMOS contains information about the configuration of the hard disk and other hardware, and also about the system's date and time settings. Information or software programs stored on a non-volatile chip (such as CMOS) is called **firmware**. The non-volatile nature of the chip insures that the information stored within the chip will not be lost after power is removed. The information contained in CMOS can be stored for several years as long as a minimal source of power such as a battery is available. Any time the battery is removed, the CMOS information is lost.

BIOS

The BIOS tests your system whenever you power-up the PC. The BIOS start-up procedure consists of these steps.

Step 1	*Low Memory Test*	If this test fails, it means the lowest bank of RAM has failed.
Step 2	*Scan for other BIOS*	Some installed boards may contain their own ROM BIOS. The system BIOS searches for any additional BIOS.
Step 3	*Yield to other BIOS*	The system BIOS yields to other BIOS it may find before it checks the main system.
Step 4	*Inventory the system*	Reads the CMOS and checks all hardware (drives, memory, etc) that it will control. This may take several minutes, so be patient.
Step 5	*Test the system*	This is the diagnostic part of the BIOS. Any failed device will generate an error message at this point.
Step 6	*Load DOS*	Before the BIOS loads the operating system, it first loads DOS. The system looks for a drive that's ready. (It looks in the boot-up sequence you've chosen in CMOS...first Drive A, then Drive C, for example.)
Step 7	*DOS loads Master Boot Record (MBR), then DOS Boot Record (DBR)*	The DBR contains the hidden files IO.SYS and MSDOS.SYS.
Step 8	*IO.SYS loads MS DOS.SYS, CONFIG.SYS, then COMMAND.COM*	CONFIG.SYS loads device drivers which can shut down a system if they have a bug. If the COMMAND.COM has been corrupted somehow (wrong version, contaminated by a virus for example), you'll get a Bad or Missing Command.Com error message and your system will not boot.
Step 9	*COMMAND.COM loads AUTOEXEC.BAT*	TSRs such as anti-virus programs, network shells, protocol stacks, disk cache programs and disk compression programs are loaded by the AUTOEXEC. BAT. Problems with any of these programs will cause your system not to boot.

Once the system checks are successfully completed, another program called the bootstrap loader looks for the operating system (in this case DOS) and loads into memory the necessary files to make it run.

- The first file loaded is **IO.SYS**. It controls the basic input/ output services DOS provides.
- **MSDOS.SYS** is loaded next, which looks for the **CONFIG.SYS** file and loads it into memory.
- The last file is **COMMAND.COM**. This file is the user interface to DOS and evaluates the validity of keyboard and batch file commands. Internal DOS commands are those commands that are built into the **COMMAND.COM** program. Examples of these commands are **DIR, COPY, CD, CLS**. As the name implies, these commands are available as soon as the **COMMAND.COM** program is loaded. External DOS commands are those that must be physically present on the hard disk. The DOS **FORMAT** and **FDISK** programs are both examples of external DOS programs.

If the presented commands are illegal, **COMMAND.COM** issues an error message on screen. **COMMAND.COM** also checks to see if the batch file **AUTOEXEC.BAT** is present in the boot directory.

Booting the Computer

The PC boot process starts when a small program within the BIOS chip looks for an active partition and loads the operating system. There are two methods for booting a computer: *cold* and *warm* booting.

Cold Boot

Cold booting occurs when the computer's power switch is turned on. The effect of a cold boot is that it brings the system to the very beginning of the boot process, beginning with the **POST**. This may become necessary when the computer stops responding to any commands, including warm boots.

Warm Boot

A warm boot bypasses the first two system tests and goes directly to the bootstrap loader (the point where DOS loads). A warm boot is triggered by pressing the *Ctrl, Alt*, and *Del* keys at the same time.

CTRL + ALT + DEL

Rebooting the computer should be used only as a last resort. Any information in open application files could be lost when rebooting takes place.

POST Audio Signal	Probable Cause
No beep, nothing happens	Bad power supply or power supply not plugged in.
Continuous beep	Bad power supply or keyboard stuck.
Repeating short beep	Bad power supply.
1 long beep, 1 short beep	System board has failed.
1 long beep, 2 short beeps	Display adapter or cable is missing or has failed.
1 short beep, no boot	Floppy drive adapter has failed.
2 short beeps (PS/2)	Configuration error.

Creating Boot Disks

Every once in a blue moon your system may refuse to boot. There are numerous reasons that could cause this. If you are prepared with an emergency boot disk for such an occasion, you will save yourself a lot of anxious moments

The steps for preparing a boot disk are as follows:

- Format a floppy disk using the **/S** switch. Put a blank diskette into your floppy drive.
- Type **format A: /S**
- Copy the **AUTOEXEC.BAT** and **CONFIG.SYS** files to the newly **/S**-formatted disk.
- Copy any files and drivers that are essential to the boot process such as **IO.SYS**, **COMMAND.COM** and other files necessary for your particular system.
- Label the disk appropriately and write-protect it by flipping the black switch on the bottom of the diskette.
- Store the disk in a safe and readily accessible spot.

By default, every time the computer is started, it searches in drive A for a bootable floppy disk. In the event that the hard drive does not boot, you are able to access the system from drive A. This allows you the opportunity to look for the problem.

Understanding DOS Files and Directories

The two primary roles of DOS (Disk Operating System) are the storing and the retrieving of data. In order to do this, DOS must provide a common platform for file storage and retrieval. This common platform allows software programs to access information easily and quickly.

DOS File System

A computer running the DOS file system is roughly analogous to a file cabinet system. The hard disk and floppy disk are used to store data electronically and use many of the same conventions used in the file cabinet system. Every file on the disk has a unique name, just like a letter in a file cabinet. The files are placed in directories on the hard disk, which makes them easier to find, much the same as a file cabinet might use a group of file folders to store individual letters.

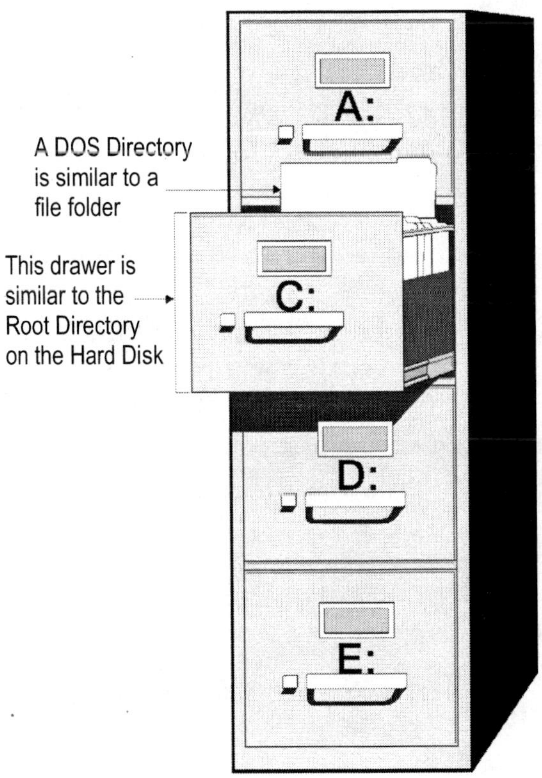

A DOS File

A DOS file is a collection of related information that is referenced by a name. The electronic file can contain various pieces of related information which is grouped in an electronic file folder referenced by the file's name. These files can serve many purposes. For example, a word processor file might hold all the sentences in a letter or a database file might contain the names, addresses and phone numbers of the customers for a business. Much like an office person would use color-coded labels to indicate the type of information contained in a folder, DOS uses file names that also indicate what kind of information that particular file holds.

DOS File Name Conventions

The DOS operating system applies rules or conventions to the way the file is named. A DOS file name consists of 1-8 characters followed by a period and an optional 3 character extension.

Examples: **install.exe, readme.txt, work.doc.**

The period and the extension are optional, but are normally used. The 8-character name portion of a file usually provides an association or description of the contents of the file. The 3-character extension after the period will traditionally describe the type of file and its format.

By default, the DOS operating system ensures that every file on your hard disk has a name. Whenever a file is created, the File Allocation Table (FAT) stores information about the file and the physical location where it can be found This is similar to a book's table of contents. The DOS operating system will also place each file in a special structure called a directory.

File Name Rules

As mentioned earlier, DOS applies certain rules for creating files. Listed below are the rules for creating legal DOS file names

- A file name can consist of the following items: a name from 1-8 characters, an optional extension of 1-3 characters, and a period between the name and the extension.
- The following characters are allowed in a file name: the letters A-Z (lower case letters are transformed into upper case automatically), the numbers 0-9, and the special characters: $ # & @ ! ( ) - { } _ .
- DOS reserves certain ASCII character codes for other uses and does not let them be part of a file name. These are called illegal characters. The following are illegal characters: any control character, the space character, and + = / [ ] " : ; ? * \ > < | .

Reserved Names

It is important to understand that certain names are used by the operating system and these names cannot be used for other purposes like a file name. Listed below are the DOS reserved file names:

com1, com2, com3, com4, con, aux, clock$, lpt1, lpt2, lpt3, lpt4, nul, prn.

Commonly Used DOS File Extensions

- A file containing executable commands will usually have an extension of **.com, .exe** or **.bat.**
- A file that the actual operating system uses will usually have an extension of **.sys**.
- A text file or a user-generated document will usually have an extension of **.txt** or **.doc.**
- A file that is a backup of another file will generally have a **.bak** extension.

DOS Commands

DOS commands that are typed into the computer from the keyboard allow the user to instruct the operating system to perform an operation. Some of these commands can be a bit overwhelming to the new user. However, with a little practice the commands can be an effective tool in managing the DOS environment.

NOTE: From a DOS command prompt you can press the **F3** function key to recall the last command typed. Later versions of DOS expanded this functionality with the **DOSKEY** program. **DOSKEY** is a TSR program that allows you to scroll through previous commands by using the up and down arrows.

DIR Command - Viewing DOS Files

The DOS **dir** command allows you to view files that have been stored on the hard disk or a floppy disk. By simply typing **dir** followed by a carriage return all of the files in the current directory will be displayed. The **dir** command can also be used to sort output based on a given search criteria, such as: extensions, file names, the size of the files, or any of the file's special attributes. To view information about the use of the DOS **dir** command, type **dir/?**. This will bring up the **dir** help screen.

TYPE Command

After locating a file using the DOS **dir** command, the **type** command can be used to read the file's contents. The proper syntax for the use of the **type** command is: **type**, space, the drive letter, followed by the path and the file name.

> *Example*: To display the contents of a file called **readme.txt** located in the **C:\procomm** subdirectory of the hard disk (C:\), type the following: **type C:\procomm\readme.txt**

The **type** command should only be used with standard ASCII files. Using this command with **.com** or **.exe** files will yield erroneous results and should be avoided.

REN Command - Renaming Files

The DOS **ren** command allows you to change the name of a file that has already been created on the disk. The rename command can be very useful when a file needs to be updated and the original version needs to be saved for backup purposes. This is often done in the case of configuration files, such as **.INI** files, the **AUTOEXEC.BAT**, and the **CONFIG.SYS**. The syntax for the rename command is: **ren**, space, the drive letter, path, old file name, space and then the new file name.

> *Example*: To rename the **AUTOEXEC.BAT** file found in the root directory of C to **AUTOEXEC.BAT** you would type **ren c:\autoexec.bat autoexec.bak**

DEL Command

The DOS **del** command allows you to remove or erase a file from a floppy or hard disk. The syntax for the delete command is **del**, space, drive letter, path, file name.

Example: To delete a file in your current directory called **helpme.txt,** you would type **del helpme.txt**.

Wild cards can also be used in conjunction with the delete command allowing for the deletion of many files with one command. Another handy option is the **/p** which can be placed at the end of the command to give the user a final chance to abort the process.

Another file which is closely related to the **del** command is the **undelete** command. As the name implies, the **undelete** command will restore any previously deleted files.

ATTRIB Command

The **attrib** command allows you to view or change a file's attributes.

Example: To use the **attrib** command to set a file called **cbt.exe**
as a "read only" file you would type **attrib +r cbt.exe**

DOS "ATTRIB" Command + extensions	Operation
ATTRIB *.*	Displays the attributes of all files in a directory.
ATTRIB +R test.dat	Assigns the *read-only* attribute to the file **test.dat**
ATTRIB +A test.dat	Assigns the *archive* attribute to the file **test.dat**
ATTRIB -R *.*	Turns off the *read-only* mode for all files in a particular directory.
ATTRIB +R A:\USERS /S	Assigns the *read-only* attribute to all files and subdirectories in **A:\USERS**
ATTRIB +H Secret.BAT	Sets the file **Secret.BAT** as a hidden file. (File will not appear in a directory listing.)

COPY Command

Occasionally the user needs the ability to copy files. The DOS **copy** command is used to copy files from one disk to another disk or from one subdirectory to another subdirectory. The format for the DOS copy command is: **copy**, space, the source drive letter, path, file name to be copied, space, destination drive letter, path.

> *Example*: The following command will copy a file named **AUTOEXEC.BAT** on the root of the C drive to the SAVE directory on the A drive: **copy c:\autoexec.bat a:\save\autoexec.bat**

Much like the other commands, wild cards can also be used with file names and the extensions. If the actual location of the source is not entered, DOS will assume that the action is to be performed in the current directory.

MOVE Command

Sometimes a file can be placed in the wrong directory or subdirectory on the hard disk. There are many ways to remedy this situation. The file could be copied to the new location, but the net result would be two copies of the same file on the hard disk. A better option is to use the **move** command. The syntax for the **move** command is: **move**, space, drive letter, path, file name, space, new drive letter, path.

> *Example*: To move a file called **report.txt** located in the **DATA** directory of the root drive C to the **ACCOUNT** directory on the same drive, you would type: **move c:\data\report.txt c:\account**.

This command would actually take the file **report.txt** and move it to the directory **c:\account**.

VER Command

Occasionally a user needs to verify the version of DOS currently in use. Usually this occurs when adding new software or confirming which commands are available. To view the version number of DOS running on a computer, from the command line, type **ver**, then press **Enter**.

CLS Command

The display of your CRT will show all previously typed commands and associated output. This clutter can be very distracting. To solve this, you can clear the screen by typing **cls**. This will clear the screen of any old information and will move the command prompt to the top of the screen.

PROMPT Command

The standard and most common command prompt shows the current drive letter followed by **:**, the actual path, and **>**. For example, if you were working in the DOS WINDOWS directory the command prompt would read as follows: **C:\WINDOWS>**

This standard prompt can be changed by the user with the use of the **prompt** command. This command can be executed either from the command line or included as part of the **AUTOEXEC.BAT** configuration file located in the root directory. The syntax for the default prompt is created by typing: **prompt=pg**

The **$p** is a DOS variable that displays the current drive letter and path. The **$g** is a variable that will display **>**. The following table shows additional variables that can be used with the prompt command:

Variable	Value
$Q	Equal sign (=)
$$	Dollar sign ($)
$T	Current time
$D	Current date
$P	Current drive letter & path
$V	DOS version number
$N	Current drive only
$G	Greater than sign (>)
$E	ASCII escape code (27)
$H	Backspace (erases last character of prompt)
$L	Less than sign (<)
$B	Pipe sign (|)
$_	Enter or linefeed

PROMPT COMMAND VARIABLES

MEM Command - Viewing Memory

Another very useful command is the DOS **mem** command. The **mem** command will display information about your memory usage. It will tell you the amount of free memory and which programs are currently loaded in memory. This information is very useful when trying to diagnose problems or when attempting to optimize available memory on your system. To execute the **mem** command, simply type **mem** at the DOS prompt and then press **Enter**.

DATE and TIME Command

A system clock is built into every PC. The system clock is responsible for recording date and time information about files and directories. Every time a file is created, saved, or modified, a date and time stamp is applied to that file. There are two commands that allow the system clock to be changed: the **date** command and the **time** command. The **date** command displays the current system date and also allows it to be changed. The **time** command displays the current time and also allows it to be changed. To execute these commands, type **time** or **date** at the DOS prompt and then press **Enter**.

Directory Commands

MD Command - Making a New Directory

The **md** command, also known as the **mkdir**, is used to make a directory or a subdirectory on a hard or floppy disk. The syntax for the **md** command is: **md**, space, directory or subdirectory name. To create a subdirectory named **programs** in your current location, you would type **md programs**

CD Command - Changing From One Directory To Another

To move into the newly created directory, you type in the DOS **cd** (change directory) command. The syntax would be **cd programs**

RD Command - Removing a Directory

The DOS **rd** command allows you to remove a directory or subdirectory from the PC's hard disk (if the directory contains NO files). The syntax for removing a subdirectory in your current location would be **rd programs**

CHKDSK Command

The DOS **chkdsk** command reports the status of a disk. It will tell you how many files are on it and how much of the disk is in use and by which files. It can also check for a lost cluster.

TREE Command

The **tree** command will display a visual representation of your hard drive directory and subdirectory structure.

VOL Command

The **vol** command will display a disk volume label.

FORMAT Command

The DOS **format** command prepares a hard disk or floppy disk to accept data. The **format** command will create sectors, tracks, and clusters on the diskette. The file allocation table, or FAT, is also created on the diskette. This table will reference the location of files and directories stored on the diskette or hard disk.

There are several options available when using the **format** command. One of the most commonly used commands is the forward slash s (**/s**), or the system option. This option places the necessary operating system files on the disk.

Example: To format the C drive, type: **format c: /s**

There are three files necessary to make a bootable diskette: **COMMAND.COM**, **MSDOS.SYS**, and **IO.SYS**. The **MSDOS.SYS** file and the **IO.SYS** file are both hidden files so they cannot be viewed using the basic **dir** command. However, these files can be viewed by using the forward slash A **(/a) option** with the **dir** command. To view these files type: **dir /a**

LABEL Command - Creating a Volume Label

At the completion of the formatting process, the DOS operating system will ask for the volume label or name to be associated with the disk. This makes for easy identification at a later date. The volume label name can be changed in the future by using the **label** command.

UNFORMAT Command

The **format** command will erase all data from the diskette. If, however, the **format** command was used inadvertently, there are several methods that can be used to restore the data.

The DOS **unformat** command will reverse the effects of a format. The **unformat** command will work as long as no changes have been made to the disk after the format. The syntax for the unformat is: **unformat**, drive letter. For example, if you wanted to unformat drive C, type **unformat C:**.

UNDELETE Command

It is also possible to recover just an individual file with the use of the **undelete** command. However, much like the **unformat**, the **undelete** should be used as soon as possible. If the space on the disk is written over by a new file, the old file cannot be recovered. The syntax for the **undelete** command is: **undelete**, drive letter, path, file name. For example, if you wanted to undelete a file named **program.txt** on drive C, type **undelete C:\program.txt**

CHKDSK & SCANDISK Command - Checking for Corrupted Disks

As a hard disk or floppy disk is used over and over again, it will eventually show signs of wear. This means that some files and directories may become corrupted. There are several DOS commands that will attempt to repair these files and directories. The two most common DOS commands for repairing corrupted files are **chkdsk** and the **scandisk.**

The **chkdsk** command will check the drive for any defective areas and display the results on the screen. The **chkdsk** command can be run a second time using the forward slash f (**/f**) option. Using the **chkdsk** program with the **/f** option will attempt to repair any defective areas on the disk.

The **scandisk** program, introduced with DOS 6.21, is a more powerful version of the **chkdsk** command. To execute either of these commands, simply type **chkdsk** or **scandisk** followed by the letter of the disk you want to check or repair. For example, if you wanted to repair a floppy disk in drive A using the **scandisk** command, type **scandisk A:**.

The **scandisk** program will display a menu allowing you to fix any errors that may have been found.

Exercise 8.1: Formatting Diskettes

OBJECTIVES

When you've completed this exercise, you will be able to:

- Format a blank diskette.
- Create a boot disk using the format system option.
- Unformat a diskette.
- Create a volume label on the diskette.

PREPARATION

Obtain a blank, high-density diskette.

Part One: *Formatting a diskette using the* FORMAT *command.*

Step 1: Change to the root directory.

- Type **cd**
- Verify your location by typing **dir**

  You should see the **AUTOEXEC.BAT** and **CONFIG.SYS** files.

Step 2: Format the diskette in drive A.

- Insert the blank diskette in drive A.
- Type **format A:**
- Press **Enter**.
- When completed, you will be asked to supply a volume name. Type in your first name. (It cannot exceed 11 characters.)
- Answer **No** to *not* format another diskette.

Step 3: **View the volume label on the newly-formatted diskette.**

- Type **dir a:** at the DOS prompt
- Press **Enter**.

Step 4: **Copy the DOSKEY.COM file from your hard disk to the floppy diskette in drive A.**

- Change to the DOS directory by typing **cd\dos**
- Press **Enter**.
- Locate the Doskey program by typing **dir doskey.com**
- Press **Enter**.
- Copy the file to a floppy diskette in drive A by typing **copy doskey.com a:**
- Verify that the file is on the diskette by typing **dir a:** Is the file listed?

Part Two: ***Formatting a diskette using the quick formatting option.***

Step 1: Change to the DOS directory.

- Type **cd\dos**
- Type **format a: /q**
- Press **Enter**.
- When prompted for a label, type **quick**
- Press **Enter**.
- Answer **No** to *not* format another diskette.

  NOTE: The quick format should have been much faster than the previous format.

- Type **dir a:**
- Examine the directory. The file that you copied to the diskette will no longer be there. Formatting a diskette erases all files on the disk.

Part Three: ***Using the* UNFORMAT *command to recover data erased by the* FORMAT *command.***

Step 1: Verify your location in the DOS directory.

- Type **cd\dos**
- Press **Enter**.
- Type **unformat a:**
- Press **Enter**.
- Answer **Yes** to update the system area.
- After the disk is unformatted, type **dir a:** The **doskey.com** file should be restored.

Part Four: *Creating a DOS bootable diskette.*

Step 1: Format the diskette in drive A using the /s system option.

- Type **format a: /s**
- Press **Enter**.
- When prompted for a volume label, type **bootable**
- Press **Enter**.

Step 2: Boot the system using the newly formatted bootable diskette.

- Restart your PC with the diskette in drive A.
- Press the **Enter** key when prompted for the date and time.

Step 3: Verify the system files on the diskette.

- Type **dir a: /a**
- Press **Enter**.
- Examine the directory. What files did the **format /s** put on the disk?

NOTE: You now have a bootable diskette that could be used to boot your PC in case something caused the boot files on your hard drive to become corrupted.

Part Five: ***Formatting a diskette using the unconditional*** **FORMAT.**

Step 1: **Remove the diskette from Drive A and reboot.**

Step 2: **Format the diskette using the /u option.**

- Type **format a: /u**
- Press **Enter**.
- When prompted for the volume label type **format.**
- Press **Enter**.
- Answer **No** to *not* format another diskette.

Step 3: **Attempt to unformat the disk.**

- Type **unformat a:**
- Press **Enter**.
- View the resulting message. Was the unformat successful?

NOTE: The unconditional format command does not allow for unformatting later.

Creating DOS Directories

The DOS operating system is capable of dividing the disk into separate storage and work areas called directories. Directories and subdirectories are roughly analogous to the folders found in a file cabinet. A directory would be like a file folder that contains several smaller related folders. These related folders would be similar to subdirectories in DOS. This allows the DOS user a system of organization on the disk that groups related data. Every disk has one main directory, called the *root directory*. The root directory is identified by a single back slash (\ ). All other directories on the disk are then subdirectories under the root directory.

The directories and subdirectories on the disk are structured much like the organization chart of a business. At the very top of the disk structure is the root directory. All successive layers of directories and subdirectories start below the root. The only limitation to the number of directories and subdirectories is the amount of disk space in your system.

The root directory and all of its subdirectories are sometimes referred to as the DOS TREE. It is this tree structure that enables the user to find a particular file on the hard disk. When trying to find a file in the DOS file system, it is not only important to know the name of the file but where the file is physically located. This location is known as the DOS PATH.

DOS Path

The DOS PATH starts from the root directory working down, one directory at a time, until the file is located. This path is represented by the name of the root and subdirectories that hold the actual file and then the file name itself. Each directory (and file) is separated by a backward slash.

For example, the path to the PACMAN directory below would be written as: C:\GAMES\PACMAN

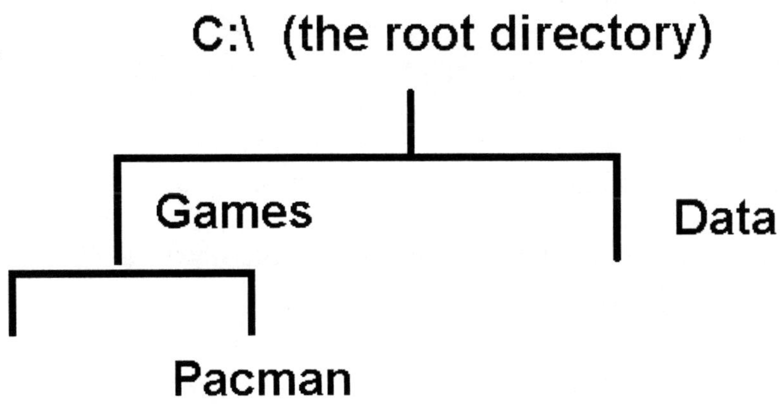

Exercise 8.2: Creating a Directory Structure

OBJECTIVES

When you've completed this exercise, you will be able to:

- Use the DOS **md** command to create directories and subdirectories.
- Use the **rd** (remove directory) command to delete directories.
- Use the **tree** command to view DOS directories and subdirectories.
- Use the **cd** (change directory) command to move into a directory.
- Copy files to a DOS directory.

PREPARATION

Change into the root directory of your hard drive by typing: **cd**

Step 1: **View the current directories on the hard disk.**

- Type **dir** to view the current directories.
- Press **Enter.**

Step 2: **Create a directory using your first name as the directory name.**

- Type **md joe** *(type in your name).*
- Press **Enter.**
- Type **dir** and confirm that the new directory is listed.

Step 3: **Move into the newly created directory.**

- Type **cd joe** *(type in your name).*
- Press **Enter.** What does your prompt display?

Step 4: **Create two subdirectories under your directory. Name them** DATA **and** GAMES.

- Type **md data** to create a new directory named DATA.
- Press **Enter.**
- Type **md games** to create a new directory named GAMES.
- Press **Enter.**
- Type **dir** to view the list of directories.
- Press **Enter** to verify that the new directories are listed.

Step 5: **Use the DOS** cd **command to move one level up the directory tree.**

- Type **cd..** to move one step up the directory tree; in this case, all the way up to the **root** directory.
- Press **Enter.**

Step 6: **Use the** cd **command to move into the newly created** DATA **directory.**

- Type **tree**
- Press **Enter** to find the data directory.
- Type **cd\yourname\data**
- Press **Enter.** What does your prompt display? It should show that you are now in the **data** directory.

Step 7: **Use the** rd **(remove directory) command to delete the** GAMES **directory.**

- Type **rd games** to remove the **GAMES** directory.

- Press **Enter.** What happened? You should get an error message telling you this is an invalid path. This is because you need to be in the directory which contains the subdirectory you want to remove in order to use the **rd** command.

- Type **cd..**

- Press **Enter.**

- Type **rd games** again.

- Press **Enter.**

- Type **dir**

- Press **Enter** to view the directory's contents. The **games** directory should no longer be listed.

Step 8: **Make a directory named** backup **and copy the** AUTOEXEC.BAT **file from the root to this directory.**

- Type **md backup** to create a new directory named **Backup.**

- Press **Enter.**

- Type **cd backup** to change to the **backup** directory.

- Press **Enter.**

- Type **copy c:\autoexec.bat** to copy the file to the **backup** directory.

- Press **Enter.**

- Type **dir** and verify that the **AUTOEXEC.BAT** file was copied to the **backup** directory.

DOS Configuration Files

When the computer is turned on and the DOS operating system starts to load, it looks for two very important configuration files, the **CONFIG.SYS** file and the **AUTOEXEC.BAT** file. These are both text files that can be created and edited with any DOS text editing program. Both files must be located in the root directory of the bootable drive to ensure that the operating system will locate them. These files are executed in a particular order.

- **CONFIG.SYS** - The first of the files to be executed is the **CONFIG.SYS** file. This file contains special commands relating to the hardware devices found in the computer, such as the mouse, the printer, the keyboard and disk drive present in the computer.
- **AUTOEXEC.BAT** -The second file to execute is the **AUTOEXEC.BAT** file. The **AUTOEXEC.BAT** file is used to customize your DOS environment. It can be used to automatically start any application, to present the user with a menu, and to set DOS environmental variables such as the **PROMPT** command.

Bypassing the Start-Up File

It is possible that something could be placed in the **AUTOEXEC.BAT** file or the **CONFIG.SYS** file that may cause the computer not to function correctly or, in some cases, not to boot at all. In this case, the DOS operating system gives you the ability to bypass both files during the booting process. Follow these steps to accomplish this:

- Boot the computer
- Press the **F5** function key immediately after the starting DOS message appears on the screen.

The above procedure allows the user to boot the computer without any of the special commands that may have been specified in the **CONFIG.SYS** or the **AUTOEXEC.BAT**. At this point, the user can try to determine what command or commands in the configuration files are causing the problem.

The **F8** key serves a similar function to the **F5** key. The main difference between the two function keys is that while the **F5** key bypasses the configuration files altogether, the **F8** key allows you to selectively bypass commands either in the **CONFIG.SYS** or the **AUTOEXEC.BAT** The user is prompted with a message asking if each step is to be performed. If the user tells DOS to bypass the command it will then proceed to the next step.

CONFIG.SYS File

The contents of the **CONFIG.SYS** file can be roughly broken down into two categories: commands and device drivers. Some of the more common **CONFIG.SYS** commands are **files** and **buffers**. The **buffer statement** tells DOS the amount of memory to reserve for information transfers to or from the hard disk. This parameter can be set between 1 and 99, with each buffer taking up approximately 530 bytes. The **Files** command specifies the number of files that can be open concurrently. The range is 8 to 255.

CONFIG.SYS Commands	
BREAK	Turns on or off extended Ctrl-Break checking.
BUFFERS	Sets the number of disk buffers used by DOS.
COUNTRY	Sets country information.
DEVICE	Loads an installable device driver.
DEVICEHIGH	Loads an installable device driver into high (UMB) memory.
DOS	Determines whether DOS will use the HMA or UMB.
DRIVPARM	Redefines the physical characteristics of an existing disk drive.
FCBS	Sets the maximum number of open File Control Blocks.
FILES	Sets the maximum number of open files that DOS will allow.
INCLUDE	Includes the commands from one CONFIG.SYS block within another.
INSTALL	Loads TSR programs into memory from CONFIG.SYS.
LASTDRIVE	Sets the maximum number of letters available to DOS.
MENUCOLOR	Sets the color of the screen for the CONFIG.SYS start up menu.
MENUDEFAULT	Sets the default menu choice in a CONFIG.SYS menu block.
MENUITEM	Sets the text and configuration block associated with menu items in CONFIG.SYS.
NUMLOCK	Sets the state of the NumLock key when the computer starts.
REM	Inserts a remark into CONFIG.SYS.
SET	Sets environment variables.
SHELL	Sets the name of the program used as a command-line shell by MS-DOS.
STACKS	Sets the number of stacks set aside for hardware interrupts.
SUBMENU	Defines a submenu in CONFIG.SYS.
SWITCHES	Sets miscellaneous control options for MS-DOS.

In addition to the **CONFIG.SYS** command, there are also a number of device driver options that can be used. For example, the **ANSI.SYS** device driver expands the ability of a system to respond to advanced video command sets. The **ANSI.SYS** driver must be loaded in the **CONFIG.SYS** file.

A device driver simply tells DOS how to control each hardware device attached to the computer. Some of the more common device drivers and their associated functions are listed in the following table.

Device Driver	Associated Function
ansi.sys	Controls screen colors and the position of the cursor.
driver.sys	Creates drive letters which are assigned to physical devices
emm386.exe	Provides access to upper memory & emulates expanded memory.
himem.sys	Manages the extended memory area.
setver.exe	Manages the DOS version table.
smartdrv.exe	File used by various hard drives.
power.exe	Advanced Power Management (APM) reduces power consumption during idle times.
ramdrive.sys	Driver that simulates a logical hard drive in RAM (memory).

Common Device Drivers

The following is an example of a **CONFIG.SYS** file.

```
device=C:\dos\himem.sys
device=C:\dos\emm386.exe
files=40
buffers=25
dos=high,umb
stacks=9,256
lastdrive=E
```

In the above example . . .

- The first line, **device=C:\dos\himem.sys,** will manage the extended memory area in the system RAM.
- The second line, **device=C:\dos\emm386.exe,** will make **emm386.exe** active so that upper memory will be available and will simulate expanded memory for programs that can use it.
- The **files=40** statement provides that 40 files can be open concurrently.
- **Buffers=25** will assign 25 buffers for transferring information to and from the hard disk.
- The **dos=high,umb** statement will load DOS into high memory and will also make upper memory blocks available.
- The **stacks=9,256** statement will provide nine 256-byte stack handlers available for use by the interrupts.
- The **lastdrive=E** statement indicates the last local drive available.

AUTOEXEC.BAT

The **AUTOEXEC.BAT** contains commands that customize a DOS installation. It runs automatically when the system is started. Listed below are some of the more common DOS commands that can be used in the **AUTOEXEC.BAT** file:

Common DOS commands in an AUTOEXEC.BAT file	
path	Sets a logical path to directories containing executable files.
set	Defines DOS variables.
prompt	Establishes and sets the command prompt.
mode	Specifies options for the monitor, printer ports and keyboard.
echo off	Instructs DOS not to display each command as it executes.
call	Will run a second batch file.
rem	Used to add a documentation statement in the AUTOEXEC.BAT file

The following is an example of a **AUTOEXEC.BAT** file.

```
echo off
cls
prompt=$p$g
path=c:\;c:\dos;c:\wp
```

In the above example . . .

- The **echo off** statement will tell DOS not to display each command as it executes.
- The **cls** statement will clear the screen.
- The **prompt=pg** command will set the user's prompt to display the current drive followed by the "greater than" sign (>).
- The DOS **path=c:\;c:\dos;c:\wp** statement in this example tells DOS to search for files in the following order starting with the root directory, the DOS directory, and finally, the **WP** directory.

DOS Batch Programs

DOS batch files or programs are short cuts that allow a user to place frequently used commands into one file. These commands will execute when the file name is typed. A DOS batch file could be very simple, issuing one or two commands, or it can be very complex, issuing an entire series of commands. Any valid DOS command can be included in a batch command or any third party application compatible with DOS can also be included as the batch file. The list below includes some of the most frequently used batch file commands:

call

goto

if then

echo

choice

pause

rem

Creating Batch Files

A DOS batch file can be created within a DOS text editing program, but the files should always be saved with a **.bat** extension. The names of the batch files should always be unique and should never be named the same as any other DOS commands. An example of a name to avoid would be **format.bat** because the DOS operating system would not have any way of differentiating between the **format.bat** and **format.com** files.

To execute a batch file, the user types the batch file name followed by the enter key. The extension is optional and does not need to be typed. The execution of the batch file may be halted by typing **Ctrl + C** or touching the **Ctrl + Break** keys. Another command that can be used to temporarily suspend the process of a batch file is the DOS **pause** command. It is very useful for troubleshooting or testing a batch file.

Exercise 8.3: Creating a DOS Batch File.

OBJECTIVES

When you've completed this section, you will be able to:

- Describe the use of DOS batch files.
- Create a DOS batch file.
- Execute a DOS batch file.

PREPARATION

DOS batch commands can be very useful and can save you time. For example, let's say that as part of your job you need to create multiple directories and subdirectories on every new machine that comes into your office. You also have to copy files to these directories. You could use the **md** and **copy** commands repeatedly each time you configure a new system, or you could create a batch file that will do this for you.

In this exercise, you will create a batch file to do the following: create five directories, copy your current **AUTOEXEC.BAT** and **CONFIG.SYS** file to a directory called **backup**, and copy all DOS files to a directory called **c:\save.**

Step 1: Change the root directory and view the directory.

- Type **cd** to change to the root directory.
- Press **Enter**.
- Type **dir** to display the contents of the directory.
- Press **Enter**.

Step 2: **Create a DOS batch file called** repeat.bat.

- Type **edit repeat.bat**
- Press **Enter**
- Enter the following commands:

```
cd\
md backup
md save
md word
md common
md test
copy c:\dos\*.* c:\save
copy c:\autoexec.bat c:\backup
copy c:\config.sys c:\backup
```

Step 3: **Now exit and save the file.**

- Press the **ALT** key.
- Press **Enter**.
- Press **X** to exit.
- Press **Enter** again when the system asks if you want to save.

Step 4: **Run the batch file you just created and view the results.**

- Type **repeat.bat** to run the batch file.
- Press **Enter**.
- Type **tree** to verify that the directories have been created.
- Move into the **save** directory.
- Type **dir** to view the contents of the directory.
- Press **Enter** to verify that you have a backup of the DOS files.

List of DOS Commands

The following is a list of common DOS commands organized by their function. A brief description of the command is included.

Directory Commands	
CD or CHDIR	Changes the current directory of a disk drive.
DELTREE	Deletes a directory, including all the files and sub-directories it may contain.
MD or MKDIR	Creates a new sub-directory on a disk.
RD or RMDIR	Deletes an empty sub-directory on a disk.
TREE	Displays the sub-directory structure present on a disk.

Batch File Commands	
CALL	Executes a batch file from within another batch file.
CHOICE	Accepts a single keystroke from the keyboard.
COMMAND	Runs a second copy of the MS-DOS command interpreter.
ECHO	Echoes text to the screen from a batch file.
FOR	FOR-IN-DO loop for batch files.
GOTO	Jumps to a labeled line in a batch file.
IF	IF-THEN decision structure for a batch file.
PAUSE	Waits for a keystroke before continuing.
REM	Inserts a remark into a batch file.
SHIFT	Shifts batch file parameters down one place.

Disk Commands	
CHKDSK	Checks a disk for errors and provides information on the amount of space in use.
DEFRAG	Defragments the files on a disk. This can cut down on the time it takes your computer to find files on your hard disk.
DISKCOMP	Compares two floppy disks to see if they are identical.
DISKCOPY	Makes an exact copy of a disk.
FDISK	Hard disk partitioning program. Prepares a new hard disk to accept DOS, or partitions a single drive into two or more logical drives.
FORMAT	Formats a hard or floppy disk for MS-DOS.
LABEL	Creates, edits, or deletes the volume label on a disk.
SCANDISK	Analyzes disks and repairs errors. The ScanDisk utility can repair DoubleSpace compressed drives as well as normal disks.
SUBST	Creates a disk drive letter that refers to a sub-directory of another drive.
SYS	Installs the MS-DOS system files on another disk.
UNFORMAT	Returns a disk to its previous state before FORMAT was run.
VERIFY	Controls whether DOS will read everything written to disk to ensure that no errors occurred.
VOL	Displays the volume label of a disk.

File Commands	
ATTRIB	Views or changes file attributes.
COPY	Copies or concatenates a file or group of files.
DEL or ERASE	Deletes a file or group of files.
DIR	Displays a listing of the files in a sub-directory.
EXPAND	Expands (uncompresses) files on the MS-DOS 6 distribution disks.
FC	Compares two files for differences.
FIND	Finds matching text in a file.
MOVE	Moves a file from one sub-directory to another or renames a sub-directory.
REN or RENAME	Renames a file or group of files.
REPLACE	Replaces or adds files to a sub-directory.
SHARE	Provides file sharing and locking capabilities for DOS.
TYPE	Displays the contents of a file on-screen.
UNDELETE	Undeletes a file or group of files.
XCOPY	Copies files and sub-directories.

Full-Screen DOS Applications	
DBLSPACE	Program that compresses information on a disk, providing up to twice the amount of space you previously had.
DEBUG	Programmer's debugger.
DEFRAG	Defragments the files on a disk. Running this program can cut down on the time it takes your computer to find files on your hard disk.
DOSSHELL	Graphical shell program for DOS.
EDIT	A full-screen ASCII text file editor.
MSAV	Checks your computer for viruses.
MSBACKUP	Backs up files on your hard disk to a series of floppy disks.
MSD	Provides information about a computer's configuration.
QBASIC	Provides access to the MS-QuickBASIC development environment, which enables users to write and run programs written in the QuickBASIC language.

Help Commands	
FASTHELP	Displays a short description of what each DOS command is for and the correct syntax for its use.
HELP	A full-screen, on-line help system that provides descriptions and examples of every DOS command.
/?	Not an actual command. If you include a /? on the command line with a DOS command, a short description is displayed of what the command does and how you can use it.

International Commands and Device Drivers	
CHCP	Changes the active country code page.
KEYB	Sets the active keyboard layout.
MODE	Configures standard DOS devices, including changing the active code page for the keyboard, display, and printer.
NLSFUNC	Contains code page switching support required by CHCP and MODE.

Miscellaneous Commands	
MEM	Displays how memory in your computer system is being used.
MEMMAKER	Utility to optimize memory usage on your computer.
APPEND	Establishes a DOS search path for data files.
BREAK	Turns on or off extended Ctrl-Break checking.
CLS	Clears the screen.
DATE	Sets or views the system date.
DOSKEY	Provides enhanced command-line editing and macros capability.
GRAPHICS	Provides support for a graphics mode Print Screen function.
MSCDEX	Provides support for CD ROMs.
MODE	Configures standard DOS devices such as serial ports, parallel ports, the display, and the keyboard.
MORE	Pauses display output when the screen is full.
PATH	Establishes a DOS search path for executable files.
PRINT	Print spooler for ASCII text files.
PROMPT	Customizes the prompt used by DOS at the command line.
RESTORE	Restores files backed up with the DOS 5 version of BACKUP
SET	Sets, clears, or displays environment variables.
TIME	Sets or views the system time.
VER	Displays the version of DOS running on the computer.
VSAFE	Resident program that watches for viruses.

Exercise 8.4 (Optional): Installing and Partitioning a Hard Disk

(Note: This is done as a group exercise)

OBJECTIVES

When you've completed this exercise, you will be able to:

- Install an additional hard disk drive.
- Edit your **CMOS** settings to accurately reflect system configuration.
- Use the **fdisk** utility to create primary and extended partitions.
- Create logical drive assignments.
- Format a hard disk drive partition.
- Use the **fdisk** utility to delete a primary partition.

PREPARATION

DOS must be available on the student machines' hard disk or through a bootable DOS diskette that contains at least the following files: **FDISK.EXE, FORMAT.COM** and **SYS.COM.**

Obtain additional hard disk drive from your instructor.

Part One: Installing an additional Hard Disk Drive.

Step 1: Power down your system.

Step 2: Install hard disk drive.

- Set jumpers on new drive to **SLAVE.**
- Place hard disk drive in an available drive bay, and fasten in place with appropriate screws.
- Connect HDD ribbon cable and power connector.

Step 3: Power up your system.

- During the boot process, observe hardware information displayed on computer screen. Were both drives discovered?

Part Two: Updating CMOS settings.

Step 1: **Reboot your system.**

Step 2: **Enter the CMOS Setup Screen.**

- Ask your instructor for the appropriate key sequence to access the CMOS Setup Screen on your computer.

Step 3: **Select Standard CMOS Setup.**

- Observe current hard disk drive configuration.
- Press **Esc** to return to main CMOS menu.

Step 4: **Select IDE HARD DISK DETECTION.**

- Select **Primary Master Option**.
- Type **Y** and press **Enter.**
- Select **Primary Slave Option**.
- Type **Y** and press **Enter.**
- Select **Secondary Master and Slave Options**.
- Type **N** and press **Enter** for each one.

Step 5: **Select Standard CMOS Setup**.

- Observe updated hard disk drive configuration.
- Press **Esc** to return to main CMOS menu.

Step 6: **Save and Exit CMOS Setup.**

- Select **Save and Exit Setup.**
- Type **Y** to confirm save and press **Enter.**
  (System will re-boot.)
- After boot process completes, observe hardware information displayed on computer screen. Are both drives now displayed?

Part Three: Creating new partitions.

Step 1: View the existing partitions on your hard disk.

- At the **C:** prompt type **fdisk** and press **Enter.**
- Choose **Option 5** from the **fdisk** main menu. How many partitions currently exist?
- Make sure Disk Drive Number **1** is selected.
- Press the **Esc** key to return to the **fdisk** main menu.

Step 2: Create an Extended DOS partition and two Logical DOS drives.

- From the **fdisk** main menu, select **Option 1** to create a DOS partition or Logical DOS drive.
- Select **Option 2** to Create an Extended DOS Partition.
- Press **Enter** to accept the default size in megabytes.
- Press **Esc** to continue.
- After a short pause, you will see the command: **Create Logical DOS Drive in the Extended DOS Partition.**

No Logical drives defined

- Type **50%** in the total space field and press **Enter** to create the first logical drive. Note which letter is assigned to the first logical drive.
- Press **Enter** to accept the total space and create the second logical drive. Note which letter is assigned to the second logical drive.
- Press **Esc** to return to the main menu.

Step 3: **Create a primary DOS partition.**

- Select **Option 5** from the **fdisk** main menu.
- Select disk **2**.
- Press the **Esc** key to return to the **fdisk** main menu.
- Select **Option 1** to create a DOS partition.
- Select **Option 1** again to create a primary DOS partition.
- When prompted with **Use the Maximum Size**, click **No** and press the **Enter** key.
- Enter **50** megabytes for the size.
- Press the **Esc** key to return to the main menu.

Step 4: **Exit the** fdisk **program.**

- Exit the **fdisk** program by pressing the **Esc** key until the system re-boots.

Part Four: Format a new partition.

Step 1: Format the new primary partition (D).

- From the **C:** prompt type **format D:**
- Press **Enter.**

Step 2: Verify that you can access the newly formatted drive.

- Type **D:** to switch to the D drive.
- Press **Enter.**
- At the warning message, type **Y** and press **Enter.**
- When prompted for a volume label, press **Enter.**
- Type **dir** to view the contents of the D drive.
- Press **Enter.**
- Type **C:** and press **Enter** to return to the root partition.

Part Five: Deleting a Primary DOS Partition.

Step 1: View the existing partitions on your hard disk drive.

- At the **C:** prompt, type **fdisk** and press **Enter.**
- Select **option 5** from the **fdisk** menu.
- Select **Disk Drive Number 2** and press **Enter.**

Step 2: Delete a Primary DOS Partition.

- Select **option 3** from the **fdisk** main menu.
- Select **option 1** to delete a Primary DOS Partition.
- Press **Enter** to select the default partition.
- Press **Enter** to accept the volume label.
- Confirm by typing **Y** and press **Enter.**
- Press **Esc** to return to the **fdisk** main menu.

Step 3: Confirm partition has been deleted.

- Select **option 5** from the **fdisk** main menu.
- Observe changes to partition table information.
- Press **Esc** until system restarts.

Summary

This section provides an overview of DOS. Introduced in the early 1980s, DOS has become the most widely used operating system in the world. Literally hundreds of thousands of programs have been written for it. This section has focused on the key concepts and functions of DOS that will prepare you for *A+ Certification.*

DOS allows the user to organize the hard drive for storing and retrieving files. It does this through a hierarchical file system that uses directories, subdirectories and files. In order to identify files, DOS follows certain rules called "naming conventions." These rules set limitations on the length of file names and the characters that can be used for naming files.

Before DOS can run on a system, the hard drive or disk that will be used must be formatted. Formatting prepares a disk to accept data by creating sectors, tracks and clusters on the disk. In addition, certain files must be present within DOS that tell the system how DOS will be configured. The two most important files for DOS configuration are the **CONFIG.SYS** and the **AUTOEXEC.BAT** files.

Review Questions

1. Choose the correct load order sequence of the following files:

    A. **CONFIG.SYS, AUTOEXEC.BAT**
    B. **AUTOEXEC.SYS, CONFIG.SYS**
    C. **AUTOEXEC.BAT, CONFIG.SYS**
    D. **AUTOEXEC.BAT, COMMAND.COM**

2. To bypass both the **CONFIG.SYS** and the **AUTOEXEC.BAT** you would type:

    A. **F6**
    B. **F8**
    C. **F5**
    D. **F3**

3. The acronym **POST** stands for:

    A. **Power On Start Test**
    B. **Power On Self-Test**
    C. **PC Over Start Test**
    D. **Power Off Self-Test**

4. Which of the following file names is invalid?

    A. **money1.txt**
    B. **com1.txt**
    C. **12345x.doc**
    D. **back.xxx**

5. What three required files are placed on a diskette after formatting it with the **/s** option?

    A. **COMMAND.BAT, IO.SYS, MSDOS.SYS**
    B. **AUTOEXEC.BAT, CONFIG.SYS, COMMAND.COM**
    C. **IO.SYS, MSDOS.SYS, COMMAND.COM**
    D. **AUTOEXEC.BAT, CONFIG.SYS, COMMAND.EXE**

6. You can always unformat a disk that has been formatted with the **/u** option.

   A. True
   B. False

7. The **himem.sys** command will manage extended memory.

   A. True
   B. False

8. What does the **$G** command do in the following statement: **PG**?

   A. Displays the path.
   B. Displays the "greater than" sign.
   C. Displays DOS.
   D. Displays the C:

Section 9

DOS Memory Optimization

Section 9: DOS Memory Optimization

Introduction

In a perfect computer world, only one configuration of DOS would be needed for all computers. In the real world, however, no two computers are exactly alike. Therefore, one default configuration is not practical.

In order to get the best performance from a computer, it is often necessary to optimize the installation. For the most part, optimization relates to memory and how it is allocated. As mentioned in the previous section, DOS and DOS programs are limited to the first 640K of memory (conventional memory), so the process of managing or optimizing memory under DOS usually involves freeing up as much of that memory as possible.

Objectives

When you've completed this section, you will be able to:

- Describe the different types of PC memory areas.
- Identify which programs are located in these areas.
- Use the DOS Memory Optimization Program (**MEMMaker**)

IMPORTANT NOTE

This section is OPTIONAL. DOS is NOT covered in the A+ Certification Exams. While DOS is not explicitly covered in the A+ Exams, knowledge of DOS commands is still extremely helpful for PC technicians and support staff. For example, when a Windows-based system does not boot correctly, a basic understanding of DOS commands will allow you to troubleshoot and recover the system.

Memory Optimization

In order to discuss memory optimization, it is first important to understand the different terms associated with the optimization of memory. These terms generally describe the different types of memory available to the PC.

The graphic below depicts the different memory locations.

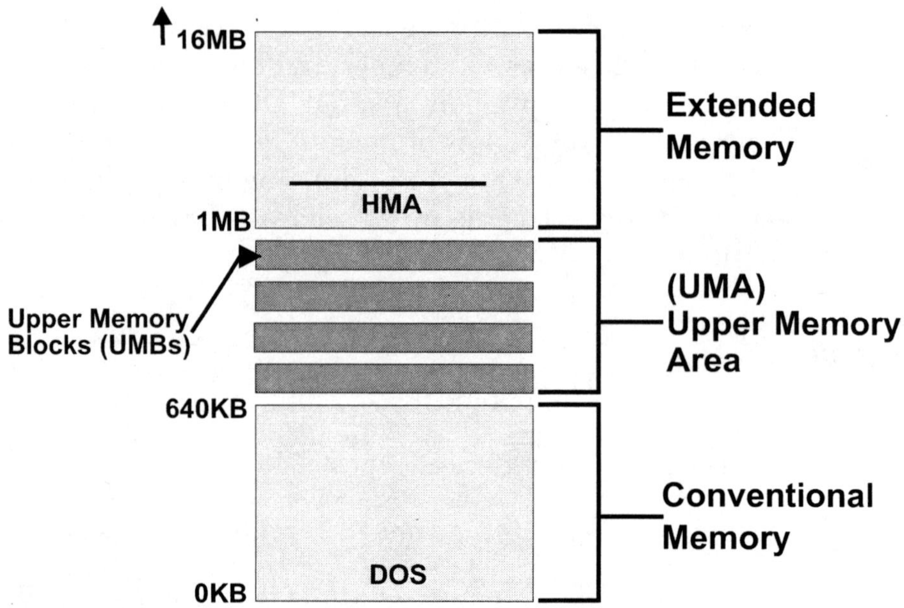

Memory Locations

Conventional Memory

Conventional memory is the first 640KB of system memory. This is all the memory DOS has for running programs. Traditionally, this was the only memory available to DOS applications. Even if your computer has 16MB of RAM, you only have 640KB in which to run DOS programs. This is sometimes referred to the 640KB barrier. In addition to DOS programs, the DOS command processor, TSR, and BIOS information table reside in this area.

Upper Memory Area (UMA)

The UMA, upper memory area, is located between 640KB and one megabyte. This area of memory contains ROM BIOS, video ROM and RAM, and device controllers. It will also contain the expanded memory page frames.

Upper Memory Blocks (UMB)

The UMB are free blocks of memory within the upper memory area. They can be used to contain things like TSR (terminate and stay resident) programs and device drivers. To gain access to the upper memory blocks, you must use **HIMEM.SYS** and **EMM386.EXE**.

Extended Memory (XMS)

The extended memory can range from 1MB to 16MB for 80286-based machines, and up to 4GB for 80386 and above based machines. The use of the extended memory requires that the **HIMEM.SYS** program be loaded in the **CONFIG.SYS** file.

High Memory Area (HMA)

The high memory area, or HMA, is the first 64KB of extended memory. DOS requires a program such as **HIMEM.SYS** to access the HMA area. This area of memory is most commonly used for loading DOS components. However, only one program at a time may reside in the high memory area.

Expanded Memory Specification (EMS)

Expanded memory is extra memory located in the PC. It was originally developed as a way of working around the limitation of DOS. It requires the use of the LIM (Lotus-Intel-Microsoft) specifications. This is generally referred to as the LIM4.0 memory manager. Very few programs will actually make use of the expanded memory area.

Managing Memory

Memory management is something unique to the DOS operating system. Other operating systems do it automatically. With DOS, you need to use an additional program. There are many products on the market that help you manage and optimize memory. Some examples are: *QuarterDeck's* QEMM, or the **MEMMaker** program that comes bundled with DOS 6.

The DOS **MEMMaker** utility will help you configure, manage, and optimize all the memory in your PC. This program will analyze all the currently loaded programs and device drivers on your PC and then determine the best possible memory configuration. The **MEMMaker** program is fairly straightforward and easy to use. Unfortunately, **MEMMaker** will not run on all systems. It requires at least an 80386 microprocessor or above and extended memory.

The **MEMMaker** program can be run in two ways. The express setup works for most systems without any problems. The custom setup may be necessary if you have a monitor or device driver that may interfere with the **MEMMaker** program.

Viewing Memory

While the DOS **MEMMaker** program allows you to optimize the system memory, the DOS **mem** command allows you to view memory usage and availability. The DOS **mem** command can be a useful tool when you need to diagnose a memory problem or for optimizing memory manually. The **MSD** (Microsoft Diagnostic Program) will also allow you to view current system memory usage.

Exercise 9.1 : Viewing and Optimizing System Memory

OBJECTIVE

View and optimize system memory usage with the DOS **mem** command and the DOS Optimize Program (**MEMMaker**).

PREPARATION

Rename your current **AUTOEXEC.BAT** and **CONFIG.SYS** to **AUTOEXEC.BAK** and **CONFIG.BAK**.

- Type **ren autoexec.bat autoexec.bak** to rename your current **AUTOEXEC.BAT** file.
- Press **Enter.**
- Type **ren config.sys config.bak** to rename your current **CONFIG.SYS** file.
- Press **Enter.**

Part One

Step 1: Create a new AUTOEXEC.BAT **file.**

- Type **edit autoexec.bat** to modify your **AUTOEXEC.BAT** file.
- Press **Enter.**
- Enter the following commands:

  echo off

  path c:\;c:\dos

  prompt PG
- Save the new file by pressing the **Alt** key.
- Press **Enter.**
- Type **X** to exit.
- Press **Enter** to save.

Step 2: Create a new CONFIG.SYS **file.**

- Type **edit config.sys**
- Press **Enter.**
- Enter the following Remark (REM) Statement **rem This is my config.sys file**
- Save the **CONFIG.SYS** file by pressing the **Alt** key.
- Press **Enter.**
- Press **X** to exit.

Step 3 - **Reboot your system.**

Step 4 - **From the C: prompt view your current memory statistics.**

- Type **msd** to start the MSD utility.
- Press **Enter.**
- Press **M.**
- Press **Enter** to view memory.
- Record the following:

Total Conventional Memory ____________

Available Conventional Memory____________

Total Extended Memory ____________

Step 5: **Exit the** MSD **program by pressing function key F3.**

Step 6: **Edit your** CONFIG.SYS **file:**

- Type **edit config.sys**
- Press **Enter.**
- Add the following line by typing:

device=c:\dos\himem.sys

- Save the file.

Step 7: **Reboot your computer by pressing** CTRL + ALT + DEL **simultaneously.**

Step 8: **Run the** MSD **program and record the amount of Available Extended Memory.**

- Type **msd** to start the MSD utility.
- Press **Enter.**
- Press **m.**
- Record the amount of Available Extended Memory ____________.
- Exit **msd** by pressing the function key **F3**.

Step 9: **Add the Expanded Memory Manager (**EMM386.EXE**) to your** CONFIG.SYS **file.**

- Type **edit config.sys**
- Press **Enter.**
- Add the following line to your **CONFIG.SYS**, immediately following the **HIMEM** line by typing **device=c:\dos\emm386.exe**

- Save the new file by pressing the **Alt** key.
- Press **F**
- Type **X** to exit.
- Press **Enter** to save.

Step 10: Reboot your computer and note the addition of Page Frame in the Upper Memory Area.

- Type **msd** to start the MSD utility.
- Press **Enter.**
- Press **m** and notice Page Frame Memory.
- Exit **msd** by pressing the function key **F3**.

Step 11: Load DOS into High Memory by adding dos=high **to the** CONFIG.SYS **file.**

- Type **edit config.sys**
- Press **Enter.**
- Add **dos=high** as the last statement in the **CONFIG.SYS** file.
- Save the changes.

Step 12: Reboot your computer to view the changes.

Step 13: View the effects of the dos=high **statement, using the DOS** mem **command.**

- Type **mem /c |more**
- Press **Enter.**
- Record the amount of **Total Conventional Memory** ____________.
- Compare this to the results of Step 4.

Step 14: Add the noems **command to the end of the** device=c:\dos\emm386.exe **statement in the** CONFIG.SYS **file.**

- Type **edit config.sys**
- Press **Enter.**
- Add **noems** to the end of the **emm386.exe** line. The line should read:

  device=c:\dos\emm386.exe noems
- Save the changes.
- Reboot your computer.

Step 15: Run the MSD Program to see your changes and note that the Page Frame is now gone.

- Type **msd**
- Press **Enter.**
- Press **m** and notice that the **noems** prevented **Page Frame** from being created.
- Exit **msd** by pressing the function key **F3**.

Step 16: Add the umb statement to the CONFIG.SYS file to create Free Upper Memory Blocks.

- Type **edit config.sys**
- Press **Enter.**
- Add the **umb** statement to the **dos=high** statement. The line should read **dos=high, umb**
- Save the changes and reboot your PC.

Step 17: Run the MSD Program and look for the creation of Upper Memory Blocks. (These are the areas designated by FF.)

- Type **msd**
- Press **Enter.**
- Press **m** and look for the Free Upper Memory Blocks.
- Exit **msd** by pressing the function key **F3**.

Step 18: Loading a program into the umb area.

- Type **lh doskey**
- Press **Enter.**. (This will load the **DOSKEY** Program into Upper Memory.)
- Type **msd**
- Press **Enter.** View where the **DOSKEY** Program was loaded. (You should see four U's in the Upper Memory Area. This is the **DOSKEY** Program.)
- Exit **msd** by pressing the function key **F3**.

Part Two*: Running the* MEMMaker Program *to optimize memory.*

Preparation

Rename your **AUTOEXEC.BAT** and **CONFIG.SYS** files to **autoexec.xxx** and **config.xxx**.

Step 1: **Create a new** AUTOEXEC.BAT.

- Type **edit autoexec.bat**
- Press **Enter.**
- Add the following lines:

```
echo off
path=c:\;c:\dos
prompt=$P$G
vsafe
doskey
```

- Save the new **AUTOEXEC.BAT** file.

Step 2: **Create a new** CONFIG.SYS **file.**

- Type **edit config.sys**
- Press **Enter.**
- Add the following line:

```
device=c:\dos\setver.exe
```

- Save the new **CONFIG.SYS** file.

Step 3: **Reboot your computer.**

Step 4: **Using the** mem **command to view and record the location (conventional or Upper Memory area) and size of the following** doskey **and** vsafe **programs.**

- Type **mem /c /p**
- Press **Enter.**

	LOCATION	SIZE
DOSKEY:	________	________
VSAFE:	________	________
SETVER:	________	________

How much Conventional Memory is Available?________

How much Extended Memory is Free? ________

How much Upper Memory is Free? ________

Part Three : *Running the* MEMMaker Program *to optimize the system. Compare the results with the information listed above.*

Step 1: **Run the MS DOS** MEMMaker **Program.**

- Type **memmaker**
- Press **Enter.**
- Choose **Custom Setup.**
- Respond **No** to **EMS Support.**
- Respond **No** to **Support Windows**.
- Toggle all the rest of the **Advanced Options** to **Yes**
- Press **Enter** to accept the **Windows Default Directory.**
- Respond **Yes** to optimize **setver** and **doskey**.
- Respond **No** to optimize **vsafe.**
- Press **Enter** to allow **MEMMaker** to **Optimize System.**

Step 2: **The computer will automatically reboot twice.**

- Press **Enter** after the first reboot.

Step 3: **If the computer boots the second time, respond** Yes.

Step 4: **Note any changes that MEMMaker has made.**

- Press **Enter** to exit.

Step 5: **View the** AUTOEXEC.BAT **and** CONFIG.SYS **and note the changes that were made.**

- Type **type autoexec.bat**
- Press **Enter.**
- Note changes.
- Type **type config.sys**
- Press **Enter.**
- Note changes.

Step 6: **Use the** mem **command to compare this to the results that you recorded in Part Two.**

Summary

In this section, we discussed the reasons for optimizing memory and conducted hands-on labs. No one memory configuration will work for all computer systems. In fact, optimizing a computer's performance is the process of finding and establishing settings that are unique to that particular system.

Most optimizing is a process that involves manipulating a computer's memory. As mentioned in the previous section, DOS and DOS programs are limited to the first 640KB of memory (conventional memory), so the process of managing or optimizing memory under DOS usually involves freeing up as much of that memory as possible.

Review Questions

1. HMA is the first 64KB of ____________ Memory.

    A. Conventional
    B. Expanded
    C. Base
    D. Extended

2. Conventional Memory starts at _____KB and ends at ________KB.

3. Which MS DOS Program will optimize your system's memory?

    A. **DOSKEY**
    B. **MEM**
    C. **MEMMaker**
    D. **MEMORY**

4. Which of the following statements from the **CONFIG.SYS** file depicts the correct load order?

    A. **DEVICE=C:\DOS\EMM386.EXE**
    DEVICE=C:\DOS\HIMEM.SYS
    B. **DEVICE=C:\DOS\HIMEM.SYS**
    DEVICE=C:\DOS\EMM386.EXE
    C. **DEVICE=C:\DOS\SETVER.EXE**
    DEVICE=C:\DOS\EMM386.EXE
    DEVICE=C:\DOS\HIMEM.SYS
    D. **DEVICE=C:\DOS\HIMEM.COM**
    DEVICE=C:\DOS\EMM386.SYS

5. Using the **NOEMS** switch with:
    DEVICE=C:\DOS\EMM386.EXE NOEMS
    will not create Page Frame Memory.

    A. True
    B. False

6. The UMA Memory Area is located between __________ and __________.

   A. 0 - 640KB
   B. 640 - 1024KB
   C. 1024 - 16MB
   D. 640 - 740KB

7. What device will manage the Upper Memory Blocks?

   A. **HIMEM.SYS**
   B. **EMM387.EXE**
   C. **EMM386.EXE**
   D. **DOSKEY**

8. Extended Memory ranges from __________ to __________on a 80286 machine, and __________to __________on a 80386 and above machine.

9. When using **MSD**, Free Memory Blocks are depicted by:

   A. BB
   B. FF
   C. UU
   D. FB

10. As a general rule of thumb, one set of optimized configuration files will work for most machines.

    A. True
    B. False

Section 10

Printers

Section 10: Printers

Introduction

A printer is a computer whose sole purpose is to convert electronic pulses into images on paper. Although printers come as a separate unit, they are an integral part of a computer system. Printer technology has kept pace with newer computers. Today's printers are able to handle increasingly large amounts of data and produce extremely high quality outputs for a variety of different applications. This section will focus mainly on electrophotographic printers (commonly called laser printers), their different components and how they produce a printed page. We will also briefly examine the other categories of printers, as there is a wide variety of printers in use today.

Objectives

When you've completed this section, you will be able to:

- Identify and describe the different parts of a laser printer
- Identify and describe the different parts of the Image Formation System.
- Troubleshoot and diagnose common printer problems
- Perform preventive maintenance

Electrophotographic (EP) Printer

The term *laser printer* has become a generic name to describe printers that utilize an electrophotographic process to produce images on paper. The fact is there are many "*laser printers*" on the market which do not use laser beams to write image data.

Instead, they utilize a bar of microscopic *light-emitting diodes (LEDs)* or arrays of *liquid crystal shutters (LCS)* to accomplish the same task. There is a big difference between *electrophotographic (EP)* printers and their more inexpensive counterparts. EP printing is a process that involves the interaction of many areas within the printer. Dot matrix and ink-jet printing, on the other hand, are the result of a single event: the printing head creating an image directly on paper.

The collection of parts that produce EP prints is known as an Image Formation System (IFS) and it consists of several distinct components:

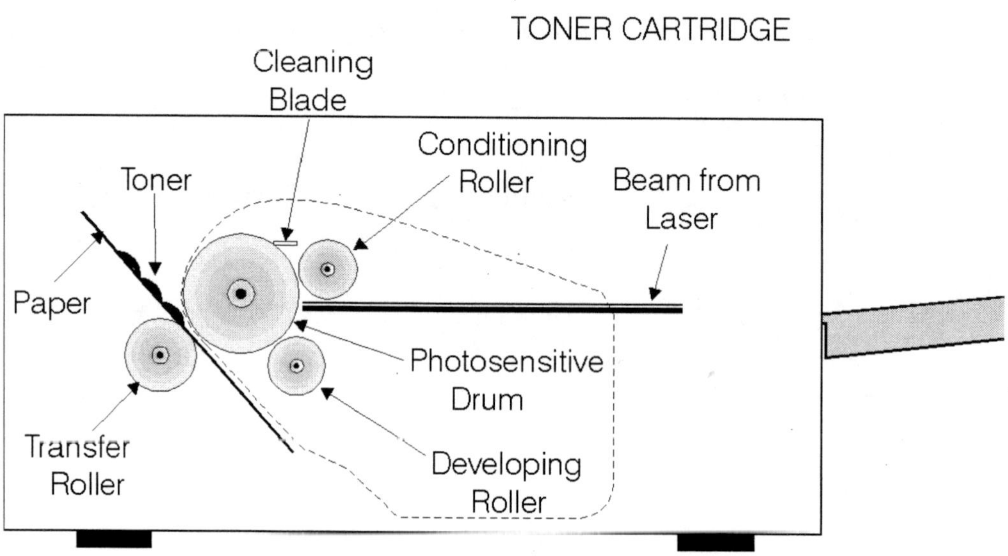

Basic Components of an Image Formation System

The Parts of an Image Formation System	
The photosensitive drum (PS drum)	An aluminum cylinder coated with a photoconductive material, which conducts electricity when exposed to light. This is a very delicate instrument. It can be permanently damaged if exposed to unfiltered light.
The erase lamp assembly	Clears or erases images from the PS drum by shining a strong beam of light across the drum's surface.
The primary corona	A thin wire located in the disposable toner cartridge. A highly negative charge is applied to the wire creating an electrical corona effect that is used to condition the PS drum. The static charges in the corona may reach -6000 Volts, making it the highest electrically charged component of the printer.
The writing mechanism	Writes images onto the PS drum by producing and directing light to its surface. There are three types of writing mechanisms for EP printers: a laser beam or scanner; bars of light emitting diodes (LEDs), or arrays of liquid crystal shutters (LCS)s.
Toner	An extremely fine powder composed of plastic resin and organic compounds bound to iron particles.
The transfer corona	Operates in the same way as the primary corona, except that this wire carries a positive charge. Its function is to place a positive charge on paper.
Fusing assembly	Consists of two rollers that apply a combination of heat and pressure to fuse toner to the paper. As the paper goes between the two rollers, heat from the top roller melts the toner while pressure from the bottom roller squeezes it into the paper fibers. A lot of heat is generated at this station. Make sure that the material you are printing on will not melt below 180°F.
Duplexer	The Duplexer allows a laser printer to print to both sides of the medium (paper).

EP Printer Components

All printers have to process electronic data to produce images. An **interface controller** is the printer's motherboard. It performs several functions:

- Communicates with the host computer via one of three installed interface ports (parallel, serial, or direct video interface).
- Manipulates incoming data for translation to the print engine.
- Monitors the control panel for user input.
- Provides information on printer status at the display and through various LED's.
- Stores configuration and font information.

The interface controller is very similar to the motherboard in the PC. It contains a CPU, memory (RAM) and a System Bus.

Electromechanical Components	
AC power supply	Provides energy for the fusing assembly heaters and the erase lamp assembly.
DC power supply	Converts AC into the various levels of DC needed to power electronics and electromechanical devices.
High-voltage power supply	Used to create and dissipate the powerful static charges (1000 V or more) needed to move toner within the printer.
Main motor	Provides the mechanical force needed to support mechanical activity within the printer.
Paper control assembly	Provides sensors that monitor and detect the presence of paper at every area in the IFS.
Main logic assembly	Consists of most of the circuitry that operates the printer and the electronics that interface with the host computer.
EP cartridge	A replaceable cartridge that contains the toner supply. It also includes delicate, wear-prone parts such as the primary corona, the EP drum, and the developer roller.
Control panel assembly	Provides the user with the means to select different printer's operating modes.

Printing Process

As mentioned earlier, printing is a series of events combined to produce a printed page. This complicated process creates sharp printed images in extremely high resolution. But it also increases the potential for problems. It is important that you understand each of the steps in the printing process, not only to prepare for the *A+ Certification* test, but also so you will be able to troubleshoot laser printers. Understanding each step in the process will enable you to more efficiently identify, diagnose and isolate potential laser printing problems.

SPECIAL NOTE:

A+ Certification candidates must know these steps.

Step-by-Step Description of the Laser Printing Process

Step 1: Drum Preparation (Cleaning)

Before a new page can be printed, the *photosensitive drum* must be cleaned. (This process could be listed as the last or the first step of the printing process.) The cleaning process is accomplished by a rubber cleaning blade that gently scrapes any residual toner from the drum. The drum is then exposed to a lamp (the erase lamp) that will completely remove the last image.

Step 2: Conditioning (Charging)

After the cleaning/erase process, the drum is no longer light sensitive and it needs charging. This is done by applying a uniform negative charge (about 6000 volts) to the drum's surface. This is accomplished by a very thin solid wire called the *primary corona* located very near the drum's surface.

Step 3: Writing

During the writing process a latent image is formed on the drum surface. The uniform negative charge from the previous step becomes discharged at precise points where the image is produced. The actual writing is done with the *laser*. Where the laser strikes the drum will now become less-negatively charged.

Step 4: Developing

After the writing process the image is no more than an invisible array of electrostatic charges on the drum's surface. The *toner* is used to develop it. When the toner is ready to be applied, it is exposed to a cylinder (*developer roller*) that contains a permanent magnet. It is here that the toner receives a strong negative charge. The areas of low charge on the drum now attract the toner from the cylinder. This will fill-in the electromagnetic image. The other areas repel the equally negatively charged toner. The drum now holds an image that is ready to be transferred to the paper.

Step 5: Transfer

At this point, the developed image is transferred to the paper. The paper is exposed to the *transfer corona* which fixes a powerful positive charge to the paper that allows it to pry the negatively charged toner particles from the drum.

Step 6: Fusing

After the transfer process, the toner image is only laying on the surface of the paper, held by a small charge. It must be permanently bonded to the paper before it can be touched. The *fuser assembly*, along with the *pressure roller*, melts and presses the image into the paper's surface.

Servicing Laser Printers

As previously stated, the *Image Formation System* of a printer consists of several distinct components. If any one of these components fails to function properly the quality of the printed material suffers. Because of the number of components involved in the printing process, the potential for problems is high. Diagnosing a problem requires some intuition, the proper equipment and a logical troubleshooting approach.

Troubleshooting Cycle

The need for a logical troubleshooting approach cannot be overstated. No matter how complex the system may be, a simple four step procedure should help you to pinpoint the cause of the printer's problems.

Step 1: Define the Symptoms

In order to diagnose an illness, a doctor must first study the symptoms. The same concept applies here. If a printer is not working properly, take a close look at what it is (or is not) doing. This will make it easier for you to trace the problem to the right cause. Remember: it is always a good idea to take notes.

Step 2: Identify and Isolate

Never assume the printer is the cause of the problem. Remember, the printer is one piece of a larger system, which includes the computer and the cable connecting them. You could try connecting the suspect printer to a different computer, or try connecting a similar printer to the computer. Once you've determined that the printer is at fault, then you can start examining the components to find the cause of the problem.

Step 3: Repair or Replace

When you determine which component(s) is failing, you will then need to determine if you should replace them, or whether you should attempt to repair them. The solution could be as simple as cleaning the component in question. Or, if the problem is more severe, it may require replacing parts.

Depending on your level of expertise and knowledge, you may decide to replace small electronic components within the different subassemblies. NOTE: This can be a risky undertaking since many small parts are only obtainable through the manufacturer who may refuse to sell to anyone other than their authorized distributors.

If you are able to obtain new parts, there is nothing wrong with replacing a defective subassembly with a new one. However, be sure to keep the pieces well organized. Labeling may be tedious but, in the long run, it will save you the anxiety and frustration of not remembering how the components should to be reassembled.

Step 4: Re-Test

After the repair is completed and the unit is reassembled, test the printer to ensure that you have successfully solved the problem. If the problem persists or new problems surface, you will need to repeat the troubleshooting process.

Things to Check Before You Open Your Tool Box

The following is a list of potential causes for printer problems to consider before performing any disassembly.

Electricity Supply

Laser printers consume a lot of energy and require a reliable and dedicated source of power. It is always a good idea to check the wiring schematic for the outlet feeding the printer to be sure it is not being shared with another device. The outlet wiring should be checked to make sure it is in good condition. Laser printers are also susceptible to device interference (electrical line pollution). Try to keep printer cables isolated.

Reset

Just as a computer may be rebooted when it stops responding to commands, the printer can be reset or powered down when it stops responding to commands. This will provide only a temporary solution. You will still need to get to the cause of the problem. When you reset the printer, any downloaded fonts or macros will be lost.

Cables

Cables that are not properly secured can be a source of problems. Any movement may loosen them enough to cause print errors. Cable length is another consideration. Parallel cables should not be longer than 10 feet. A serial cable, on the other hand, can extend up to 50 feet. If the printed material shows typographical errors that do not appear on screen, it may be due to a break in a parallel cable data pin. Switching cables should correct the problem.

Environment

Much of the energy a printer consumes is transformed into heat, so it is important to place it in a well-ventilated area to allow the heat to dissipate. Ventilation is also important to dissipate small amounts of ozone gas produced during the printing process. Aside from being a mild irritant to humans in small concentrations, ozone is also an oxidizer which may corrode components. Light is another factor that could shorten the life of the printer. The light used to write the image on the PS drum is red filtered. Do not expose the PS drum directly to light unless you intend to replace it.

Paper

Every printer manufacturer will recommend a specific type of paper to be used with the printer. Follow these recommendations. Using a cheaper lower grade paper may cause paper jams and distortion problems. Do not forget that damp paper may also affect the quality of the printout. Make sure to keep paper dry.

Preventive Maintenance

Shipping

Never ship a printer with a toner cartridge still inside. Depending on how the printer is handled during shipping, there may be a lot of toner to clean upon arrival. Toner is very difficult to remove from clothing. You may want to try cold water and soap to remove toner stains. Strong chemicals or hot water (heat) may only cause the toner to bond to the cloth fibers.

Periodic Cleaning

The following parts require some periodic cleaning:

Corona wires - A long cotton swab, some alcohol, and a good deal of care and patience are required to clean the coronas. Above all, be very gentle with the wires.

Registration and feed guide assemblies - Most of the time, the only thing that may collect on these assemblies is residual toner and paper fragments. A damp cloth should be enough to do the job.

Fusing assembly - Things have a tendency to stick to the fusing assembly due to the amount of heat generated by it. You must remove all contaminants very carefully to prevent scratching the surface of the roller. Use a little bit of alcohol and a soft cloth to clean the fusing assembly. (Let the assembly cool down before you clean it.)

Separation pawls - The pawls facilitate the separation of the paper from the fuser. They have a claw-like appearance and are located behind the fuser assembly. Contaminants attach to them creating a buildup that may scratch the Teflon-coated surface of the fuser assembly rollers. Once again, a cotton swab dipped in alcohol should be enough to remove any buildup.

Common Printer Problems and Solutions

Vertical White Streaks On The Page

This is a problem that generally occurs when any part of the two corona wires is covered with toner. Since the job of the coronas is to transfer an electric charge, any toner covering the wire will cause uneven charges to be transferred to the drum or the paper. The drum's surface would be improperly conditioned to attract sufficient toner, or, in the case of the transfer corona, the paper would be inadequately charged to bring about a full toner transfer, causing the vertical streaks on paper. A simple solution to this problem is to clean the corona wires. Some printers come equipped with a small brush or attachment specifically for this purpose.

Horizontal Streaks

Take a look at the printed material. If the lines appear at regular intervals, then the problem lies with one of the rollers the paper passes by. To identify which roller, measure the distance between the marks and use that as an indication of the circumference of the roller is causing the problem

Smearing

Remember that toner remains loose on paper until it reaches the fusing rollers. Smearing could be the result of the roller not applying enough heat to fuse the toner. Although the fusing roller is covered with a Teflon-like substance to prevent anything from sticking to it, sometimes it may get scratched or something may get baked onto it. A good way to get rid of the problem is to inspect and clean the rollers with a soft cloth and some alcohol. Keep in mind that the roller generates heat (a lot of it) and alcohol is a flammable fluid. When heat and a flammable fluid socialize, they produce fire. Let the rollers cool down before you attempt to clean them. Smears can also be caused by trying to print on both sides of the same paper. Not all printers are designed to do this.

Faded Prints

This is another problem caused by a dirty corona wire. Simply clean the coronas as described previously.

Printer Picks Up Multiple Sheets

In this case the problem may lie with the paper in use and not the printer. Dry, good quality laser printer paper is required for a proper feed. Also, if paper is exposed to humidity, chances are that it will not work very well with the printer. Always store paper in a dry area.

Paper Jams

There are various causes to this problem. Double-sided printing is one cause or you may be using the wrong side of the paper to print. There are two different sides to a sheet of paper, the wax and the wire sides. The paper wrapper has an arrow indicating which side to print first. Again, it is always best to follow the manufacturer's suggestion to use specific paper types. Low grade paper may also cause jams. Check the paper wrapper or label to make sure that it is suitable for laser printer use.

Error 20 Appears On The Control Panel Display

This is an insufficient memory error. Adding memory to the printer is generally a good solution, but don't overlook the possibility that this may be a software-related problem.

Error 55 Appears On The Control Panel Display

This is an error flag that appears during start up. This problem can be traced to two circuit boards inside the printer, one that controls the charging and discharging of the corona wires (the *DC controller board*), and one that controls the serial and parallel interfaces (the *interface controller board*). When the printer starts up, the two boards run a communications test; if the test fails, the error signal is displayed. This may be an indication of a bad interface controller board that will need to be replaced. Before replacing the controller, try connecting the printer to a different outlet. Power noise is strong enough at times to cause interference between the two boards, and this may also trigger an error message.

Stalled Print Spooler

Windows creates a temporary file called a "spool" file on your hard disk where it stores the document information prior to printing the document. If the printer becomes stalled for some reason (out-of-paper, printer offline,etc.), click on the **Print Manager** icon on your desktop (Windows 3.x) or the **Printers** folder (Windows 95). The stalled printer should be clearly identified. Click **Resume** to clear and jump-start the printer to resume printing.

Wrong Printer Driver

If you receive an "*incompatible printer driver*" error message, contact your software manufacturer to obtain the most current driver for your particular printer if your printer is not listed when you installed the printer. To update the driver, follow these steps:

Windows

- Click **Start** > **Settings**.
- Click **Printers** (or, from the **Control Panel**, click the **Printers** folder).
- Double-click the **Add printer** icon and the **Add Printer Wizard** will appear.
- Click **My Computer** to make changes to only *your* printer configurations not for the entire network.
- Click **Next**
- Click the box next to the port the printer is directed to.
- Click **Next**
- If your printer is not listed and you wish to install the printer driver from a disk, click **Have Disk**.
- If the correct drive is displayed, click **OK**. Otherwise, type in the letter for your floppy drive, then **OK**.

The new printer driver will be installed into the correct Windows directory.

Other Printers

Laser printers are not the only type of printer that you will encounter in the real world. There are at least two more categories of printers you will need to be aware of as an A+ Certified Technician. These two categories are impact printers (dot matrix) and non-impact printers (ink jet).

Dot Matrix Printers

Dot matrix printers fall under the broad heading of impact printers. This is the family of printers that uses a print head containing pins (generally 9 to 24) that are forced to strike an inked ribbon against the paper to form a character. The character is actually formed by a series of dots. The more dots, the better the print quality. This is why a 24-pin printer will cost more than a 9-pin printer.

Just as with laser printers, dot matrix printers have various components that are more likely candidates for failure than others. Some of the most common components that are prone to fail are listed below:

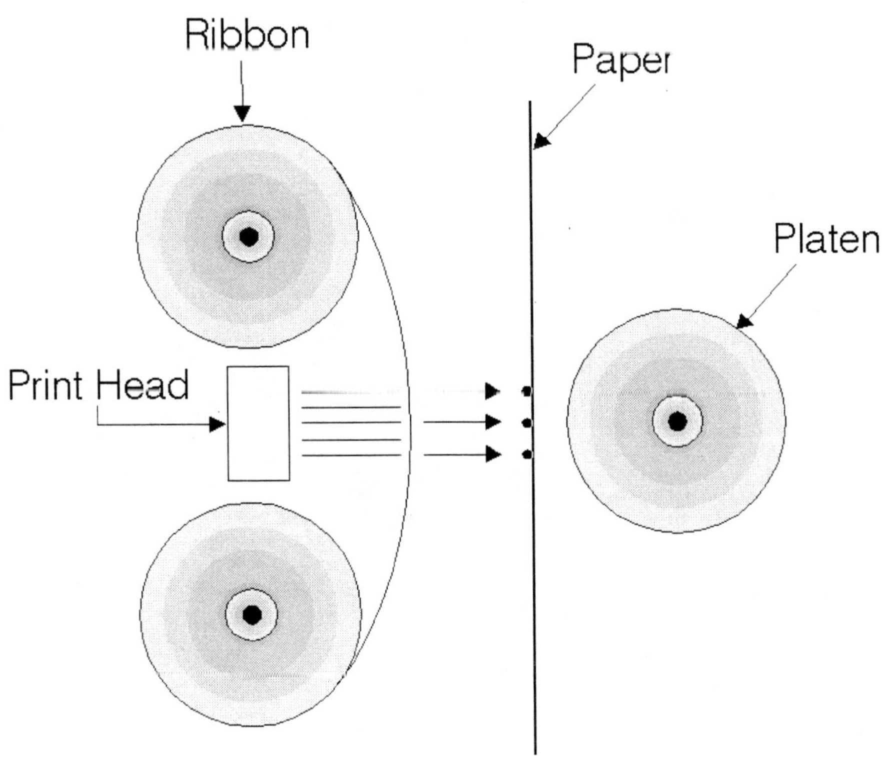

DOT-MATRIX PRINTER (IMPACT PRINTER)

COMMON DOT-MATRIX PROBLEMS	
Problem	**Possible Cause**
Light then dark print.	Most likely caused by a defective ribbon drive motor.
Consistent light, patchy print.	Could be caused by a dry or old ribbon.
Printer shuts down after getting hot, then restarts after a short while.	Replace the thermistor, a device that will shut down the printer after it reaches a certain temperature.
Characters not fully formed.	Could be a defective print head or broken pin.
Printer does not print.	Check to see if the printer is on-line and connected to the PC.
Prints continuously on the same line.	Check and replace the stepper motor (linespace).

Non-Impact Printers

Unlike impact printers, nothing is forced against the paper in non-impact printers. For the most part, non-impact printers use a technology called ink-jet to form the image on the paper. The print head in this case actually sprays a narrow stream of ink on the paper. Generally, ink-jet printers will yield a more fully-formed character than the dot-matrix. They are also much quieter than impact printers.

A disadvantage of ink-jet printers is that the cartridges tend to clog resulting in partial or no print at all. Another potential problem is that there is little warning when the cartridge is running out of ink. An ink-jet printer can go from perfect print to no print in just a few lines. With the dot-matrix, the ribbons progressively get lighter, giving you a little warning.

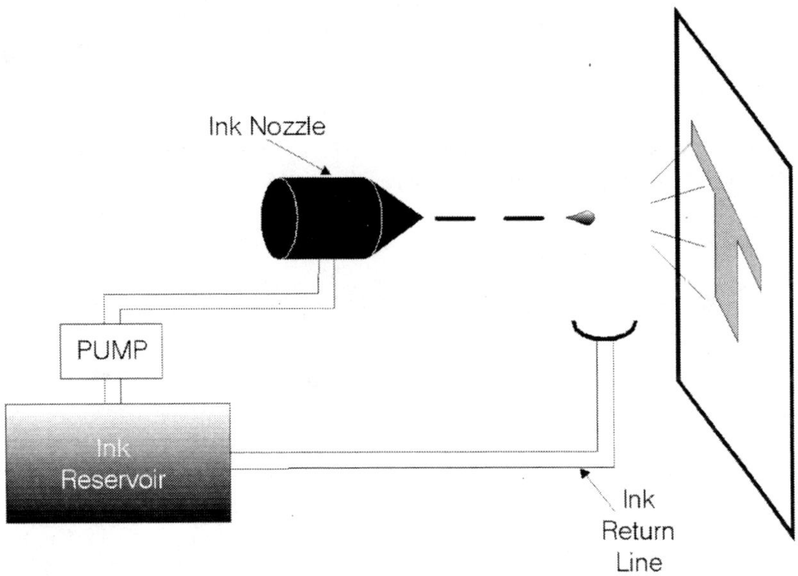

NON-IMPACT PRINTER

Summary

A printer is a computer in itself that converts electronic pulses into images on paper. Printers are an integral part of a computer system. Today's printers are able to produce extremely high quality outputs for a variety of different applications. Laser printers are perhaps the most common in the business environment. It is important that you understand the components integral to the laser printer and the electrophotographic process. Regardless of the brand, most laser printers use this six-step process to produce the image on the paper:

- Cleaning
- Conditioning (charging)
- Writing
- Developing
- Transfer
- Fusing.

Laser printer technology is not the only process for printing. There are also two other categories of printers:

- Impact (dot-matrix)
- Non-impact (ink-jet).

Both of them have advantages and disadvantages over the other. When choosing between them, it is important to define what type of print jobs that you will be doing.

Review Questions

1. Which laser printing step puts a uniform negative charge on the drum's surface?

   A. Cleaning
   B. Developing
   C. Conditioning
   D. Transfer

2. During the laser printing process, what happens in the transfer stage?

   A. Residual toner is removed.
   B. The image is transferred to the drum.
   C. A negative charge is transferred to the drum.
   D. The image is transferred to the media.

3. In a laser printer, which component will least likely cause a paper jam?

   A. The drum
   B. The fuser roller
   C. The sheet feeder
   D. The laser scanner unit

4. Which laser component should never be exposed to sunlight?

   A. The photosensitive drum
   B. The corona wire
   C. The toner cartridge
   D. The paper

5. Which of the following laser components should be cleaned or replaced during preventive maintenance?

   A. Scanner
   B. Cleaning blade
   C. Ozone filter
   D. Toner cartridge

6. Light then dark print on a dot-matrix printer would typically be caused by:

   A. Print head alignment
   B. Print head overheating
   C. Erratic ribbon drive advancement
   D. Paper advancement

7. During preventive maintenance you should never lubricate:

   A. Paper advancement gears
   B. Print head pins
   C. Print head pulley
   D. Gear bus hinge

8. Your printer's power lamp LED is on, but the printer will not print. What should you do first to attempt to correct the problem?

   A. Replace the fuse.
   B. Replace the ribbon.
   C. Ensure printer is on-line.
   D. Turn the printer off.

9. Which of the following printers would be the best choice for printing on multipart forms?

   A. Ink-jet
   B. Dot-matrix
   C. Thermal
   D. Bubble-jet

10. When storing laser paper which of the following should be considered? (Choose all that apply.)

   A. Location
   B. Temperature
   C. Humidity
   D. Ream size

Section 11

Preventive Maintenance

Section 11: Preventive Maintenance

Introduction

Have you ever heard the saying, "An ounce of prevention is worth a pound of cure?" This saying certainly holds true for computer equipment. Electronic equipment is delicate. If you want it to last and provide you with peak performance during its life, then you need to maintain it properly and protect it from potential harm. The focus of this chapter is two-fold. First, we will talk about things you can do to minimize or eliminate damage from outside sources. Then we will outline the steps for developing a good Preventive Maintenance program.

Objectives

When you've completed this section, you will be able to do the following:

- Recognize harmful external influences for computer equipment
- Understand the possible damage that could be caused by stray electromagnetism, power-related problems, water and other liquids and corrosive elements
- Run a comprehensive preventive maintenance program
- Review the recommendations for cleaning the parts of a PC

Harmful Influences

In order to better understand what steps to take to better care for a PC, we need to know what things affect it adversely.

Internal Heat

Chips and other internal components are continuously generating heat. This is why most computers are equipped with fans. The fan helps to dissipate heat as quickly as possible. If the fan fails, the heat continues to build and there is a strong likelihood that the chips will suffer damage. Computer manufacturers spend large amounts of time and money engineering case design to create optimal air flow. Always replace slot covers over empty slots. The air flow may change enough to cause heat related problems if the slots are left open.

Heat from Direct Sunlight

If the computer sits under direct sunlight, it adds an additional heat source for the fan to combat. It may cause the fan to fail, or it may cause the system to overheat. Hardware manufacturers recommend specific operating temperature ranges for their products. A typical range would be a minimum of 60° F and a maximum of 85° F. Individual components are rated for much higher temperatures. Circuit boards, for example, are rated for a maximum of 125° F and hard drives for 110° F These may sound like safe numbers, but typically the interior of a computer will run approximately 40° F higher than the room temperature. On a hot summer day, you may well exceed the operating range for these parts.

Thermal Shock

Thermal shock occurs as a result of rapid cooling or rapid heating of computer components. This occurs most often during the winter months when an office computer may be exposed to cold temperature settings during a weekend and then rapid heating as the office is heated again during the week.

Dust

When dust settles on a surface it may act as a thermal insulator, helping to create a larger heat build up. It may also permeate sensitive areas like the space between the disk drive heads and the disk, causing mechanical failure.

Magnetism

Magnetism could cause you to loose data on the hard drive or on floppy disks. The following is a list of common objects in an office that are a source of magnetic fields:

- Small electric motors from office equipment.
- Magnetic screwdrivers.
- Magnetic clip holders.
- Magnetic paper holders.

Stray Electromagnetism

Electromagnetic Interference (EMI)

Electromagnetic interference is particularly problematic in network environments. Wires carry electronic pulses that produce magnetic fields as a side effect. When two or more wires are in close proximity to each other, their magnetic fields cross and produce additional electronic pulses or echoes. These echoes are then carried by the wires causing interference.

Radio Frequency Interference (RFI)

Radio frequency interference is radiation emitted in the frequency range of radio waves. Have you ever taken a portable radio into a car and heard it hum in synch with the engine? This is radio frequency interference. Additional sources are:

- High speed digital circuits (like the ones in your computer)
- Nearby radio sources
- Cordless telephone
- Power line intercoms
- Electric motors

Power-Related Problems

Electric utility companies are supposed to provide users with a constant and regular supply of energy all the time. But for many reasons, the energy that comes out of your outlet does not always flow evenly. Power suffers very brief variations in the form of drops (sags) and surges. These power fluctuations cause very harmful effects on your PC, both in the short-term and over time.

Voltage Surges and Sags

Surges and sags in voltage are the most common type of power-related problems. The nature of surges may be such that they slip past the built-in protection in your computer's power supply and go directly to the chips. Damage may not become evident the very first time a voltage surge passes into your system. More than likely it will have a cumulative effect that will slowly destroy one or more components.

Sags, on the other hand, have a different effect, especially if they endure for an extended period. Extended drops in voltage are commonly known as brown-outs. When these occur, the power supply tries to compensate for the loss of voltage by drawing more current. This causes chips and other components to heat up and may even cause them to overheat.

Electrostatic Discharges

We've already talked about the causes and dangers of ESD. But since the subject is a very critical one, here are a few more tips on how to control electrostatic potential build up.

- Install a static-free carpet.
- Raise the humidity level in a room through the use of an evaporative humidifier, (ultrasonic humidifiers create dust) or by adding some plants to the environment.
- Make use of anti-static mats under your PC.

Water and Other Liquids

Most liquid damage caused to computer equipment occurs when the computer user spills a beverage on the keyboard, the mouse, or even the monitor. The computer case has a nice flat surface that some people may find suitable for resting a soda or cup of coffee. These and other fluids will oxidize and corrode metals, and can diminish their conductive properties.

A second, more hazardous problem occurs when fluids mix with electricity. At the very least, this combination could cause a component to short. The most dangerous effect of combining water and electricity is the possibility of electric shock. Remember, the system is plugged into an electrical outlet!

The best way to avoid fluid damage is to provide a secure spot for the computer. Rest the case on a stand above the floor to preclude the possibility of flood damage. The keyboard can be protected by covering it with a plastic "keyboard skin."

Corrosive Elements

The major problem with corrosion is that it affects the conductive properties of metals. Household cleaners contain chemicals such as ammonia, various acids, sulfurs, etc. that have a corroding effect on any metal they come in contact with. Mist particles from spray bottle cleaners may find their way inside a computer case, causing some damage. When cleaning your computer, use a damp cloth with a mild mix of soap and water. You may also want to dust off components with compressed air. However, be careful not to do it in the vicinity of other equipment otherwise you'll be moving dust from one component to the other.

Implementing a Preventive Maintenance Program

Let's summarize the previous section by outlining the steps necessary to provide a safe environment for PCs.

- Preferably, computers need to be in a cool, constant environment. But if changes in temperature are inevitable, take steps to ensure that the maximum operating temperature does not exceed 110° F and does not fall below 65° F.
- Eliminate the possibility of dust buildup on components. Regular internal component cleanups may help to alleviate this problem. Another way would be to utilize power supplies that come equipped with a filtered fan. This type of fan creates an opposite airflow pattern by filtering the air first, compared to regular fans, which filter the air after pulling it through the fan.
- Remove any magnetic sources from the computer's vicinity.
- Instruct computer operators on ESD damage and prevention. Provide an environment less conducive to ESD and make use of anti-static materials around the computer.
- Make sure the computer does not share the same electrical line that may supply energy to large electric motors such as the ones found in refrigerators or air conditioners and other smaller appliances. This may have the effect of causing power sags and surges as the appliances and motors turn on and off.
- Instruct operators on the potential dangers of liquid spills.
- Remove corrosive chemicals from the list of suitable computer cleaners and provide some other options.

Troubleshooting/Repair Tools & Maintenance Procedures

Cleaning Tools

Your troubleshooting/repair toolbox should contain the following to clean and maintain computer equipment:

- Can of compressed air
- Dust-free cloth
- Glass cleaning liquid (Windex, etc.)
- Small brush
- Cotton swabs
- Hand-held vacuum cleaner
- WD-40 or teflon-based lubricant like Tri-Flow to lubricate the head rails of floppy drives
- A commercial connector cleaning product, such as TexWipe, to clean contacts and connections

Wear and Tear

Dust can clog air-intake areas which will result in excessive wear and heat-buildup within the CPU. Dust can also clog spaces such as the area between the floppy disk drive head and the disk. When you're installing a new peripheral card or performing other tasks inside the CPU, take the time to blow out the interior of the case with compressed air, being careful to aim the compressed air away from the machine. Otherwise, you're blowing the excess dust right back into the system.

PCs attract dust -- much the same as your television screen does. Don't smoke around your PC and be sure users are warned about consuming food or beverages while working at the computer. Nothing can damage a keyboard quicker than a spilled "Big Gulp" or that morning cup of coffee. A plastic skin can be used over a keyboard to protect it in high traffic areas where spills may occur.

To control ESD and EMI, don't plug heating elements into the same outlet as the PC. Keep the PC away from any vibration source, such as an impact printer.

When transporting or storing circuit boards or other components, always use anti-static protective tubes or bags. Be careful not to touch the fragile pins on a circuit board.

Preventive Maintenance/Cleaning Recommendations

- **System Case -** Clean the system case, inside and out, on an annual basis. Wipe the case with a damp cloth but don't spray cleaning liquids directly on the case. Clean the inside by either blasting with compressed air or using a small vacuum with a PC cleaning attachment. Be sure to replace any slot covers that may have been removed. Slot covers are a good way to keep dust from the interior of the case.

- **Power Supply** - The main enemy of a power supply is overheating caused by excessive dust and dirt clogging the fan and coating the components. Inspect the fan regularly to ensure it is providing good ventilation and is not dirty. Clean it with the vacuum or compressed air. Also check the power protection devices to see that they are working properly.

- **Motherboard** - As part of the annual cleaning, clean the motherboard and expansion cards with a vacuum or compressed air to improve the cooling of the motherboard components. DO NOT clean the gold contacts on expansion cards with a pencil eraser. Over time, the abrasion can cause damage. Check the board for connectivity problems. Are all cards and cables making good contact. On older boards, check for "Chip creep" - chips that work their way out of their sockets due to repeated thermal expansion and contraction. Back up the system BIOS settings as a part of your annual maintenance routine.

- **Processor** - The system processor requires no maintenance, however, during the annual cleaning, touch the edge of the processor (or the edge of the heat sink as close to the processor as possible). If it's too hot to leave your finger on for more than a second, it's too hot. Consider adding a larger heat sink or a better cooling fan to improve the cooling level. Inspect and clean the heat sink and fan with a vacuum or compressed air.

- **System Memory** - SIMMs and DIMMS do not require maintenance, other than as part of the overall cleaning of the inside of the system. Check to be sure all memory modules are seated correctly in their slots.

- **Video Cards** - Clean the video card just as you did the expansion cards on the motherboard, with a vacuum or compressed air.

- **CRT** - Clean the monitor's screen weekly. Just like on a TV, the screen accumulates dust more quickly because of the static charge generated by the CRT. Wipe it with a soft cloth. Using the wrong cleaner can damage the special coatings used on many newer screens to reduce glare and improve image quality. Some cleaners may also leave smudges and streaks. Never use an abrasive cleaner on the screen. A damp, soft cloth is the best choice. Clean the outside of the CRT including the vents to prevent the cooling vents from becoming clogged with dirt.

- **Hard Disk Drives** - Newer hard drives generate a lot of heat. Be sure the system's interior has adequate cooling and ventilation. The annual general cleaning will reduce excessive dust buildup on the sealed hard drive unit. When the case is opened, check the hard drive for excessive vibration and heat. (Be sure the PC has been running for at least a half-hour before you open the case.)

- **Floppy Disk Drives** - Unlike hard disk drives, floppy drives are not sealed and are thus exposed to the outside air. Clean these drives quarterly, or more often if they are used often. Clean the read/write heads with either a Q-tip and alcohol or a special cleaning kit. Clean the inside of the drive with a vacuum or compressed air, just as you did the other components. Also check and adjust the alignment of the drive. A misaligned drive will lose its ability to read and write data.

- **CD-ROM Drive** - Most CD-ROMs can tolerate a good deal of dirt and dust. If you are experiencing errors reading disks that can be read in other CD-ROM drives, you can use a CD-ROM lens cleaner.
- **Peripheral Ports** - Clean and check all connections as you perform the annual cleaning.
- **Keyboards** - Over time, dirt and the natural oils from fingers accumulate on the keycaps and dirt and debris fall between the keys. Clean the keyboard with compressed air and/or the PC vacuum at least annually. Check for cable and connector damage.
- **Mouse** - Clean the mouse on a monthly basis, including the mouse ball and the rollers on the inside of the unit. Check for cable and connector damage.

Safety/Environmental Repair Considerations

High-Voltage Equipment

NEVER attempt to repair a monitor or a power supply. If you were to open a power supply or a monitor while the computer was plugged in (even if the power was OFF), you could receive a charge of the full 120 volts. Even if the PC is OFF, the capacitors store power and can shock you.

Laser Beams

When repairing a laser printer or other component that uses laser technology, avoid looking directly at the laser beam. Lasers have the potential to cause blindness.

Disposal of Used Materials

Consult your city's environmental regulations for the proper disposal procedure for potentially harmful materials such as batteries, monitors, toner kits/cartridges, circuit boards, cables and chemical cleaning solvents. You should always check your local laws concerning disposal of batteries or toxic cleaning supplies.

Material Safety Data Sheets (MSDS)

Ask the vendor or manufacturer of a cleaning solvent or other chemical product you use regularly for the product's MSDS. These sheets provide specific handling procedures and safety precautions to minimize the risk to health and environment when they are used and disposed of in the workplace.

Summary

Computer equipment is delicate and expensive. If you want it to last and function properly, you need to conduct regular maintenance on your equipment. Take steps to protect it from potential harm. By recognizing those elements which may damage or interfere with a PC's performance, you will be able to create a safe operating environment for your computer.

Review Questions

1. What is the term for the rapid cooling or rapid heating of computer components?

   A. Shock
   B. Hot/cold transfer
   C. Thermal shock
   D. Thermal reduction

2. Magnetic screwdrivers are very helpful and safe when working with computer components.

   A. True
   B. False

3. When some electrical equipment produces undesirable magnetic fields, it is called what?

   A. EMB
   B. EMI
   C. Field Shock
   D. Stratus noise

4. Electronic components are not sensitive to dust because they are hermetically sealed.

   A. True
   B. False

5. Which of the following describes the sudden drop of voltage on an AC line?

   A. Sag
   B. Drop
   C. Surge
   D. Null

Section 12

Networks

Section 12: Networks

Introduction

A network is a group of computers linked together for the purpose of sharing resources. Due to the expansive growth of the Internet and Internetworking technologies, most PCs in the world today are connected to a network. Businesses not only need to share resources among personnel, but also need to manage and protect data by controlling and limiting access to information. Networks address these needs in various ways. In this chapter we will discuss different network set-ups and look at the parts that combine to form a network.

Objectives

When you've completed this section, you will be able to explain the following concepts:

- Define a Local-Area Network
- Identify the components of a network
- Describe the LOGON process
- Identify the types of networks
- Identify topology

LAN (Local-Area Network)

A Local-Area Network is a group of computers that share information and other resources through a system of cables and network interface cards that links them together. As the name implies, a LAN links computers that are located relatively close to each other, as would be the case with a group of computers located in offices in the same building. Networks with widespread coverage linking cities or even countries are known as Wide-Area Networks (WAN). Networks address the need to share data and resources and also allow for the protection of data by controlling and limiting access to the information contained in them.

Components of a Network

Networks consist of two major areas, a physical and a logical. The physical network is the collection of hardware and peripherals linked together to build the network. The logical network is the software that manages the information going through the physical network. Here is a look at some of the components:

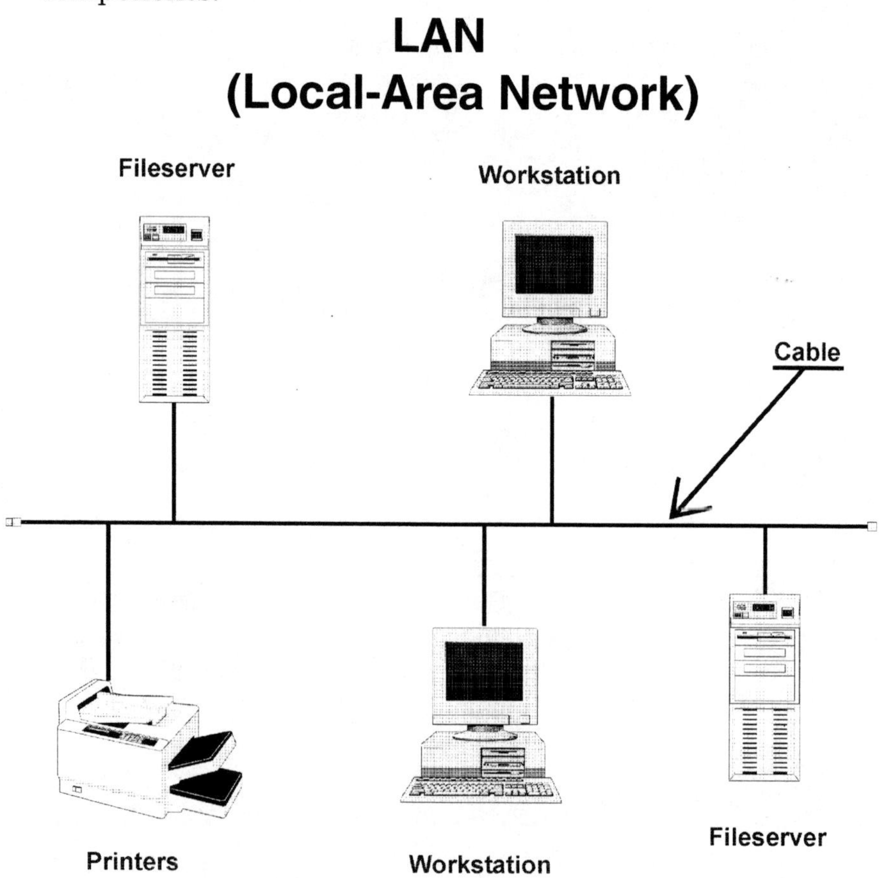

COMPONENTS OF A LOCAL-AREA NETWORK

Physical Components

Server

The server could be any computer on the network that provides services. These services might include print and file sharing, email, communications and other functions. The server is responsible for acknowledging and responding to user requests for network resources.

Typically network servers will have larger hard disk capacity, more RAM and faster processors than the average network user's computer. Often, network servers will also be configured with a redundant hard disk for extra fault tolerance. This multiple hard disk configuration is generally refered to as a RAID system, discussed in more detail later in this course.

Most servers in today's networks are "dedicated" to the function of just providing services. They are service providers, if you will. However, in some smaller networks, a server may be "non-dedicated." In this role, the server acts as both a service requester as well as a service provider. This type of arrangement is called a peer-to-peer networking environment.

Workstation

The workstation could be any computer in the network other than the server. The workstation, sometimes referred to as a "client", fulfills the role of service requester. This is the computer that you would typically see on most people's desktops. An individual uses this client machine to access the network services and resources.

Network Interface Cards (NICs)

The NIC is an expansion board that allows the workstation or server to attach to a common cabling system. Most network interface cards provide for more than just one cable type. The most common connection types are twisted pair (RJ45), coax (BNC) connector and fiber optic connections.

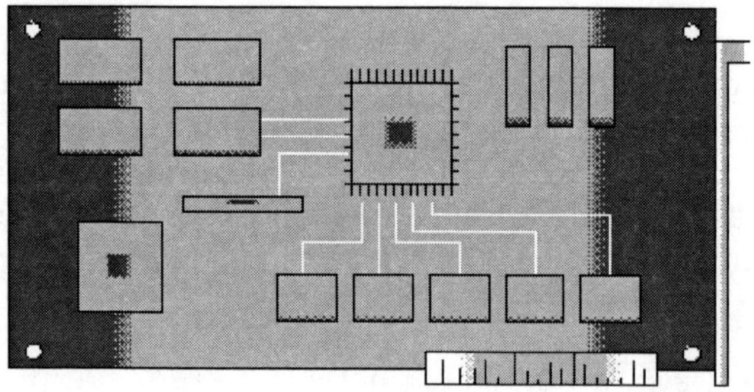

Transceivers

A transceiver is a network component that is usually built into the network interface card. Its primary responsibility is to convert a digital signal to match the appropriate signal needed for transmission on a particular media (cable). If the transceiver is built into the NIC, it is called an internal transceiver. An external transceiver can be used to convert between different media types. An example of this would be a NIC that only has an old style **Attachment Unit Interface** Ethernet connector and you need to convert it to a RJ-45 connector making it suitable for a 10base-T network.

Hubs and Concentrators

A hub, often referred to as a concentrator, provides a common multi-point connection for the network computers to attach to. This cabling configuration is called a star topology. The term **active hubs** apply to those that have the ability to act not only as a central connection point but also can boost signal strength if needed.

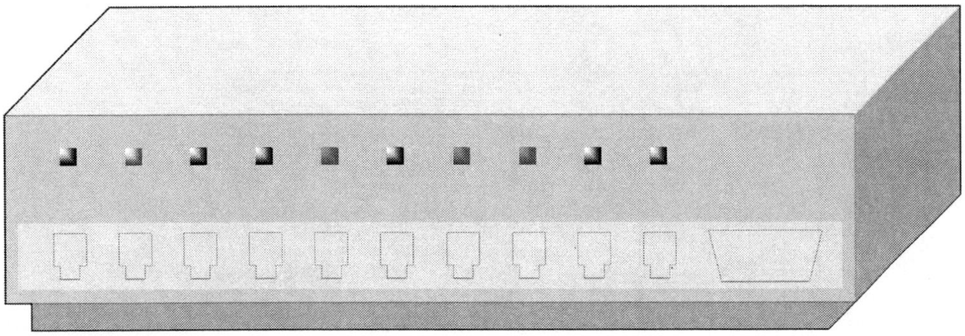

Switches

A switch is very similar to a hub or a concentrator in that it is a network device that connects multiple segments. Unlike a concentrator, it can guarantee full or maximum bandwidth on or across each port.

MAUs

The MAU (multi-station access unit) is very similar to a hub; however, it was specially designed for the IBM token-ring environment. The MAU can be distinguished from the hub by the unique ring in/ring out ports that are used to daisy chain multiple MAUs together. The typical MAU has eight connection ports plus the ring in/ring out port.

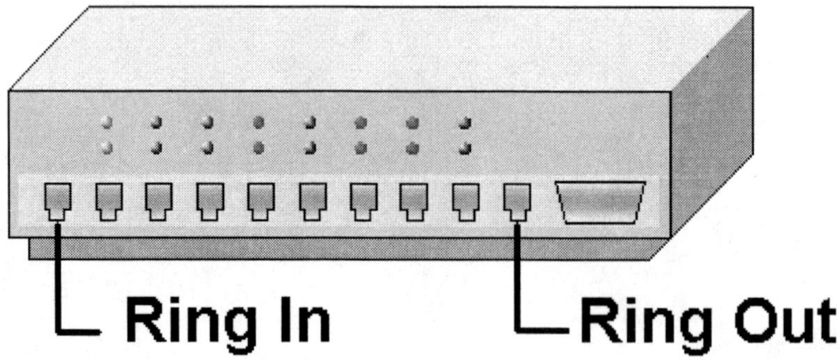

Repeaters

A repeater is a signal amplification device. So, just what does that mean? Simply stated, as an electronic signal travels down a wire it weakens in strength. In electronic jargon this is known as attenuation. It's much like a marathon runner getting tired and weak as the race progresses. Repeaters are place at predetermined points along the cable and act to boost and retransmit the signal, like giving the runner a power bar or drink at crucial points in the race.

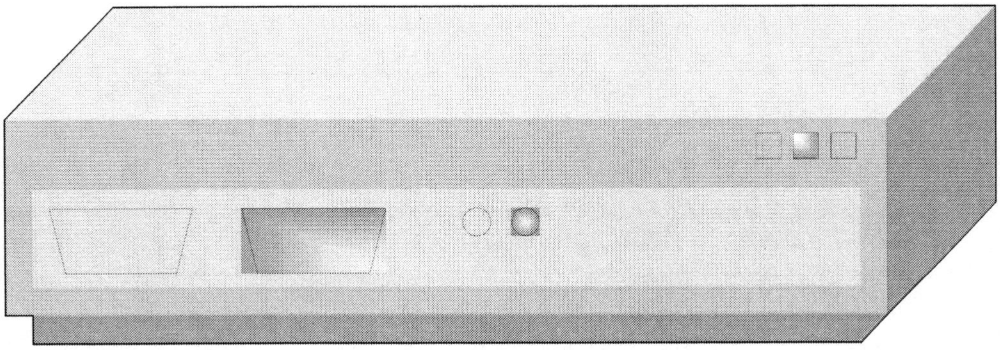

Bridges

The bridge is a hardware device that segments a **single** network into two or more pieces for the purpose of isolating network traffic. It's like a drawbridge that lets people in or keeps people from passing through. The network bridge performs the same function in a network environment. The bridge will either pass network traffic or deny network traffic based on the destination address. If the intended address is on the local segment the bridge will block the traffic. On the other hand, if the destination address is on another segment the bridge will allow the traffic to pass through.

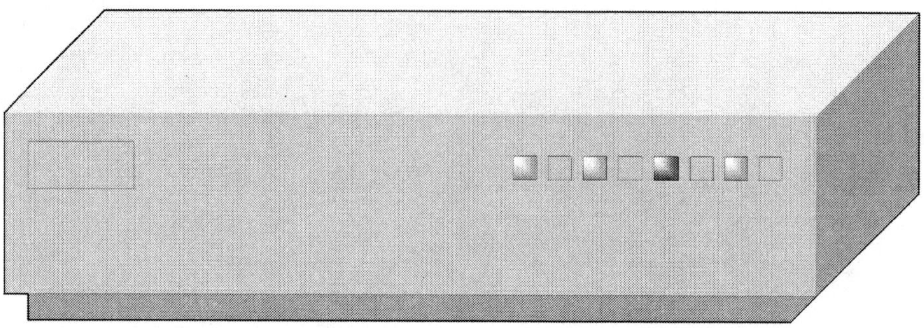

Routers

The router is considered to be an intelligent networking device. It performs basically two functions. First, it provides the physical connection between two or more different networks. The second and major function is to route packets of network information between different networks, hence the name "router." The router also has the intelligence built in to dynamically adapt to changes in the network configurations and route traffic around downed links.

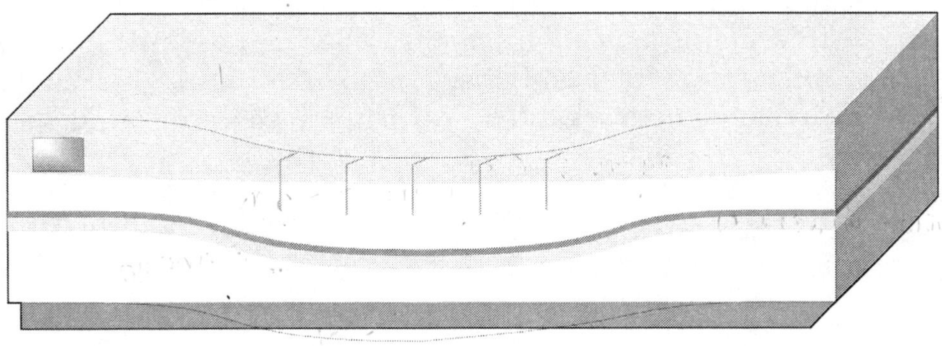

Gateways

If a router is considered an intelligent networking device, the gateway would be considered the device with a PhD. The gateway basically provides all the functionality of a router and acts as a translator as well. The router is a protocol-independent device, meaning it doesn't really care what language a computer speaks, it is just interested in getting the message from one machine to another. The gateway performs the routing function as well as translating between different computer languages (protocols). An example of this could be the connection between a Windows NT/2000 network and an IBM mainframe environment. The word **default gateway** refers to a router on the network that sends all TCP/IP packets to remote networks. The key point here is any or all packets are sent which are not destined for the local network!

Because of the translation and other overhead involved, the gateway is the least rapid (slowest) of the Internetwork connection devices.

Network Cables and Connectors

Perhaps the most important network components are the media and connectors used to attach computers to the system. The word "media" simply refers to the physical pathway on which network data travels. In most cases, this media is some type of cable. We refer to these cables as bounded media. Within the networking environment, many different types of bounded media are used. Each of these have very different characteristics such as speed, maximum length and connection types. The following is a list of the most common type of cables:

- Coaxial (Coax) Cable
- Twisted Pair
- Fiber Optic

Coaxial Cable (Coax)

Coaxial cable, typically called **coax** cable, uses a center core conductor that is insulated and surrounded by either a braided or solid thin foil aluminum shield. Coax cable is very similar in appearance to the type used by television cable companies in your home; however, it should be noted that these are not the same and can not be interchanged. Due to the amount of shielding, coax cable is very resistant to crosstalk (interference from adjacent wires) and EMI (electromagnetic interference). The graphic below shows that a coax cable is composed of an outer jacket, an outer shield, an insulator and the center conductor.

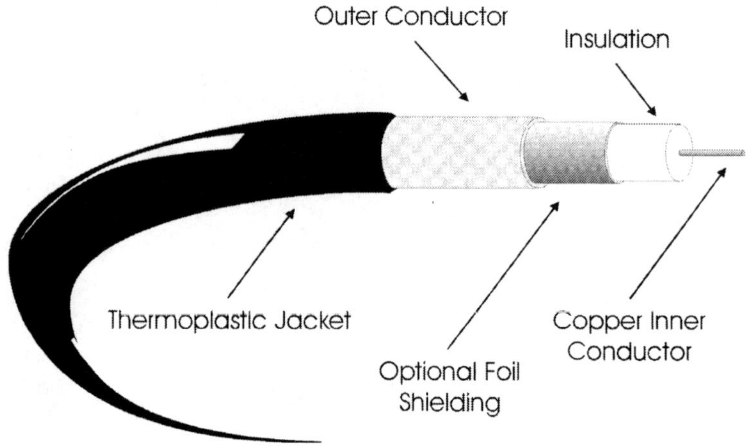

The coax cable uses a BNC-type connector. The BNC connection consist of three different components: the BNC connector itself, a T-connector and a matching terminator (resistor) that is used on both ends of a coax segment. See the graphic below:

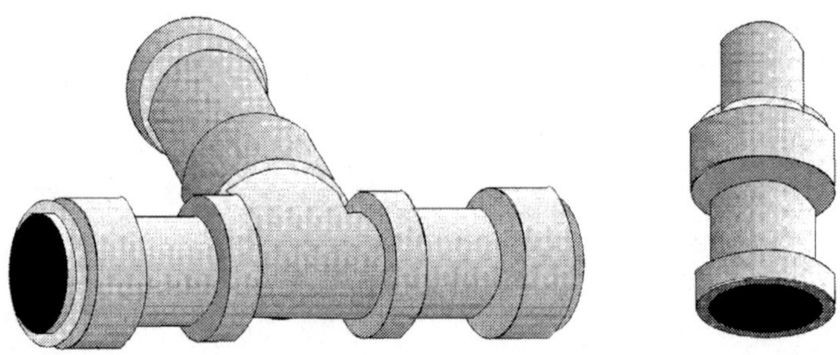

Twisted Pair Cable

Twisted pair cable consists of at least two insulated wires twisted together to reduce the effects of crosstalk. There are two broad categories of twisted pair cables. They are UTP (unshielded twisted pair cable) and STP (shielded twisted pair cable).

STP cable is very resistant to environmental factors like EMI because of the added layer of shielding that surrounds the twisted wires. STP cable tends to be more expensive than UTP and is also harder to work with than the thinner unshielded variety. The most common implementation of STP is for IBM Token ring cables.

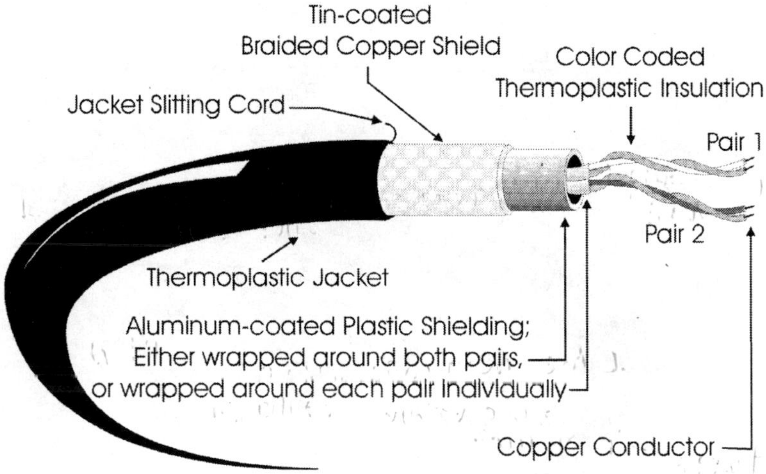

UTP, as the name would imply, does not have an added layer of shielding and is therefore thinner and cheaper to manufacture. UTP cable is rated in categories: Category 3 and 5 are the most common for data grade transmissions. The CAT 3 cable was dominant in the early years of networking but has been replaced by CAT 5 wiring because CAT 5 is better able to create a stable platform for data transmissions greater than 10 Mbps. The CAT 5 twisted pair cable can support speeds of 100 Mbps. The main physical difference between CAT 3 and CAT 5 cable is the number of twists per inch. The CAT 5 cable has many more twists than CAT 3, eliminating most crosstalk. UTP cable closely resembles the cable used by telephones in your home. The graphic below shows a UTP cable.

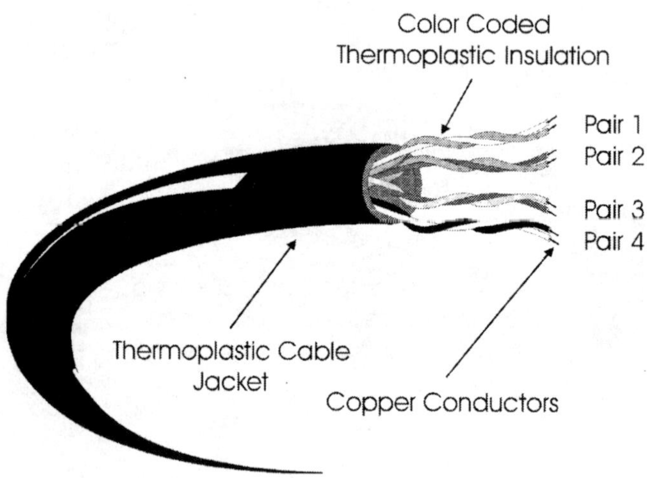

Twisted Pair Connectors

Twisted pair cables (UTP) use an RJ-45 connector. This connector looks very much like the connector used by telephone wires in your home. The telephone connector is called a RJ-11 and typically has two or three pairs of wires, while the RJ-45 data connector supports up to eight wires or four pairs. The graphic below shows an RJ-45 data connector.

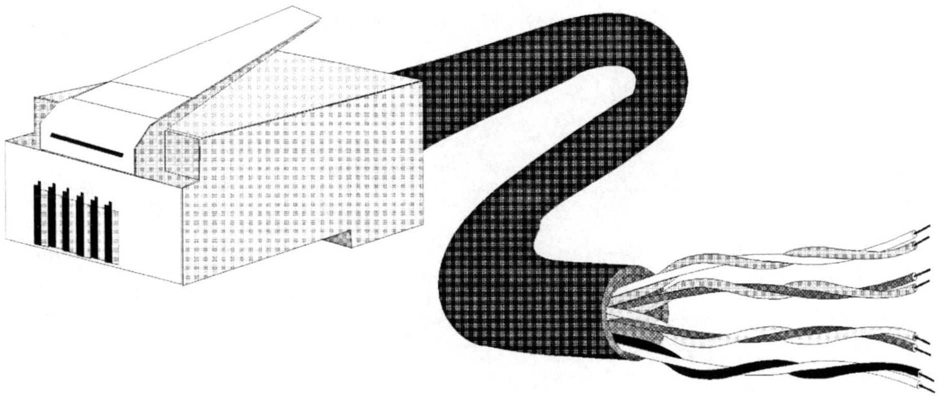

Fiber Optic Cable

Fiber optic cable uses a small strand of glass or plastic, instead of copper, as the core of the cable. It consists of a glass center core surrounded by a plastic sheath and a layer of gel or wire stands. Fiber optic cable offers a major advantage over copper wire. It is almost completely immune to EMI and does not suffer from attenuation (loss of signal strength over distance) like copper cable. Fiber cable tends to be very expensive as compared to copper wire; however, this cost variance should decrease as more companies choose to implement this technology. The graphic below depicts two types of fiber optic configurations:

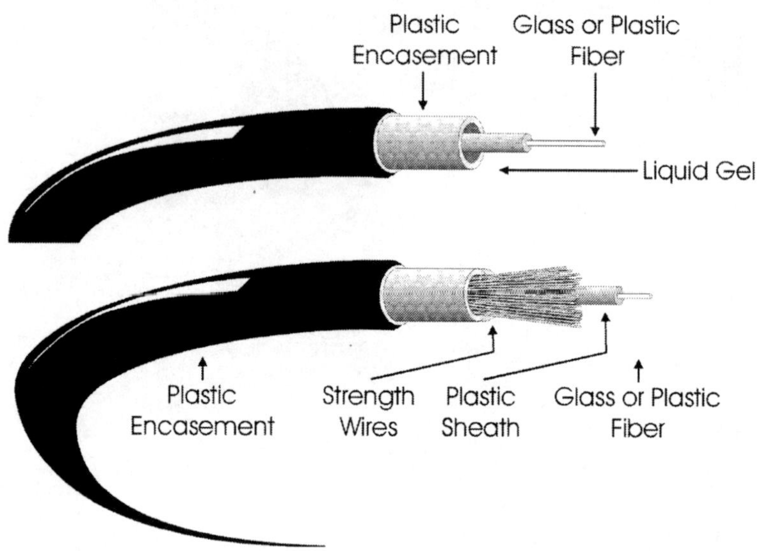

PVC and Plenum

Networking components, like cable, not only must adhere to networking specifications but also must meet strict fire code standards as well. Generally speaking, there are two types of coverings used in the manufacturing of computer networking cables: PVC (polyvinyl chloride) and plenum-grade cables. PVC is an inexpensive plastic coating that is very suitable as an insulator and cable covering. It is most often used in exposed open areas of office buildings.

Plenum-grade cables are required anytime they are to be used in a confined air space. Generally this means the space between a false ceiling and the floor space above. The technical word for this air space is **PLENUM,** hence plenum-grade cable. The air in the plenum typically circulates throughout the building and standard PVC-type cable gives off poisonous fumes when burned. For this reason, PVC **can not** be used in the plenum air space. You must use a plenum-grade cable instead. The plenum-grade cable is certified to be fire-resistant and produces a minimum amount of fumes. As one might expect, plenum-grade cable is more expensive than PVC cable. As a rule of thumb, when in doubt, install plenum-grade. It's cheaper than having to re-cable.

Cable Restrictions

Not only do cables have limitations placed on their use by networking committees and fire codes, but different cables have inherent limitations due to the physical properties of copper and glass. These physical limitations include factors like the speed and distance that specific cables can support. An example of this is the fact that copper cables suffer far more **attenuation** (loss of signal strength over given distance) than does fiber cable. The table below compares some common cable types:

Physical Topology	Maximum Distance	Minimum Distance	Data Rate	Description
10Base2	185 meters	0.5 meter	10Mbps	Thinnet coax cable, sometimes called Cheapernet.
10Base5	500 meters	2.5 meters	10Mbps	Thick Ethernet cable.
10BaseT	100 meters	0.6 meter	10Mbps	UTP (unshielded twisted pair cable).
100BaseTX	100 meters	0.6 meter	100Mbps	Uses only two pair of CAT 5 twisted pair wires.
100BaseFX	2.5 kilometers	1 meter	100Mbps	Fiber optic cable.
100BaseVG	100 meters	0.6 meter	100Mbps	Sometimes called 100BaseVG-AnyLan, supports both Ethernet & Token ring packets.

Protocol

Before any communication can take place between computers, they first must agree upon a common language to speak. In the world of networks, this is referred to as the *protocol*. Some common LAN protocols are:

NetBEUI (Net BIOS Extended User Interface)

NetBEUI, unlike TCP/IP, is called a non-routable protocol and is not suitable for large networks. However, NetBEUI is a fast, reliable choice for small networks and workgroups. NetBEUI support is built into Microsoft's networking products.

IPX (Internetwork Packet Exchange)

IPX is Novell's default protocol choice for its networking products.

TCP/IP (Transmission Control Protocol/Internet Protocol)

TCP/IP is the major language used to communicate across the Internet. It is ideal for this task because of its ability to cross routers and connect different networks together.

The TCP/IP Protocol Suite

An important point to keep in mind when discussing TCP/IP is that it is actually a suite of protocols. We often just refer to TCP/IP as a single protocol but it is really composed of a number of different protocols that all work together to facilitate network communication. Listed below are some of the most important protocols of the TCP/IP suite:

- TCP
- UDP
- IP
- POP3
- SMTP
- SNMP
- FTP
- HTTP

TCP

The main function of TCP is to establish and monitor connections between the sending and receiving devices. TCP is responsible for providing reliable connection-oriented data delivery. TCP functions at the Transport layer of the OSI model. When you are using TCP, you basically have an acknowledgement between sender and receiver that is maintained the entire length of the data transmission.

UDP

If you don't require the reliability of TCP, UDP (User Datagram Protocol) would be the protocol of choice. UDP provides a connectionless-oriented service and has much less overhead than TCP. The receiving computer need not acknowledge the receipt of every packet. The UDP protocol also operates at the Transport layer of the OSI model.

IP

Internet Protocol provides the mechanism for Internet addressing. IP functions at the Network layer of the OSI model. There are basically two parts to an IP address; the first part defines the network a device is attached to, and the second portion identifies the actual device itself.

An IP address can be assigned by the network administrator or assigned by a DHCP (Dynamic Host Configuration Protocol) server.

POP3

The POP3 (Post Office Protocol) version 3 is used to download email from various servers to an email client. Microsoft's *Outlook Express* is an example of a client-side software that uses POP3 technology. Most ISPs (Internet Service Providers) that provide home service also use the POP3 protocol. This enables the ISP to download messages to the individual user's computer rather than having to store them on the ISP's servers.

SMTP

SMTP (Simple Mail Transfer Protocol) provides a mechanism to send email between dissimilar operating systems. It is SMTP's ability to send email between different operating systems that makes it so useful on the Internet. An example of this would be composing an email message from a Windows 98 client, forwarding that to a local Microsoft Exchange Server which could then send it via the Internet to a server running the UNIX operating system.

SNMP

Management software applications that collect data about the condition of the network use SNMP (Simple Network Management Protocol) to gather and send this information. This combination of software/hardware management devices can collect information like the internal temperature in the server to the status of a router or the condition of a server's hard disk. That information is then stored in that device's database, the MIB (Management Information Base). This is all facilitated by the use of SNMP protocol.

FTP

FTP (File Transfer Protocol) is somewhat unique in that it is both a protocol and a program. It is usually associated most closely with the UNIX environment. As the name would indicate, it is used to transfer files. It is very powerful and flexible in its use. It can be configured to let users take files but not transmit them. This could be very advantageous in the case of limiting the transfer of files that may contain a virus. There is also a stripped down version of FTP called **TFTP** (Trivial File Transfer Protocol) which lacks some of the functionality of FTP in particular the ability to browse for files. **Most FTP access is granted using "anonymous" user account.**

HTTP

HTTP (Hypertext Transfer Protocol) is in widespread use today. HTTP is used to transfer Web pages from a Web server to a local Web browser. Those Web pages are created as HTML (Hypertext Markup Language) documents. HTTP also has a sister protocol called **HTTP(S),** which allows for secure transfer of documents. While HTTPS is slower due to the overhead generated by encryption methods, most would agree that it is essential for e-commerce and on-line banking transactions.

Topology

The topology is the cabling pattern used to form the network. Examples of topologies are:

- Bus
- Star
- Ring

Bus Topology

The bus topology will typically consist of one main cable, referred to as the *backbone*. The individual computers and components of the network are attached to this main cable via shorter cables, called drop cables. It's important to note that if the cable breaks anywhere, the entire network will be affected. Each end of the main cable must include a device called a *terminator* to remove any signals from the wire after passing all workstations.

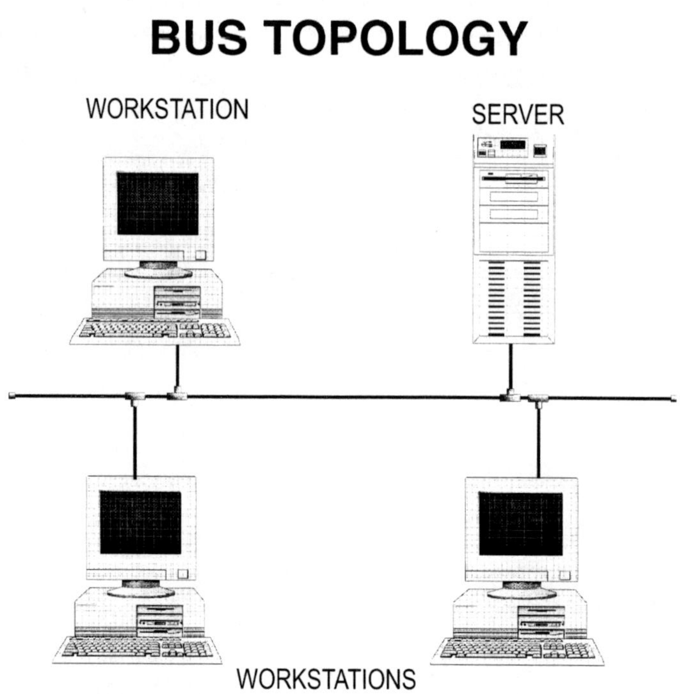

Star Topology

A star topology uses a central wiring device to connect all the individual computers to the network. Each device is connected to the network by a cable from the PC to a central device called a *hub* or *concentrator*. Multi-hubs and concentrators can be linked together to accommodate growth. A key advantage of the star topology as compared to the Bus is if a cable breaks between the PC and the hub, only that station is affected. This also facilitates the troubleshooting process.

A star topology is typically implemented in conjunction with 10BaseT technology (twisted pair cabling).

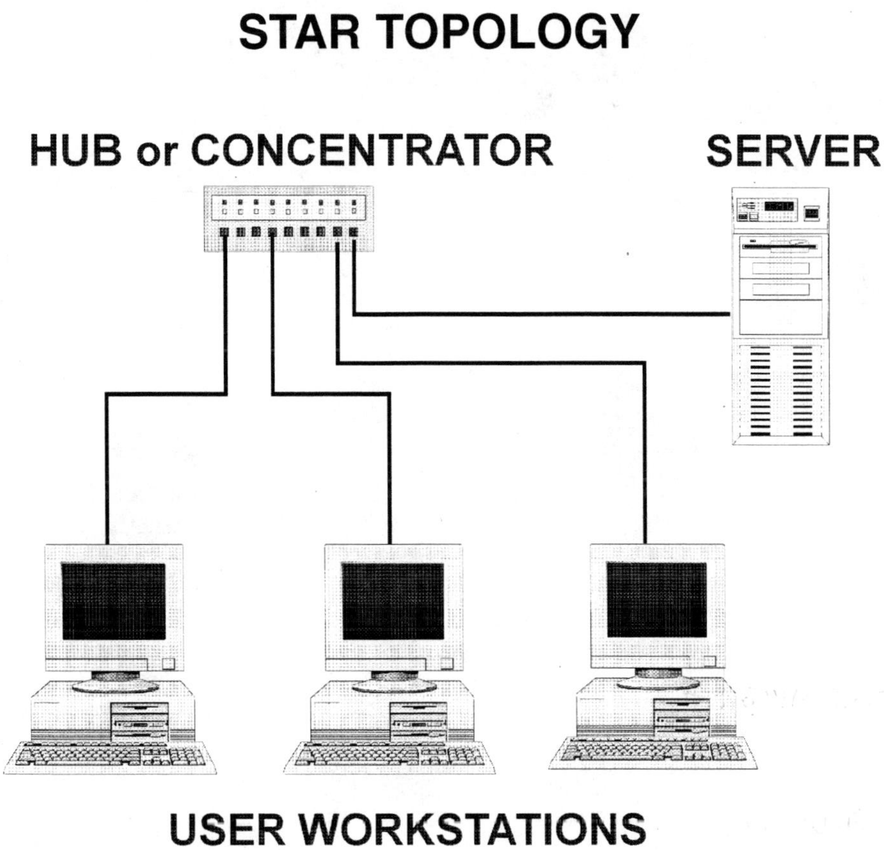

Ring Topology

As the name would imply, the ring topology connects the devices of the network in a circular fashion. Each network device connects directly to the ring or indirectly via a drop cable. Unlike a Bus topology, where the electrical signal can pass in both directions, the ring topology passes the signal from one device to the next, in one direction only.

RING TOPOLOGY

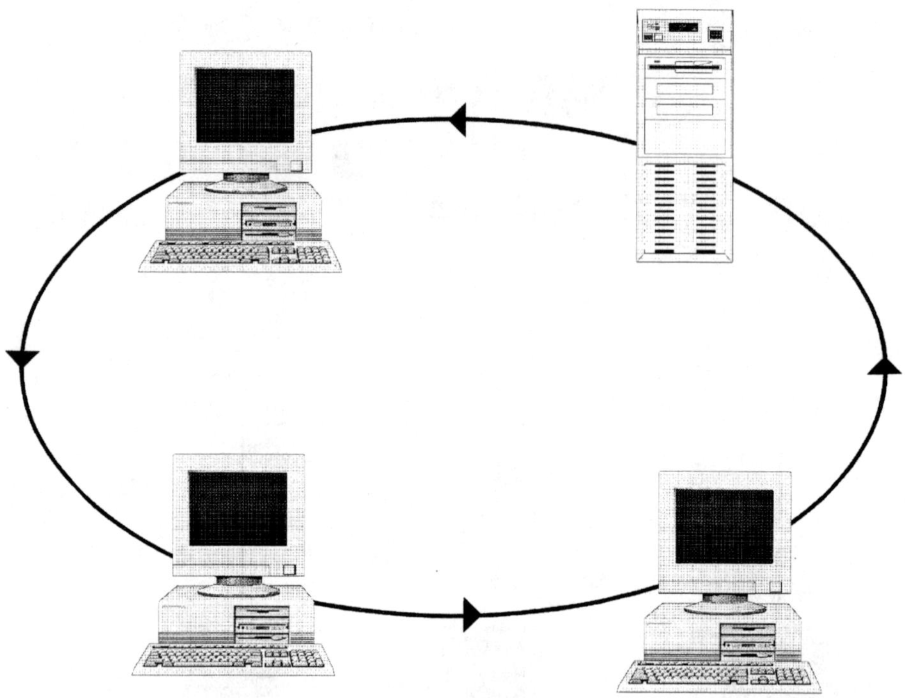

Logical Components

Network Operating System

A Network Operating System (NOS) is a group of programs that run on networked computers. It can be divided into two areas: *server* and *client* software.

Server Software

The *server software* has various functions: it manages the network, it prioritizes the applications' requests for network hardware resources, and it provides network security by controlling access to files. The NOS is also responsible for the *Logon* process. It's during the *Logon* process that a user sitting at a workstation will enter his/her unique *user ID* (*Logon name*) and *password* to gain initial access to the resources of the network.

LOGON

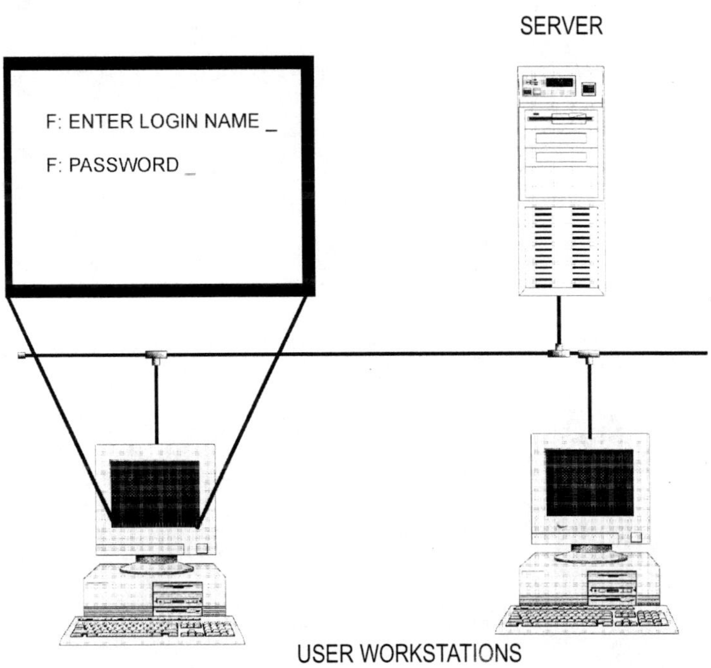

Client Software

The softwareloaded on the user's individual workstation is called the *client software.* Unlike the server software that controls overall access to the network, the client software is just responsible for making the connection between the workstation and the server.

The following are some of the different network operating systems available in today's market:

AppleShare	**LAN Manager**
IBM LAN Server	**LANtastic**
Banyan VINES	**Novell NetWare**
MS Windows 95/98	**MS Windows NT**
MS Windows 2000	

Different Types of Networks

Server-Based LAN

The concept behind a server-based LAN is that a single, dedicated computer provides all server functions to the network. The server runs a specialized multitasking operating system and stores the files and applications the workstations use. Information is retrieved or written to one or many hard drives inside the file server. This centralized approach allows the server to offer security and excellent data management. It also provides an almost unlimited capacity for expansion. Because of their complexity, server-based LANs represent a considerable investment in equipment, software and training. Novell and Microsoft both provide this type of platform.

Peer-to-Peer Networks

This type of network is simple and economical. Peer-to-peer networks utilize the resources of existing hardware to create the network. Instead of relying on one centralized server, peer-to-peer networks rely on many computers to provide server functions. All of the computers in the network share their resources (files, hardware and peripherals) with others. Windows 95/98 and *Artisoft's* LANtastic are both examples of peer-to-peer networks.

Summary

A LAN (Local-Area Network) is a group of computers that communicate through a cabling system. The goal of local-area networking is to provide a means of sharing common resources such as hard drives, files, printers and applications.

The LAN can be broken down into two major components: the physical (hardware) component, and the logical (software) component. The network hardware is made up of the server and workstation PCs, and peripherals such as printers and modems. The network operating system and the client software, along with any applications, comprise the logical components of the network.

The two basic types of networks are the server-based network and the peer-to-peer network.

Review Questions

1. A LAN is a group of dumb terminals attached to a mainframe.

   A. True
   B. False

2. The acronym NOS stands for:

   A. Network On System
   B. Net Op System
   C. Network Operating System
   D. New Operating System

3. Which of the following are networking topologies: (Choose all that apply.)

   A. Ring
   B. Open
   C. Star
   D. Bus
   E. Road

4. The ________determines the language that the server and workstation will use to communicate.

   A. Rule
   B. TCP
   C. Protocol
   D. Topology

5. The letters TP, when used in reference to computer cabling, stand for:

   A. Two Pair
   B. The Pair
   C. Twisted Pair
   D. Three Pair

6. *Microsoft's* Windows 9x would be an ideal choice for this type of workgroup:

    A. Client server
    B. WAN
    C. Peer-to-peer
    D. MAN

7. This type of topology connects every device to the network via a point-to-point connection to a central HUB or concentrator:

    A. BUS
    B. RING
    C. RANG
    D. STAR

8. The LOGON process typically would require the user to enter a unique:

    A. number and password
    B. phone number
    C. name
    D. user-name and password

9. A Novell client server network would most likely use which of the following protocols?

    A. TCP/IP
    B. NetBEUI
    C. SOFAST
    D. IPX

10. The maximum distance for a 10Base2 segment is:

    A. 185 meters
    B. 500 meters
    C. 100 meters
    D. 2.5 kilometers

Section 13

Network Support & Maintenance

Section 13: Network Support & Maintenance

Introduction

Perhaps the most intimidating and challenging job facing any Network Administrator is that of maintaining the network. After all, it is not a matter of if a network component will fail but rather when! The task of the Network Administrator is one of monitoring, anticipating and planning in the event of a major network failure. This section will discuss those technologies and procedures that help the Administrator support and maintain the network environment.

Objectives

- Create Emergency Repair Diskettes
- Discuss Backup Procedures
- Define Fault Tolerance
- Discuss Virus Protection Methods

Emergency Repair Diskettes

As was mentioned in the introduction, it's not IF something like a disk will fail but WHEN it will occur. One of the easiest ways to recover from a disk failure is to plan and prepare for it. That plan should include doing periodic backups and creating emergency repair diskettes.

Most backup utilities will restore critical data in the event of a hard disk failure, but getting the data back is only half the problem. What about those registry settings like passwords, user accounts? The emergency repair diskette will restore those settings after the data and operating system have been restored by the backup utility.

The Windows NT/2000 operating system comes with a utility that allows the Network Admin to create individual emergency repair disks. It should be noted, that if you use the emergency repair diskette to recover system information, this information is time-sensitive. Information like the user name and passwords will revert to the time that the ERD was created. This means that any passwords that have been modified since the disk was created **will not** be reflected in the restore. For this reason, it is important the disks are updated after any significant changes have been made. Another critical piece of information concerning the emergency repair disks is that they are unique and machine-specific. So a separate disk is required for each computer.

Note: Windows 95/98 machines refer to this disk as a ***Startup Disk.***

Backup Procedures

The technologies used today in the manufacture of hard disks have certainly reduced the occurrence of disk failure over the years. However the key word is *reduced,* not eliminated hard disk failure. A hard disk will fail at some point and if it is the one that contains your company's critical data, you had better be prepared with a good backup or a good resume! Not all backups are the same. It is up to the Network Admin to choose the backup strategy that is best suited for their particular network. There are three basic backup types that can be combined to create a viable network backup strategy. They are:

- Full backup
- Incremental backup
- Differential backup

Full Backup

The full backup, as the name indicates, means that you back up all data regardless of when or if it has been backed-up before. The full backup is the easiest to configure and will backup all files on the hard disk to tape. When files are created, modified or changed they are tagged with what is known as an **"archive bit"** this tells the backup software that the file is new and has never been included in prior backups. A full backup will **clear** the **archive bit** during the backup procedure. Succeeding full backups will again copy all files to tape regardless of the archive bit status.

Incremental Backup

The Incremental backup type will backup files that have been created or modified since the last full or incremental backup. The incremental backup is able to track this via the status of the archive bit. The archive bit is **cleared** during an incremental backup. The incremental backup can be combined with a weekly full backup for a complete solution. An incremental backup is one of the fastest ways to backup your data to tape; however this method takes the longest to restore of the three methods. To restore a weekly full/daily incremental requires every daily tape plus the weekly full tape to get a complete restore.

Differential Backup

The differential backup will copy files that have been modified since the last full backup. The **archive bit** is **not cleared** during a differential backup. The differential can be combined with a weekly full backup. To restore, one would only restore the full backup along with the most recent differential.

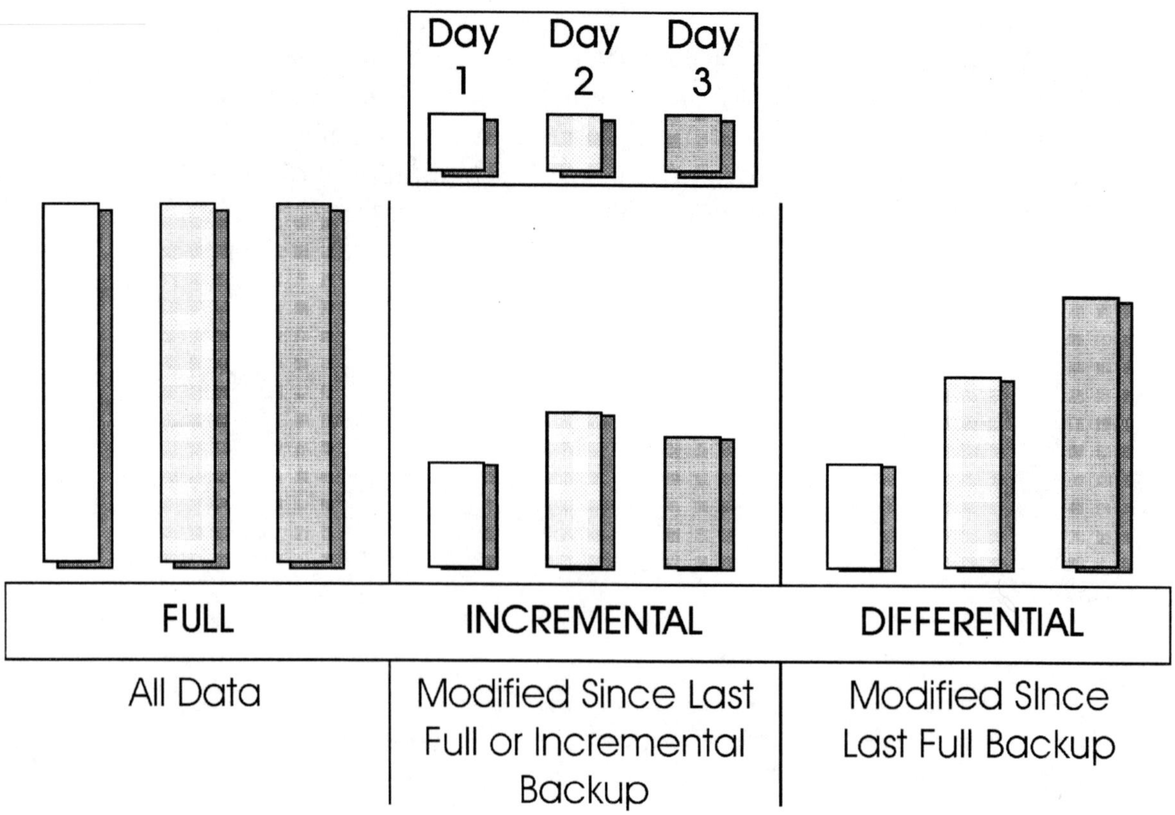

Fault Tolerance

As a Network Administrator, knowing you have a solid backup policy in the event of failure is nice. But restoring data from a tape backup can be very time-consuming. The idea of introducing fault tolerance into the network can drastically reduce that downtime. Perhaps one of the most effective fault tolerant methods is the use of **RAID** technologies. RAID (Redundant Array of Inexpensive Disks) incorporates a method of using multiple hard disks that work together to store network data. In a nutshell, RAID uses two or more disks to form a single logical disk to store data. One level of RAID called "disk mirroring" combines two hard disks: a **primary** and a **secondary**. All data written to the primary is also copied (mirrored) to the secondary as well. If the primary disk fails the secondary disk will automatically take over. Under ideal conditions down time is reduced substantially. An example of RAID Level 1 "disk mirroring" is shown below:

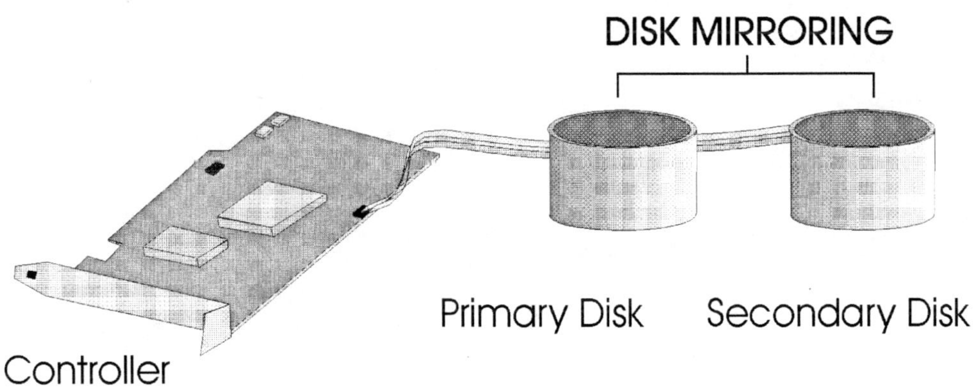

RAID Levels

RAID technology comes in many different configurations, which are referred to as levels. While the main goal of all these configurations is to achieve data redundancy, a by-product is that array technology can also improve disk I/O performance as well. The most popular RAID protection levels are compared below:

RAID 0

The data is spread across all disks during the write process. The operating system views the multiple disks (array) as just one logical disk. RAID 0 is sometimes referred to as "**data or disk striping**." This level of RAID provides **NO** fault tolerance. Since all the disks together form one logical disk, a failure of any one disk will shut down the system. Because RAID 0 doesn't worry about writing **parity information** (that information needed to rebuild lost data) it tends to be the fastest level of RAID. The major advantage of striping is the high level of I/O performance.

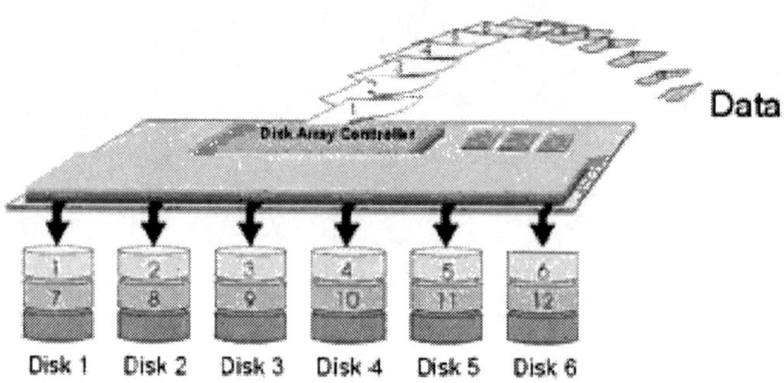

RAID 1

RAID level 1 is typically referred to as **disk mirroring**. This level of RAID incorporates two disks: a primary and a secondary. Each drive holds duplicate information. If the primary fails, the secondary will take over. This level of RAID can be further enhanced by putting each disk on its own controller. This method of one controller per disk is called "**disk duplexing**". RAID 1 provides a very high level of data reliability.

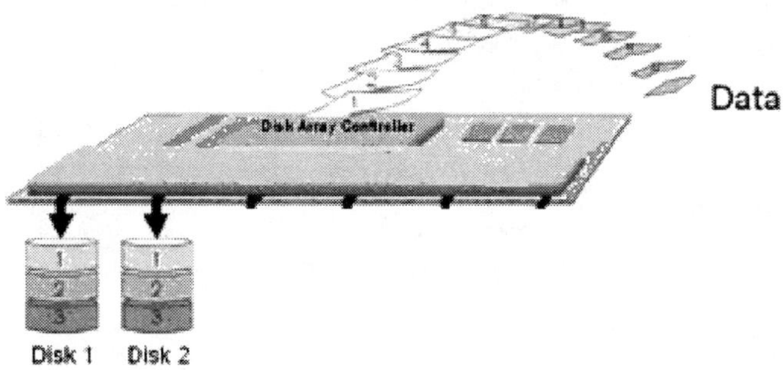

RAID 3

Data is striped (written) across multiple disks, with one disk dedicated solely for parity information. The parity drive is only used for error correction and recovery.

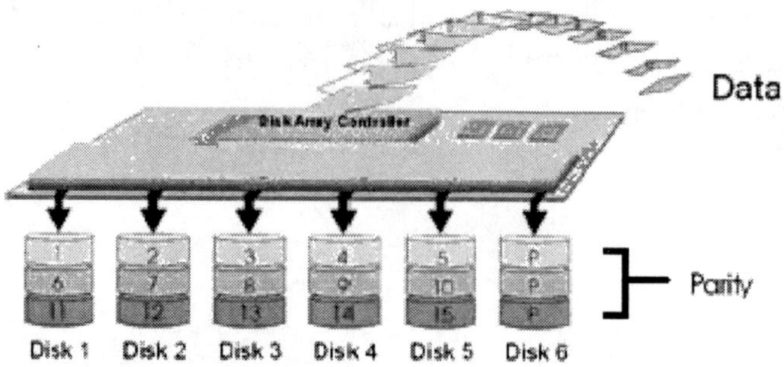

This system of RAID offers high data reliability as well as very high data transfer rates.

RAID 5

This system of RAID technology provides good operational performance while still providing adequate fault tolerance. Both the data and the parity information are striped across multiple disks. In case of a disk failure the system will still function without loss of data. This method of RAID requires a minimum of three drives. RAID 5 is the most often used configuration in the LAN environment.

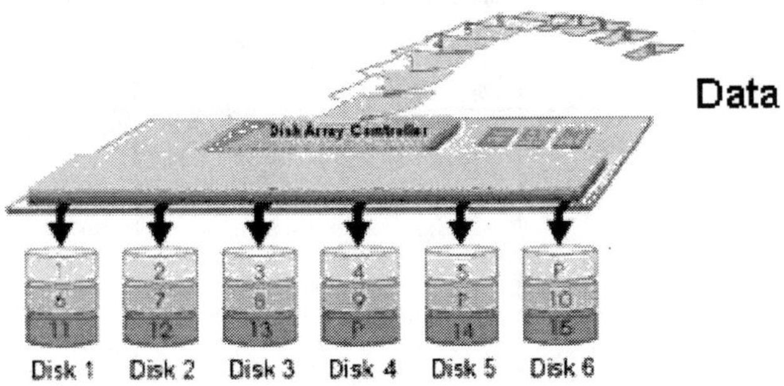

P = Parity

RAID 0+1

This level of RAID combines the advantages of both striping and mirroring, without parity. RAID 0+1 does require twice the number of disks, like RAID 1.

Summary of RAID Levels						
Name	**RAID Level**	**Description**	**Capacity**	**Data Transfer Rate**	**Data Reliability**	**Minimum Disk(s) Required**
Disk striping	0	Data distributed across the disks in the array. No redundant information provided.	(N) disks	Very High	Low	Two (2)
Disk mirroring	1	All the data is duplicated	One Disk	High	Very High	Two (2)
Parallel transfer disks with parity	3	Data is subdivided and distributed across all data disk(s).Redundant information stored on a dedicated parity disk.	(N-1) disks	Highest of all listed	Very High	Three (3)
Independent access array without parity	5	Data is distributed as with disk stripping, redundant information is interspersed with user data.	(N-1) disks	Very High	Very High	Three (3)
Diskstriping and Diskmirroring	0+1	Combination of data striping and mirroring, without parity. Fast data access and single drive fault tolerance	(N/2) disks	High	Very High	Four (4)

Virus Programs

Viruses can be anything from a cute smiley face that appears on your monitor to a catastrophic loss of all your data. There are literally thousands of different viruses that can attack the systems on your network. It is very important to insure that your entire network is protected from viruses. Often times Network Administrators will install virus protection software on their network servers while forgetting all about the peripheral equipment. The workstations, firewalls and routers are all susceptible to virus attack. Remember, that chain is only as strong as the weakest link!

Installing a virus protection program is only half the battle. Keeping it updated is the other part of the equation. There are new or modified versions of viruses being written every day. Virus protection programs search for known signatures (somewhat like a virus fingerprint). The key here is **known**. Since viruses are created and changing daily, it behooves the Network Administrator to update the virus detection program as often as possible, once a month at a minimum.

Summary

In this section, we discussed the challenging job of maintaining the network. We said that it is not a matter of if a network component will fail but rather when! This section defined the task of the Network Administrator as one of monitoring, anticipating and planning in the event of a major network failure. We discussed those technologies and procedures that help the Administrator support and maintain the network environment.

Review Questions

1. Which level of RAID provides disk mirroring?

   A. 0
   B. 1
   C. 3
   D. 5

2. Which tape backup method clears the archive bit? *Choose all that apply.*

   A. Full
   B. Differential
   C. Incremental
   D. Supplemental

3. The following are all examples of backup strategies except for:

   A. Full
   B. Half
   C. Incremental
   D. Differential

4. Which RAID technology does not provide any fault tolerance?

   A. 0
   B. 1
   C. 3
   D. 5

5. Typically virus detection programs need only to be installed on the servers.

   TRUE
   FALSE

6. Disk mirroring combines two hard disks called the ____________ and the ______________.

7. Which type of RAID technology is not typically used in a LAN environment?

   A. 0
   B. 1
   C. 2
   D. 5

8. In RAID technology, parity is used to ________________ the lost data.

Section 14

Diagnosing and Troubleshooting Hardware

Section 14: Diagnosing & Troubleshooting

Introduction

Diagnosing and repairing a computer problem can seem overwhelming until you learn to trust your instincts and approach the problem systematically.... and above all, Don't Panic! In this section, you'll learn how to approach computer hardware troubleshooting in a clear, logical fashion. A deliberate approach is necessary to avoid overlooking an obvious, simple solution to a problem.

Objectives

When you've completed this section, you'll understand:

- The seven steps of PC troubleshooting
- The common problems that occur in the various parts of the PC and peripheral devices
- How to recognize common error codes and start-up messages and use them to diagnose problems

Seven Steps of PC Troubleshooting

Step 1 Check for User Error.

Users are the primary cause of most PC problems. Your communication skills may be the most valuable tool in your repair kit. Learn to ask simple questions in a kind, non-threatening manner and then remember to LISTEN carefully. Don't assume the user has your level of technical knowledge and expertise.

Step 2 Is Everything Plugged In?

Check power strips, the PC power cord connected to the computer, every cable connection, the wall switch and the wall outlet.

Step 3 Check the Software.

For keyboard, screen, disk and timer conflicts with TSR programs, software may be the source of the problem. Applications and driver programs may have "bugs." Software may generate errors when it looks for hardware that isn't connected or activated such as: trying to print to a nonexistent printer or a printer that is offline; trying to display graphics on a monochrome monitor; or trying to run a program that requires more memory than is available.

Step 4 If the PC was once working properly, what was done differently? What is new?

Ask if a board was recently added to a system or perhaps a software program was added which was contaminated with a virus.

Step 5 Be observant and write down external signs on the PC.

What do the indicator lights show? Are all the modem lights on? Is the printer's "ready" light on? Is the monitor's image distorted? Are the hard drives grinding or making unusual sounds?

Step 6 Run a Diagnostic Program.

While not entirely useful for most problems (the system has to be running to run the program!), a diagnostic disk may buy you some repair time. Each time the PC boots, the system is tested by the POST for memory, conflicts, controllers, video, adapters, monitor, keyboard, drives, parallel ports, etc. Record what the POST displays on the screen for helpful clues to the problem.

Step 7 Take PC Apart, Clean, Check Connections & Reassemble.

Open the PC, clean the connectors carefully with a cleaning compound or a clean white eraser and push all chips into their sockets. Are boards securely installed on the motherboard?

Common Problems

Processor/Memory Symptoms

To discover if your system has a memory problem you could:

- Receive a memory error message 201 during POST.
- Run a memory test periodically.
- Get a **PARITY CHECK** error in the middle of an application. **PARITY CHECK 1** indicates a problem on the motherboard; **PARITY CHECK 2** indicates a problem on an expansion board.

Each time you power up your computer, the POST runs a memory test. The error message will contain the type of error as well as the location of the bad memory chip (its "address").

Memory is very power-dependent and needs a clean power source to function properly. Even a slight power surge can generate a memory error when, in fact, the memory is not bad. The problem is power-related. Likewise, ESD or a failing power supply can also result in false memory errors.

How do you determine between a true memory problem and a false memory error? Check the memory address in the error message. The same address will appear repeatedly if the chip has indeed failed. If the errors report different locations, the problem is most likely caused by power – either by an interruption or insufficient power

Keyboard

Before spending time repairing a keyboard, keep in mind that new keyboards have come down in price in the past several years. A new enhanced keyboard can be purchased for as little as $25 in many markets.

To determine if the keyboard has failed, first check...

- Is the keyboard plugged into the correct port? The keyboard port and the mouse port look identical on many PCs.
- Are several keys malfunctioning or only one key? If only one key, then you can replace the key spring easily.

Mouse

When troubleshooting a mechanical mouse...

- Check to see that the mouse driver is set up correctly.
- Clean the mouse. On the bottom of the mouse, remove the retaining ring by turning it in the direction of the arrows. The ball will drop out. Clean off any dust and debris that may be on the ball. The ball moves against small white wheels on either side. These tend to accumulate a black buildup of dirt, which can be easily cleaned with a Q-tip and a bit of alcohol.
- Check to be sure the mouse is plugged into the mouse port, not the keyboard port.
- On an optical mouse, polish the sensors with a soft cloth and keep the mouse pad clean so the grid lines are visible to the mouse.

Floppy Drive

When a floppy drive fails, you may receive one of these error messages when you attempt to read a disk.

Data error reading Drive A: or **General error reading Drive A:**

- Retry the procedure at the prompt.
- Remove the diskette, then reinsert it again. Sometimes it's a hub-centering problem.
- Try the diskette in another drive. Is the floppy the right size for the drive? You may be trying to read a 5.25" high-density diskette in a double-density drive, or a 3.5" 2.88MB diskette in a 1.44MB drive.
- Does the drive read other diskettes? The diskette may have been written by a drive with a misaligned head.

Drive won't operate

- Check for a **Drive A: 601** error message during POST. This would indicate the system is not configured properly to see the drive; the controller failed; Drive A failed; or the cable failed.
- Try to format another diskette. If the newly formatted diskette is unreadable by other drives, then the head of your floppy drive is misaligned.
- Remove the case and check to see that the controller is seated snugly and that all cables are secure and nick-free.
- Swap out the controller, cable and drive one at a time. If the problem doesn't go away after each swap, put the component back.

During POST, the Drive A light stays on...

- The floppy drive cable is most likely backwards if the floppy drive light comes on and stays on during POST. The error could also mean there is insufficient memory if you are trying to load a program from a floppy.

Parallel Ports

Once parallel ports are installed and configured they seldom fail. If a problem occurs, the POST may report an **Error Code 423: Parallel Port Failed**. First, troubleshoot the particular device attached to that port. Printers – most often attached to LPT ports – are often the source of the problem. Also look for a device conflict. Check to see that two devices are not configured for the same LPT port and reconfigure the boards if necessary.

When a PC boots up, BIOS checks the LPT ports. If it doesn't find LPT 1, it looks for LPT 2, then LPT 3. If you've configured your PC for a LPT 2 port but not LPT 1 port, the BIOS will convert the LPT 2 to LPT 1 and a device conflict might occur.

Scanner

Some scanners work off a SCSI host adapter and others work off a proprietary interface card. To troubleshoot a scanner;

- Check for a device conflict with another device configured for the same LPT or COM port.
- Is the scanner cable securely inserted into the board and is the cable connector tight?
- Was the scanner recently moved? If the scanner is a flat-bed type, check to be sure the movable head is not locked.
- Is the scanner software installed correctly?

Tape Drive

If you plan to backup your PC's data regularly, a tape drive is a wise investment. When purchasing a tape drive, consider an external drive rather than an internal drive so you can use the device to backup more than one PC. Some tape drives use the floppy controller which limits their speed to that of your floppy drive, which may be too slow to be efficient. Higher capacity drives usually run off the SCSI interface but some drives require their own interface card.

When buying tapes, purchase the pre-formatted variety because formatting can take up to an hour.

To troubleshoot a tape drive, first look for a device conflict, then check the manufacturer's documentation for procedures to diagnose or repair problems with your particular tape drive.

Hard Drive

There are two types of hard disk drive errors:

- *Hard Errors* - The disk surface itself cannot record data. Hard errors are usually caused by a manufacturing defect in the disk or abuse of the disk. A low-level format will record hard errors, marking them in the bad track table so data is not recorded there. If the drive just stops working, it may be a physical problem with the drive. The coating on the disk that stores data may have rubbed off or the drive arm may wobble and not reach a particular part of the disk.
- *Soft Errors* - Data has faded on the hard disk to the extent it cannot be read. Soft errors are intermittent. A bad sector may be recorded once and then skipped on subsequent tests of the sectors. A recovery effort is needed to restore lost data (regular backup is strongly recommended).

When a sector has lost its ID, you'll receive a **Sector Not Found** error. When the data in a sector is unreadable or otherwise unreliable, you'll receive a **Data Error Reading Drive** error. To troubleshoot these problems:

- Try to low-level format the disk to restore the IDs. Remember that the low-level formatting process may salvage the drive but will destroy all existing data.

Hard Drive Crash Procedure

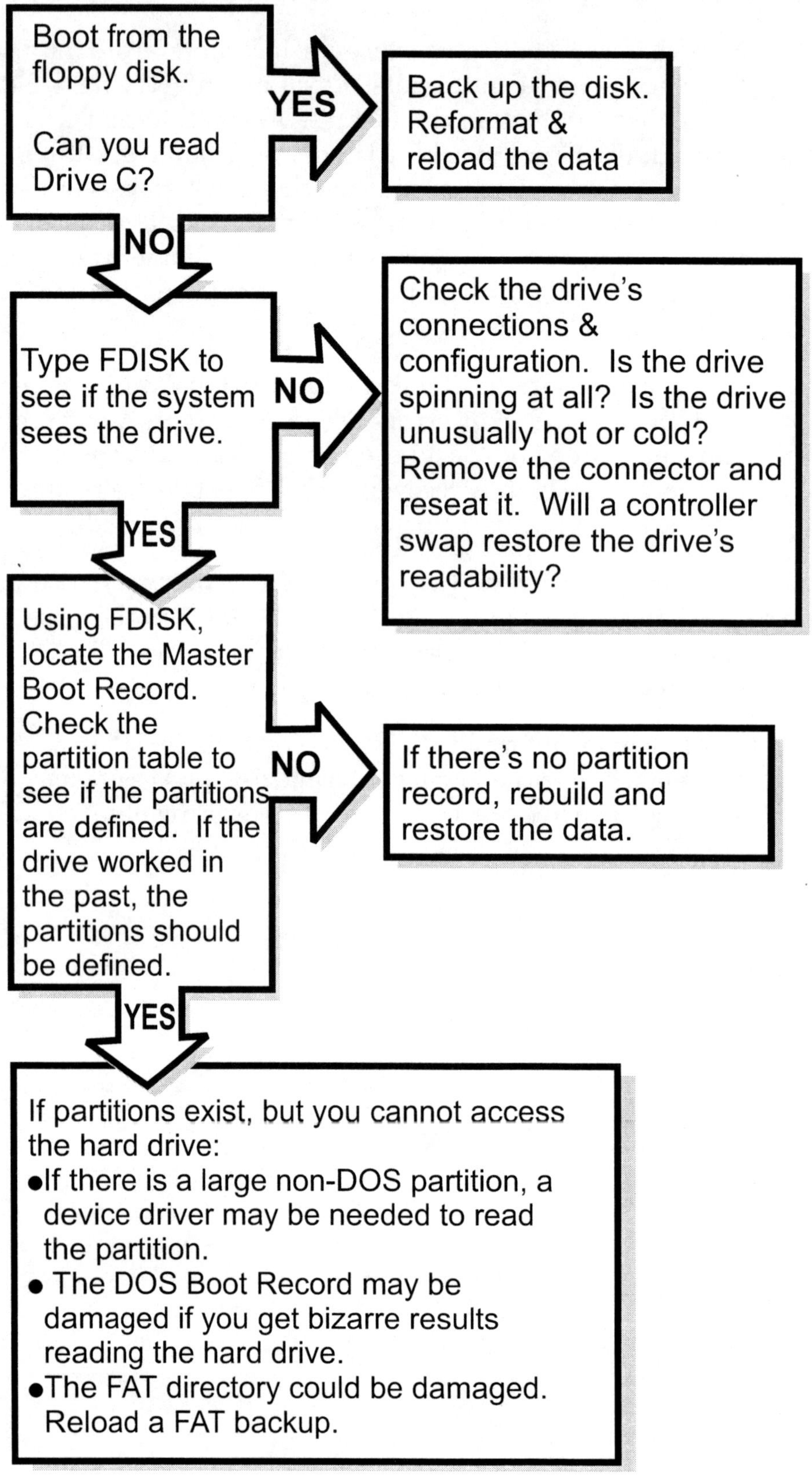

Sound Card (Audio)

If you are having difficulty with receiving sound (audio) from your PC, check the obvious first. Are the speakers plugged into the correct outlets at the back of the PC? Are they connected to a power source? If you suspect the problem is your sound card, check the card's configuration. Most sound cards require three I/O addresses, two DMA channels and an IRQ.

> NOTE: Get in the habit of writing down all the jumper and switch settings whenever you install any type of new card.

Monitor (Video)

Before you attempt to take apart a monitor - STOP. If you were to open a monitor while the computer was plugged in (even if the power was OFF), you could receive a shock. Even if the PC is OFF, the capacitors store power and can shock you.

If the monitor is malfunctioning, follow these troubleshooting steps.

- Check the simplest things first. Is the monitor turned ON? Check to see that the brightness or contrast controls are not turned way down. Is the monitor plugged correctly into the PC, as well as into the power source?
- Check the DIP switch and jumper settings on a multiple display board. Also check the DIP switches on the motherboard to see if your display adapter is configured correctly.
- If you heard a POST audio error code of one long and two short beeps, it could mean a problem with the video card.
- If you determine the problem lies with the video card, check the card's seating, clean the edge connector and the video connector and then retry the monitor.

When troubleshooting a monitor, it's best to use the VGA mode. Load the VGA drivers and see if the problem disappears. If so, then you had a driver problem. Make sure you have the most up-to-date drivers and a board that matches your monitor.

If you suspect the Graphics acceleration setting is causing problems with your PC, check the **Advanced Graphic** settings in **System Properties**. This area tells Windows how to interact with your graphics hardware. It can be very useful when troubleshooting display related problems.

Modem

The most common problem with communication devices is software. Both ends of the communication channel, the sender and the receiver, must have the same communication settings,parity, number of data bits, number of stop bits, and local echo ON or OFF.

- If you cannot connect to another computer's modem or if you get garbage letters when you do, most likely the speed or data bits are set incorrectly.
- If you connect and are able to receive a response from the receiving modem but cannot see what you've typed, the **Local Echo** setting is incorrect. Set **Local Echo** to ON to display the characters you type. If you get double characters as you type, set the **Local Echo** to OFF.
- If you suspect the problem is hardware-related, check the phone jack connection both at the PC and at the wall outlet. Make sure the modem's cable is connected securely. Check the phone line. Do you get a dial tone on other phones on that line? If you use an electronic phone system, check the required dial-out procedures. Also check the quality of the line for exceptional "noise." The problem may be with your phone wiring or the call-waiting feature may be interrupting the session.

BIOS

The BIOS tests your system whenever you power-up the PC. The BIOS start-up procedure consists of these steps.

Step 1	*Low Memory Test*	If this test fails, it means the lowest bank of RAM has failed.
Step 2	*Scan for other BIOS*	Some installed boards may contain their own ROM BIOS. The system BIOS searches for any additional BIOS.
Step 3	*Yield to other BIOS*	The system BIOS yields to other BIOS it may find before it checks the main system.
Step 4	*Inventory the system*	Reads the CMOS and checks all hardware (drives, memory, etc) that it will control. This may take several minutes, so be patient.
Step 5	*Test the system*	This is the diagnostic part of the BIOS. Any failed device will generate an error message at this point.
Step 6	*Load DOS*	Before the BIOS loads the operating system, it first loads DOS. The system looks for a drive that's ready. (It looks in the boot-up sequence you've chosen in CMOS...first Drive A, then Drive C, for example.)
Step 7	*DOS loads Master Boot Record (MBR), then DOS Boot Record (DBR)*	The DBR contains the hidden files IO.SYS and MSDOS.SYS.
Step 8	*IO.SYS loads MS DOS.SYS, CONFIG.SYS, then COMMAND.COM*	CONFIG.SYS loads device drivers which can shut down a system if they have a bug. If the COMMAND.COM has been corrupted somehow (wrong version, contaminated by a virus for example), you'll get a Bad or Missing Command.Com error message and your system will not boot.
Step 9	*COMMAND.COM loads AUTOEXEC.BAT*	TSRs such as anti-virus programs, network shells, protocol stacks, disk cache programs and disk compression programs are loaded by the AUTOEXEC. BAT. Problems with any of these programs will cause your system not to boot.

POST Audio Messages

POST Audio Signal	Probable Cause
No beep, nothing happens	Bad power supply or power supply not plugged in.
Continuous beep	Bad power supply or keyboard stuck.
Repeating short beep	Bad power supply.
1 long beep, 1 short beep	System board has failed.
1 long beep, 2 short beeps	Display adapter or cable is missing or has failed.
1 short beep, no boot	Floppy drive adapter has failed.
2 short beeps (PS/2)	Configuration error.

Motherboard

Double-check all cable connections, BIOS settings, and jumpers if you suspect a motherboard problem. Often, what appears to be a faulty motherboard, may be simply a hardware configuration problem.

All system components meet and connect at the motherboard, so a motherboard problem can affect any part of the computer. However, motherboard failures are rare. Usually the problem is the motherboard has been configured incorrectly or there is a failure with a component connecting to it. Try to avoid swapping out the motherboard. Exhaust all other possibilities before you take that drastic step.

- If the system isn't booting at all, make sure all components are inserted correctly into the motherboard. Partially inserted memory modules can often cause bizarre behavior.
- Remove all optional devices (expansion cards, external peripherals) to see if the problem is corrected.
- Double-check all jumper settings. Check the processor type, Bus speed, clock multiplier and voltage jumpers. Make sure the CMOS is clear and flash BIOS jumpers are in the normal default position. Reset all BIOS settings to default. Set all cache, memory and hard disk timing as slow as possible. Turn off BIOS shadowing and then see if the problem goes away
- Check the inside of the case to see if any components may be overheating.
- Inspect the motherboard for cracks, broken pins or broken components on the board. Check for any socketed components that may be loose in their sockets.
- Is the keyboard inserted correctly into the motherboard?

- A failed cache module or the wrong type of cache module may cause a motherboard problem. Troubleshoot the secondary cache.
- Troubleshoot the processor.
- Memory problems are often mistaken for motherboard problems. Troubleshoot the memory.
- Troubleshoot the video card or replace it with a simple, straight VGA card that you know works correctly.
- Replace an underrated power supply (less than 200W) especially if you've added new drives to the system.
- Check your BIOS manufacturer's technical support to see if there are any known bugs with your motherboard.
- Check your motherboard's manufacturer's hotline for additional troubleshooting hints.
- Last resort, swap out the motherboard with another board to see if the problem is resolved. If it is, then the original motherboard may have indeed been faulty or it could have been misconfigured or incorrectly installed.

CMOS

Record the current CMOS settings *before* you change any hardware in a system. If, after adding a piece of hardware, your CMOS has cleared, follow these steps to restore settings:

- Reboot the system and start the **CMOS** setup (consult the BIOS manufacturere for the specific way to enter the CMOS setup for your particular BIOS).
- Select **Load Bios Default Values.**
- Set the system date and time, floppy drives, keyboard and display type. These settings will be on the first CMOS setup screen or they may be listed under **Standard CMOS Setup**.
- Set up your hard drive parameters. If your CMOS setup provides an auto-detect function for the hard drive, use it. If it doesn't, enter the hard-disk settings manually: cylinders, heads and sectors. (See your hard drive documentation for this data.).
- Select **Save** and exit.
- Let the system reboot with the new BIOS settings.

Getting Troubleshooting Information From Customers

Most of the work in fixing a computer for a customer is diagnosing the problem. When you're working to solve a computer malfunction, Rule No. 1 is L.I.S.T.E.N. The user has firsthand knowledge that may help you unearth the problem.

- Watch for verbal cues - Ask the customer if the device was working prior to the problem? What was the customer doing just before the computer malfunctioned? Collect as much information as possible. *Warning:* Be careful not to make users feel stupid or they will react defensively and may withhold vital information that could help you solve the problem. If you're working over the phone with the user attempting to solve the problem, have the user perform the steps necessary to rectify the problem if at all possible.
- Respond sympathetically to the customer's situation. Empathize with the customer's frustration, but don't be afraid to say "I don't know what the problem is, I need more information."
- Users learn from their errors, especially if they can fix the problem themselves, with your coaching of course. Speak slowly when giving instructions and anticipate the user's technical level when explaining the repair procedure. You may have to break down the information into less technical terms so the user can fully understand the process.

Common Error Codes & Startup Messages

Incorrect DOS Version

This message will appear when the system boots up if you attempt to run the wrong version of DOS with a particular program. The file that contains the command you just entered is from a different version of DOS such as trying to use **DEFRAG** while running Windows.

For example, some versions of **MSCDEX.EXE** for a CD-ROM drive may require an earlier or later version of DOS than is currently on your system. Many programs designed to run with a previous version of MS-DOS will run correctly with Windows 3.1 or 95.

The version table indicates to the program that it is running with the MS-DOS version for which it was designed, even though it is running in the MS-DOS subsystem.

SETVER can be used to modify the version table. By interpreting MS-DOS version 6.0, for example, as the earlier version, the program will probably run correctly; however, using **SETVER** will not solve the problem if the program is not compatible with Windows.

Adding the following line to your **CONFIG.SYS** file will load the version table into memory.

DEVICE=C:\DOS\SETVER.EXE (if the DOS commands are located in the \DOS subdirectory)

To view the version table, at the **DOS** prompt, type:

C:\DOS\SETVER (or indicate the drive and path where you indicated in the **CONFIG.SYS** line)

After you've added or deleted entries, you must restart the system before the changes will take effect. As you update existing entries, when you specify a filename that is already in the version table, the new entry replaces the existing entry.

Bad or missing COMMAND.COM

If the boot record on the hard drive is corrupted or has been deleted, you will get this error message when you boot up the system. Use the **SYS** command or reload DOS to restore the boot record to the hard drive, then restart the system to see if the problem is solved. Also, make sure the hard drive is identified correctly in CMOS.

HIMEM.SYS not loaded

The file **HIMEM.SYS** did not load properly so it cannot make extended memory or high memory area (HMA) available to your system. Without this file, Windows 3.x is unable to use extended memory and DOS will not be able to load into the HMA. This problem often occurs because **HIMEM.SYS** did not correctly identify your type of PC, or if the **/CPUCLOCK** or **/MACHINE** switches need to be added to the **DEVICE=** line in your **CONFIG.SYS** file.

Swapfile corrupt

This error message means that your swap file has been damaged and you've lost your virtual memory. You don't have enough memory left to run a particular program.

Information is moved in blocks from memory to a swap file that Windows creates on the hard disk. This swap file can either be permanent or temporary. When all of the virtual memory (RAM) is in use, idle programs and data will be loaded into the swap file to make more actual RAM available.

A device referenced in SYSTEM.INI could not be found.

The computer is looking for a device that is listed in your System Initialization file. Perhaps the device driver isn't finding its hardware, an icon was deleted or a device was physically removed from the PC and the line wasn't removed from the initialization file. When Windows asks the drive to locate its hardware, the hardware must be there and be operational or Windows will generate an error message.

Missing or corrupt HIMEM.SYS

If you get this error message, check your **CONFIG.SYS** file. Using a text editor such as Notepad, open the **CONFIG.SYS** file. If the **HIMEM.SYS** line is missing, add the following line:

DEVICE=HIMEM.SYS

Save and close the **CONFIG.SYS** file. Restart the PC.

Safe Mode

Sometimes after a system crash, the PC will boot into **Safe Mode.** If you don't want your system to automatically boot into **Safe Mode** after a crash, disable this option in the system BIOS CMOS. We will learn more about Safe Mode in the *A+ Operating System Technologies* course.

System Lock-Up

A system lock-up means that the system boots up but the boot process stops. As the operating system software comes up, the system locks up, or a system could lock up in the middle of an application. There are several potential causes for a system lock-up:

- Do you have the most current BIOS for your motherboard? If not, call the motherboard manufacturer to obtain a copy of the latest BIOS.
- Are the BIOS settings correct? After booting your computer, enter the BIOS setup by pressing the **Delete** key. Try loading the BIOS defaults. Save the changes and exit. Reboot your computer to see if the system still locks.
- The problem may be with a fragmented hard disk. Run **DEFRAG** and/or **SCANDISK** to see if the problem corrects itself.
- Does your processor have the correct CPU fan and heat sink installed and working properly? A small fan should be on top of a heatsink that covers the entire surface of the processor.
- Are all the adapter cards seated properly? Remove the cards and reinstall them.
- Is the processor seated properly? The processor should be firmly and evenly down into the socket.
- Is the voltage setting correct for the motherboard?
- Is the motherboard set to the right speed? If a processor is running faster than its megahertz rating, the computer may not boot up.
- Are all peripheral devices on and functioning properly? The application you're working in may try to write to a peripheral that is offline, not initialized or not functioning.
- Has the operating system been reinstalled? Sometimes the Registry will become corrupted and only reinstalling Windows will fix the problem.

After you've worked through this checklist and the system still locks up, try swapping out the components one by one. Older and slower devices can cause the system to lock up.

Illegal Operation

DOS halted the system because it ran out of space to hold the necessary data to process hardware interrupts. The default amount of stack space being reserved is too low. To increase the amount of DOS stack space, add the following line to your **CONFIG.SYS** file:

STACKS=X,YYY	(X is the new number of stacks, and YYY is the size of each one in bytes -- Recommended values are: **STACKS=12,256.)**

If the problem recurs, increase the values. A particular application may have a bug that is causing the problem. Contact the application's technical support for help.

Summary

Repairing a computer hardware problem is not an exact science. Learn to trust your instincts and follow the systematic approach outlined in this chapter and you'll have a good start at solving computer problems.

Review Questions

1. A customer attached an external drive to his notebook computer but the computer is not recognizing it. What should be considered? Select all that apply.

   A. The cables are attached firmly.

   B. The external drive has been pre-loaded with the appropriate software.

   C. The external drive was attached before the computer was turned on.

   D. The external drive is turned on.

   E. All of the above.

2. After displaying the directory of a floppy disk, a different floppy is inserted in the drive. The contents of the original floppy continue to display regardless of the directory requests on the other floppies placed in the drive. You remove the drive in question and install it into your test system, and it does not exhibit the problem. What is your next step?

   A. Replace the system's floppy drive device driver.

   B. Replace the original IDE controller.

   C. Replace the floppy drive ribbon cable.

   D. Replace the system's power supply.

3. What questions could be asked to determine if a problem is software or hardware related? (Select all that apply.)

   A. Does the computer BEEP during the boot phase?

   B. Did peripheral devices initialize, i.e. printers?

   C. Will hardware components pass diagnostics?

   D. Determine how many serial ports are installed in the system.

4. Which of the following would be a logical first step in troubleshooting a PC?

   A. Check the computer CMOS.
   B. Define the circumstances of the problem.
   C. Call the vendor.
   D. Define what applications are being used.

5. What DOS command could be used to view the existing version table?

   A. **DOSVER**
   B. **SETVER**
   C. **TABLE 1V**
   D. **GOVER**

Section 15

Customer Service

Section 15: Customer Service

Introduction

When was the last time you walked out of a business saying, "***WOW,*** that was really great service!"? Now think back—did you tell anyone else about your experience? Chances are pretty good that you did. This is actually what good customer service is all about. This sounds pretty easy. So why are there so many horror stories about rude sales clerks, or phone systems that keep you on perpetual hold with no chance for human contact? The reason is that businesses and the people who run them often have no idea what the real product is!

The truth is, the product not only includes the actual widget or service, but also everything else that goes into the sale: the greeting at the front door, the smiling face, attention to small details, and the follow-up service. These are all factors that bring people back a second time and prompts them to sing your praises to others.

Objectives

When you've completed this section, you will be able to:

- Define customer service
- Identify good customer service habits
- Understand conflict management skills
- Understand effective telephone support

Customer Service

If you ask most people what customer service is, they would probably say it's to give the customer ***good*** service!

So what does that really mean? Try to picture in your mind a business (grocery store, restaurant, hobby shop) that you enjoy doing business with. Then ask yourself what it is that makes the experience enjoyable. Chances are, you will come up with words like friendly, attentive, courteous, and knowledgeable. That's good customer service in a nutshell.

Now try to remember the last time you were standing in a long line at the Motor Vehicle Department waiting to renew a driver's license. You were probably asking yourself questions like: "How much longer can it possibly take?," and, "Who are all those people behind the counter, and why aren't they helping me?" This is the other side of the proverbial coin. Ironically, it takes no more time to create a good customer service environment than a negative one.

Customer First

The idea that the customer is always right is not a new idea, but may be considered the "Granddaddy" of all good customer service habits. It's our customers who provide for our paychecks, bonuses and vacation. Placing the needs of your customer first gives them a feeling of importance and tells them they are valued as your customer.

Follow-Up

When customers are asked what upsets them the most when dealing with their service providers, the overwhelming response is that many service people do not follow through on their promises. This is an especially sensitive area in a service-oriented business. The bottom line here is simple: If you promise to do something, then **do it**! Always keep your customer informed even if it's only to tell them you haven't received the information they need, but you are still working on it. Your future credibility with the customer depends on it.

Give the Extra Effort

Always show your customers you are more than willing to go that extra mile for them. This might include helping them locate a telephone number or making a copy of a piece of lost documentation for them. This little extra effort can go a long way in establishing good rapport with your customer.

Empathy

So now your company has established the best possible customer service program possible. Well, there will still come a point in time when you are faced with a customer who is less than happy! Empathy is nothing more than trying to place yourself in your customer's position and viewing the situation from their vantage point.

You may not always agree, but at least this helps you better understand why they might be responding in a certain way. The best approach here is to use phrases such as: "I can see why you feel that way," or, "Yes, I can see your point of view." The next step is to develop a plan to remedy the situation.

Promise Less - Deliver More

Often times in our enthusiasm to deliver a product or service to our customers, we tend to overstate or promise more than what we can actually deliver. The key here is to promise only those things you are sure you can deliver, and not base it on those things that might happen. Your customer will be much happier if you are conservative up front, and then, if possible, deliver more in the end.

Have you ever been promised something would arrive the next day, only to receive it the next week? Not a very warm feeling. On the other hand, having someone tell you it would take about a week and then receiving it the next day tends to imply someone really cared about your business.

Extend Options

There will always be that time when you cannot deliver exactly what the customer wants or requires. When faced with the situation of not being able to give the customer what they ask for, try to have alternative options available. This approach of giving options as opposed to just saying "No," tends to lessen the customer's initial disappointment.

To avoid a potential pit-fall, do not offer too many options. Like a shoe sales person offering the same shoe in more than two colors, it only tends to confuse the customer. Try to limit possible alternatives to a couple of choices.

Conflict Management Skills

Up to now we have discussed some of the habits you can use to establish a good customer service environment. Although even the best plans can blow up from time to time, it is also important to know how to manage conflict when a situation goes astray.

"Just be calm."

Telling an already angry customer to calm down will only add fuel to a bad situation. Try telling them you are sorry the event occurred and you understand their frustration.

"Let me find someone to help you."

Often times you will be asked to do or say something is outside your scope of expertise or authority. In these cases, try to direct the customer to someone who can address the problem.

"I can find out for you."

No one expects you to know everything. Tell the customer you will find out for them!

"I'll be with you soon."

Every customer thinks that he or she is your most important client. Telling them you're too busy for them is like saying, "Go away, you're bothering me." Try something like, "I'll be with you just as soon as I finish this."

Telephone Support

Very often in the business world, the telephone is the customer's first contact with a company. This makes what you say and how you say it very important to your company's overall customer service policy. Knowing something about proper telephone etiquette is an inexpensive way to improve service to your customers and create an immediate positive impression.

Establishing good telephone policies and procedures need not be rocket science. The following suggestions will ensure your customers will be greeted politely and efficiently over the phone.

Answering the phone

The first step to any telephone conversation is to answer the incoming call. Generally, you should always try to answer the telephone within three rings. Anything past the third ring and your customer will conjure up all sorts of negative pictures of your company. "Don't they care about my call?," or, "Are they overworked and understaffed?"

The second part of answering the call is the greeting, or the start of any conversation. Always start by saying, "Good morning," or "Good afternoon," before identifying yourself or your company.

Placing the caller on hold

Placing someone on hold is always an inconvenience, so always ask the caller's permission to put them on hold. Be sure to tell your customer why you're putting them on hold—for example: "I have to check with the shipping department to find out about your order." Giving your customer a time frame also will help lessen any apprehension about being on hold. This could be as simple as saying, "This will just take a couple of minutes." Finally, after picking up the line again, thank the customer for their patience.

Transferring calls

Perhaps the fastest way to get on your customer's bad side is to transfer them multiple times. Passing customers from one person to another gives them the impression there is no one willing to handle their call. As with placing a customer on hold, always ask the caller's permission to transfer them. Be sure there is someone at the other end to pick up the call and inform the customer to whom they are being transferred.

Phone messages

Good message-taking skills start with giving the caller a feeling of confidence the message will get to the intended person. Always verify the information you are taking is correct. Nothing is worse than incomplete or missing information. Verify things such as the spelling of names, telephone numbers and prefixes.

Ending the conversation

Always thank the person for their call and ask them if there is anything else you can do for them. Let the customer hang up the phone first to prevent prematurely hanging up on them. After the call is complete, write down any information about the call immediately. This will prevent you from getting distracted by something else and forgetting the information.

Summary

In this section, we discussed various techniques and habits for improving and establishing a good customer service environment. However, when all is said and done, you must do more than just know these techniques. You must make a conscious effort to practice these habits on a daily basis.

Remember, good customer service is not simply giving customers what they want. It should also include giving that little extra and displaying empathy when necessary. Going the extra mile for your customer is what it's all about!

Review Questions

1. Which of the following is *NOT* a characteristic of good customer service?

   A. Empathy for the customer
   B. Follow-up on the customer's needs
   C. Get your work done first
   D. Extend the customer's options

2. Never let the customer know that you don't have all the answers.

   A. True
   B. False

3. A good company policy dictates the phone should be answered within 3 rings.

   A. True
   B. False

4. You answer the phone and the customer asks for Darcy, one of the sales reps. You know that Darcy is on her phone at the moment. What should you do to best help the customer?

   A. Tell them that she is busy and hang up.
   B. Ask the customer if they would like to hold until Darcy is available.
   C. Transfer them to the accounting department.
   D. Tell the customer that she is busy and they should call back later.

5. You promised a client that you would get back to their office within one week with a new part for their laser printer. After eight days your supplier tells you the part is on back-order. What should you do? Choose all that apply.

   A. Call the customer and inform them of the delay.
   B. Wait and hope the part comes sooner than expected.
   C. Leave on vacation.
   D. Try to find an alternate source for the part.

Appendix A

Decimal-to-Binary Chart

Decimal	Binary	Decimal	Binary	Decimal	Binary
0	0000 0000	51	0011 0011	102	0110 0110
1	0000 0001	52	0011 0100	103	0110 0111
2	0000 0010	53	0011 0101	104	0110 1000
3	0000 0011	54	0011 0110	105	0110 1001
4	0000 0100	55	0011 0111	106	0110 1010
5	0000 0101	56	0011 1000	107	0110 1011
6	0000 0110	57	0011 1001	108	0110 1100
7	0000 0111	58	0011 1010	109	0110 1101
8	0000 1000	59	0011 1011	110	0110 1110
9	0000 1001	60	0011 1100	111	0110 1111
10	0000 1010	61	0011 1101	112	0111 0000
11	0000 1011	62	0011 1110	113	0111 0001
12	0000 1100	63	0011 1111	114	0111 0010
13	0000 1101	64	0100 0000	115	0111 0011
14	0000 1110	65	0100 0001	116	0111 0100
15	0000 1111	66	0100 0010	117	0111 0101
16	0001 0000	67	0100 0011	118	0111 0110
17	0001 0001	68	0100 0100	119	0111 0111
18	0001 0010	69	0100 0101	120	0111 1000
19	0001 0011	70	0100 0110	121	0111 1001
20	0001 0100	71	0100 0111	122	0111 1010
21	0001 0101	72	0100 1000	123	0111 1011
22	0001 0110	73	0100 1001	124	0111 1100
23	0001 0111	74	0100 1010	125	0111 1101
24	0001 1000	75	0100 1011	126	0111 1110
25	0001 1001	76	0100 1100	127	0111 1111
26	0001 1010	77	0100 1101	128	1000 0000
27	0001 1011	78	0100 1110	129	1000 0001
28	0001 1100	79	0100 1111	130	1000 0010
29	0001 1101	80	0101 0000	131	1000 0011
30	0001 1110	81	0101 0001	132	1000 0100
31	0001 1111	82	0101 0010	133	1000 0101
32	0010 0000	83	0101 0011	134	1000 0110
33	0010 0001	84	0101 0100	135	1000 0111
34	0010 0010	85	0101 0101	136	1000 1000
35	0010 0011	86	0101 0110	137	1000 1001
36	0010 0100	87	0101 0111	138	1000 1010

Decimal	Binary	Decimal	Binary	Decimal	Binary
37	0010 0101	88	0101 1000	139	1000 1011
38	0010 0110	89	0101 1001	140	1000 1100
39	0010 0111	90	0101 1010	141	1000 1101
40	0010 1000	91	0101 1011	142	1000 1110
41	0010 1001	92	0101 1100	143	1000 1111
42	0010 1010	93	0101 1101	144	1001 0000
43	0010 1011	94	0101 1110	145	1001 0001
44	0010 1100	95	0101 1111	146	1001 0010
45	0010 1101	96	0110 0000	147	1001 0011
46	0010 1110	97	0110 0001	148	1001 0100
47	0010 1111	98	0110 0010	149	1001 0101
48	0011 0000	99	0110 0011	150	1001 0110
49	0011 0001	100	0110 0100	151	1001 0111
50	0011 0010	101	0110 0101	152	1001 1000
153	1001 1001	189	1011 1101	225	1110 0001
154	1001 1010	190	1011 1110	226	1110 0010
155	1001 1011	191	1011 1111	227	1110 0011
156	1001 1100	192	1100 0000	228	1110 0100
157	1001 1101	193	1100 0001	229	1110 0101
158	1001 1110	194	1100 0010	230	1110 0110
159	1001 1111	195	1100 0011	231	1110 0111
160	1010 0000	196	1100 0100	232	1110 1000
161	1010 0001	197	1100 0101	233	1110 1001
162	1010 0010	198	1100 0110	234	1110 1010
163	1010 0011	199	1100 0111	235	1110 1011
164	1010 0100	200	1100 1000	236	1110 1100
165	1010 0101	201	1100 1001	237	1110 1101
166	1010 0110	202	1100 1010	238	1110 1110
167	1010 0111	203	1100 1011	239	1110 1111
168	1010 1000	204	1100 1100	240	1111 0000
169	1010 1001	205	1100 1101	241	1111 0001
170	1010 1010	206	1100 1110	242	1111 0010
171	1010 1011	207	1100 1111	243	1111 0011
172	1010 1100	208	1101 0000	244	1111 0100
173	1010 1101	209	1101 0001	245	1111 0101
174	1010 1110	210	1101 0010	246	1111 0110
175	1010 1111	211	1101 0011	247	1111 0111

Decimal	Binary	Decimal	Binary	Decimal	Binary
176	1011 0000	212	1101 0100	248	1111 1000
177	1011 0001	213	1101 0101	249	1111 1001
178	1011 0010	214	1101 0110	250	1111 1010
179	1011 0011	215	1101 0111	251	1111 1011
180	1011 0100	216	1101 1000	252	1111 1100
181	1011 0101	217	1101 1001	253	1111 1101
182	1011 0110	218	1101 1010	254	1111 1110
183	1011 0111	219	1101 1011	255	1111 1111
184	1011 1000	220	1101 1100		
185	1011 1001	221	1101 1101		
186	1011 1010	222	1101 1110		
187	1011 1011	223	1101 1111		
188	1011 1100	224	1110 0000		

Appendix B

Standard ASCII Character Set

Item Number	Symbol	Meaning	ASCII in Decimal Representation	ASCII in Binary Representation	ASCII in Hex Representation
1	.	Null	0	0000 0000	0
33	b/	Space	32	0010 0000	20
34	!	Exclamation Point	33	0010 0001	21
35	"	Quotation Marks	34	0010 0010	22
36	#	Number Sign	35	0010 0011	23
37	$	Dollar Sign	36	0010 0100	24
38	%	Percent Sign	37	0010 0101	25
39	&	Ampersand	38	0010 0110	26
40	'	Apostrophe, prime sign	39	0010 0111	27
41	(	Opening Parenthesis	40	0010 1000	28
42	)	Closing Parenthesis	41	0010 1001	29
43	*	Asterisk	42	010 1010	2A
44	+	Plus Sign	43	0010 1011	2B
45	,	Comma	44	0010 1100	2C
46	-	Hyphen, minus sign	45	0010 1101	2D
47	.	Period, decimal point	46	0010 1110	2E
48	/	Slant	47	0010 1111	2F
49	0		48	0011 0000	30
50	1		49	0011 0001	31
51	2		50	0011 0010	32
52	3		51	0011 0011	33
53	4		52	0011 0100	34
54	5		53	0011 0101	35
55	6		54	0011 0110	36
56	7		55	0011 0111	37
57	8		56	.0011 1000	38
58	9		57	0011 1001	39
59	:	Colon	58	0011 1010	3A
60	;	Semicolon	59	0011 1011	3B
61	<	Less than sign	60	0011 1100	3C
62	=	Equal sign	61	0011 1101	3D
63	>	Greater than sign	62	0011 1110	3E
64	?	Question Mark	63	0011 1111	3F
65	@	Commercial at sign	64	0100 0000	40
66	A		65	0100 0001	41
67	B		66	0100 0010	42
68	C		67	0100 0011	43

APPENDIX B

Item Number	Symbol	Meaning	ASCII in Decimal Representation	ASCII in Binary Representation	ASCII in Hex Representation
69	D		68	0100 0100	44
70	E		69	0100 0101	45
71	F		70	0100 0110	46
72	G		71	0100 0111	47
73	H		72	0100 1000	48
74	I		73	0100 1001	49
75	J		74	0100 1010	4A
76	K		75	0100 1011	4B
77	L		76	0100 1100	4C
78	M		77	0100 1101	4D
79	N		78	0100 1110	4E
80	O		79	0100 1111	4F
81	P		80	0101 0000	50
82	Q		81	0101 0001	51
83	R		82	0101 0010	52
84	S		83	0101 0011	53
85	T		84	0101 0100	54
86	U		85	0101 0101	55
87	V		86	0101 0110	56
88	W		87	0101 0111	57
89	X		88	0101 1000	58
90	Y		89	0101 1001	59
91	Z		90	0101 1010	5A
92	[	Opening Bracket	91	0101 1011	5B
93	\	Reverse Slant	92	0101 1100	5C
94	]	Closing Bracket	93	0101 1101	5D
95	^	Caret	94	0101 1110	5E
96	_	Underscore	95	0101 1111	5F
97	`	Acute Accent	96	0110 0000	60
98	a		97	0110 0001	61
99	b		98	0110 0010	62
100	c		99	0110 0011	63
101	d		100	0110 0100	64
102	e		101	0110 0101	65
103	f		102	0110 0110	66
104	g		103	0110 0111	67
105	h		104	0110 1000	68

Item Number	Symbol	Meaning	ASCII in Decimal Representation	ASCII in Binary Representation	ASCII in Hex Representation
106	i		105	0110 1001	69
107	j		106	0110 1010	6A
108	k		107	0110 1011	6B
109	l		108	0110 1100	6C
110	m		109	0110 1101	6D
111	n		110	0110 1110	6E
112	o		111	0110 1111	6F
113	p		112	0111 0000	70
114	q		113	0111 0001	71
115	r		114	0111 0010	72
116	s		115	0111 0011	73
117	t		116	0111 0100	74
118	u		117	0111 0101	75
119	v		118	0111 0110	76
120	w		119	0111 0111	77
121	x		120	0111 1000	78
122	y		121	0111 1001	79
123	z		122	0111 1010	7A
124	{	Opening Brace	123	0111 1011	7B
125	|	Split Vertical Bar	124	0111 1100	7C
126	}	Closing Brace	125	0111 1101	7D
127	~	Tilde	126	0111 1110	7E

Appendix C

Acronyms

APPENDIX C

Acronym	Meaning
ANSI	American National Standards Institute
API	Application Programming Interface
ARPA	Advanced Research Projects Agency
ARPANET	Advanced Research Projects Agency Network
ASCII	American Standard Code for Information Interchange
BIOS	Basic Input/Output System
BNC	British Naval Connector
bps	Bits per second
Bps	Bytes per second
CCITT	Consultative Committee for InternationalTelephony and Telegraphy
CD	Change Directory
CD	Compact Disc
CDFS	Compact Disc File System
CD-R	Compact Disc-Recordable
CD-ROM	Compact Disc Read-Only Memory
CMOS	Complementary Metal-Oxide Semiconductor
CNE	Certified NetWare Engineer
CPU	Central Processing Unit
CRC	Cyclic Redundancy Check
CSMA/CD	Carrier Sense Multiple Access/Collision Detection
DHCP	Dynamic Host Configuration Protocol
DNS	Domain Name System
DoD	Department of Defense
DOS	Disk Operating System
EBCDIC	Extended Binary Code Decimal Interchange Code
EEPROM	Electrically Erasale Programmable Read-Only Memory
EPROM	Erasable Programmable Read-Only Memory
FAT	File Allocation Table
FDDI	Fiber Distributed Data Interface
FS	File Server
GB	Gigabyte
Gbps	Gigabits per second
GBps	Gigabytes per second
GUI	Graphical User Interface
HPFS	High Performance File System
IC	Integrated Circuit
IDE	Integrated Drive Electronics
IEEE	Institute of Electrical and Electronic Engineers
I/O	Input/Output
IP	Internet Protocol
IPX	Internetwork Packet Exchange
IPX/SPX	Internetwork Packet Exchange/Sequenced Packet Exchange
IRQ	Interrupt Request
ISDN	Integrated Services Digital Network
ISO	International Standards Organization
ISP	Internet Service Provider

Kb	Kilobit
KB	Kilobyte
Kbps	Kilobits Per Second
KBps	Kilobytes Per Second
LAN	Local Area Network
LLC	Logical Link Control
MAC	Media Access Control
MAN	Metropolitan Area Network
Mb	Megabit
MB	Megabyte
Mbps	Megabits Per Second
MBps	Megabytes Per Second
MCP	Microsoft Certified Professional
MCPS	Microsoft Certified Product Specialist
MCSE	Microsoft Certified Systems Engineer
MCT	Microsoft Certified Trainer
MD	Make Directory
MHz	Megahertz
MIDI	Musical Instrument Digital Interface
MODEM	Modulator/Demodulator
MSAU	Multi-Station Access Unit
MS-DOS	Microsoft Disk Operating System
NetBEUI	NetBIOS Extended User Interface
NetBIOS	Network Basic Input/Output System
NIC	Network Interface Card
NOS	Network Operating System
NT	New Technology
NTFS	New Technology File System
OEM	Original Equipment Manufacturer
OS	Operating System
OS/2	Operating System/2
OSI	Open Systems Interconnection
PC	Personal Computer
PCMCIA	Personal Computer Memory Card International Association
POSIX	Portable Operating System Interface eXtension
PROM	Programmable Read-Only Memory
PSTN	Public Switched Telephone Network
RAID	Redundant Array of Inexpensive Disks
RD	Remove Directory
RFC	Request for Comments
RIP	Router Information Protocol
RJ	Registered Jack
SMP	Symmetric Multiprocessing
SNMP	Simple Network Management Protocol
SPX	Sequenced Packet Exchange

SQL	Structured Query Language
Tb	Terabit
TB	Terabyte
Tbps	Terabits Per Second
TBps	Terabytes Per Second
TCP	Transmission Control Protocol
TCP/IP	Transmission Control Protocol/Internet Protocol
THz	Terahertz
TR	Token Ring
URL	Uniform Resource Locator
USL	Unix Systems Laboratory
WAN	Wide Area Network
WINS	Windows Internet Name Service
WORM	Write Once, Read Many
WYSIWYG	What You See Is What You

Appendix D

Beep Codes

APPENDIX E

AMI BIOS Beep Codes

Beep Codes	Translation
1 beep	Fail to Refresh
2 beeps	Memory (Parity Error)
3 beeps	Base Memory Error Fail (first 64K)
4 beeps	Timer Not Responding
5 beeps	CPU Error
6 beeps	Gate A20 Failure
7 beeps	Processor exception interrup error
8 beeps	Video memory read/write error
9 beeps	ROM checksum error
10 beeps	CMOS error
11 beeps	Cache Memory Failure

Phoenix BIOS Beep Codes

Beep Code	Translation
1-1-3	CMS read/write failure
1-1-4	ROM BIOS checksum fail
1-2-1	Programmable interval timer fail
1-2-2	DMA initialization failure
1-2-3	DMS page register failure
1-3-1	RAM refresh verification failure
1-3-3	First 64K RAM chip failure
1-3-4	Odd/even logic failure (first 64K)
1-4-1	Address line failure in first 64K
1-4-2	Parity failure (base memory)
2-1-1 thru 2-4-4	First 64K base memory failure
3-1-1	Slave DMA register fail
3-1-2	Master DMA register fail
3-1-3	Master interrup mask fail
3-1-4	Slave interrup mask fail
3-2-4	Keyboard controller test failure
3-3-4	Screen Initialization failure
3-4-1	Screen retrace failure
3-4-2	Search for video ROM in progress
4-2-1	Timer interrup test failure
4-2-2	Shutdown test failure
4-2-3	Gate A20 failure
4-2-4	Protected mode (unexpected interrupt)
4-3-1	RAM test
4-3-3	Interval timer failure
4-3-4	Clock (time of day) test failure
4-4-1	Serial port failure
4-4-2	Parallel port failure
4-4-3	Math co-processor failure

Review Answers

GLOSSARY

Glossary

GLOSSARY

A

Abend
Contraction of Abnormal END. A message issued by an operating system when it detects a serious problem.

ACK
Abbreviation for acknowledgment. In communications, ACK is a control code.

Active Partition
The partition on a hard drive that is read at computer start-up. This partition should have the operating system files that are needed to boot the operating system.

ADB
Apple Desktop Bus.

Address
An identifying number that specifies the location of a computer resource such as a node, a process, or a memory allocation.

Advertising
The process by which services on a network inform other devices on the network of their availability.

AFP
AppleTalk Filing Protocol.

Alpha Processor
A type of computer processor that typically offers better performance than Intel processors. NT is the main operating system that takes advantage of Alpha processors. Some versions of Unix also use Alpha processors.

American National Standards Institute
An organization that seeks to develop standardization within the computing industry. ANSI is the American representative to the ISO, or International Standards Organization.

American Standard Code for Information Interchange
A 7-bit coding scheme that translates symbolic characters into the ones and zeros that are stored as data on a computer. Extended ASCII uses an 8-bit coding scheme.

Amplitude
The size or magnitude of a voltage or a waveform.

Amplitude modulation
Changing the voltage or level or amplitude of a carrier frequency to transmit digital or analog signal.

Analog data
Data that varies continuously on some interval.

Analog signal
A continuously varying electromagnetic wave.

ANSI
American National Standards Institute, responsible for the ASCII code set (American Standard Code for Information Interchange).

Application Layer
The layer of the OSI model responsible for supporting file and print services. It also manages whether requests are processed locally or remotely.

Architecture
A logical structure for network communications. It is constructed of protocols, formats and operation sequence.

ARPANET
Acronym for Advanced Research Projects Agency Network. A research network funded by the defense Advanced Research Projects Agency.

ASCII
American Standard Code for Information Interchange.

Asynchronous
When used to define a code set, character codes that contain start and stop bits. When used to define data transmission, a signal that does not need a separate clock synchronization signal for data reception. Asynchronous transmission is also called start-stop transmission because one character is sent at a time.

Asynchronous Communication
Begins transmission of each character with a start bit and ends transmission of each character with a stop bit. This method of communication is not as efficient as synchronous communication but is less expensive, because no clocking hardware is needed.

Attenuation
Loss of signal energy characterized by a weakening signal.

AUTOEXEC.BAT
A DOS batch file that, if present, is automatically executed during boot-up.

B

Backbone
A portion of a network that manages the bulk of the traffic. The backbone may connect several different locations or buildings, and other, smaller networks may be attached to it.

Backups
Copy all of your data to a secondary storage option. If your storage option becomes unavailable, you can use backups to restore the operating system, application, and data files.

Backup Domain Controllers
This is used in NT domains and get read-only copies of the PDC accounts database. BDCs server two primary functions. They offload logon authentication requests from the PDC, and they provide fault tolerance. If the PDS fails, the BDC can be promoted to PDC.

Balun
A contraction of BALanced Unbalanced. A small device used to connect a balanced line I.E. twisted pair cable to an unbalanced line (coaxial cable). The balun matches the impedance between the two media.

Bandwidth
The size of the transmission channel (width). The difference expressed in hertz (frequency) between the highest and lowest frequencies of a band. In modern usage, bandwidth defines the maximum specified throughput of a communication channel.

Baseband
A signal transmitted at its original frequency. In modern usage, baseband refers to a transmission system where the original signal uses up all the channel's available bandwidth.

Base Memory
The reserved area in memory where devices can store data so that the processor can directly access the data. Some devices need this allocated memory range located in the system RAM. The area is typically located in the upper area of RAM called the Upper Memory Area(UMA).

Basic Input/Output System
A special collection of services that are included on a ROM chip. The services enable the operating system, hardware, and software used with the computer.

Baud
The number of signal level changes per second. Each signal level contains one (or more) bit of information.

BDC
See Backup Domain Controllers

Beaconing
In a Token Ring network, the process of informing other nodes that token passing has been suspended due to a very severe error condition, such as a broken cable.

Binary
A method of representing information. It relies on two states: an "on" or "off" state.

Binary Synchronous Communication
Developed by IBM in the 1960s, Binary Synchronous Communication is a data link control procedure for use with synchronous transmission.

BIOS
Basic Input Output System.

Bisync
Binary Synchronous Communications.

Bit
Binary Digit. The smallest unit of information. All digital information is composed of bits.

Bit-oriented protocol
Data transmission protocol that moves one bit of information at a time without regard for the bit's meaning.

Block
Set of continuous bits and /or bytes that contain definable information.

Bootable Diskette
A disk that contains the boot files of an operating system and is used to "boot" the computer.

Boot Partition
The partition on a hard drive that contains the operating system files.

Bottleneck
The weakest or slowest link in a communications chain; commonly the cause of a slowdown in a network environment.

bps
Bits per Second. Measure of the number of bits of information transmitted per second.

Bridge
Hardware and software used to connect networks. It is normally used in connecting LANs of identical communication methods, mediums, and topologies.

Broadband
A transmission channel able to simultaneously carry multiple signals.

Broadband Signaling
A signaling scheme that splits the signal into multiple channels to send an analog signal.

Browser Service
In NT networks, broadcasts the availability of network services such as network shares or printers.

Buffer
Temporary data storage area located in a computer's memory.

Bus
A common set of communication channels connecting parts of a system.

Bus Topology
Uses a physical linear segment to connect all network devices. Each end of the bus is terminated, and devices typically connect to the bus through T-connectors.

Byte
Generally, a set of eight continuous bits making up the smallest addressable item of information in a computer system.

C

Cable Modem
Allows high-speed access to the Internet over cable TV(CATV) lines. The cable modem needs two connections: one to the cable outlet and the other to the computer. Cable modems are more economical than ISDN, and you do not need to install an additional phone line. There is no need to dail; it is always active.

Carrier
An analog signal whose frequency, amplitude, or phase which has been altered to allow it to represent data.

CSMA/CD
Carrier-Sense Multiple Access/Collision Detection. A technique of transmitting over a local access network where only one transmitter may use the line at a time.

CCITT
Consultative Committee on International Telegraphy and Telephony. An international standards group.

CD
See Compact Disk

Central Processing Unit
The microprocessor that is the brain of the computer. It uses logic to perform mathematical operations that are used in the manipulation of data.

Channel
A path used for data communications.

Character
A single element from a particular character set.

Checksum
A block check character or block check sequence computed by adding the bits of the block by simple binary addition.

Chip
An integrated circuit, sometimes called an IC, containing many electronic circuits, transistors, switches, etc. in a single silicon wafer.

Chooser
An Apple menu utility which allows you to select printers.

Circuit
An electronic path allowing communications between two devices.

Circuit switching
Data transmission technique that directly connects a sender and receiver in an unbroken path.

CISC
See Complex Instruction Set Computing

Client
The computer on the network that requests network services.

Client-Server Networks
Use a dedicated server to centralize user and group account management. Users log on to servers where they have user accounts and access resources on the server to which their user account has permission.

Clock
A device which generates a high-speed synchronizing signal.

Clock Cycles
The internal speed of a computer or processor expressed in megahertz(MHz). The faster the clock speed, the faster the computer performs a specific operation.

Clock Signal
Controls the rate at which synchronous data is transmitted.

Cluster
The smallest unit of disk space for data storage, typically 512 bytes in size.

Coaxial cable
Transmission media (cable) composed of two shielded conductors that share the same axis and are separated by a non-conducting element.

Code
A set of rules specifying the representation of characters. A code set is formally known as an alphabet.

Cold Boot
Restarting a computer's operating system by turning the computer off and then back on.

Common carrier
A transmission facility available to the public that must abide by public utility regulations.

Communication
The transfer of information between devices.

Communication medium
A physical entity that hosts communications. It may be bounded, such as coaxial wire or twisted pair cable, or unbounded, such as air waves.

Compact Disc
An optical disk that stores data. Most CDs can be written to one time but can be read many times.

Complex Instruction Set Computing
The most common type of processor produced. CISC is composed of a full complement of instructions used by the processor. Intel processors are currently based on this standard.

Concentrator
A network device that connects several computers. The terms concentrator and hub are often used interchangeably. Normally, hub is a more generic term, and concentrator is associated with 10BASET Ethernet networks.

Config.sys
A DOS user-created text file that contains parameters read during start-up, located in the root directory.

Connectivity
The logical or physical linking of network workstations or devices.

CPS
Characters per second. The number of characters transmitted per second.

CPU
Central Processing Unit. The part of the computer where the data is processed.

CRC
Cyclic Redundancy Check. An error checking procedure using a predefined mathematical divisor to check the integrity of a transmitted block of data.

CSU
Channel Service Unit. A device that functions as a certified safe electrical circuit, acting as a buffer between the customer's equipment and a public carrier's wide area network equipment.

D

Databases
Collections of data organized so that users can easily add, edit, or access data. Databases can be created for personal use on a desktop computer or can exist as distributed databases throughout a network.

Data communications
The transmission of data between network dev

Data-Link Layer
The layer of the OSI model that includes information about the source and destination hardware addresses of the communicating devices. It also specifies lower-layer flow control and error control.ices.

Data packet
A logical group of data

Data Path
Represents the largest number of instructions that can be transported into the processor chip during one operation..

Decibel
A numerical expression of the relative loudness of sound.

Dedicated line
Medium used solely for data transmission between two locations. It is sometimes referred to as a "leased line"or a "private line."

Dedicated Server
A special computer that acts only as a server and does not perform any other tasks.

De Facto
Commonly accepted, as in "*de facto* standard."

Defragmentation
The process of reorganizing your files on a disk so that they are arranged contiguously. This process better uses disk space.

De Jure
As specified by law, as in a "*de jure* standard."

Demodulator
The section of a modem that converts analog signal to digital signal.

Desktop Publishing
Software that produces high-quality page designs. This popular application integrates word processing and graphics programs.

DHCP
Dynamic Host Configuration Protocol. Automates the assignment of IP configuration information.

Differential Backup
A backup of all files with the archive bit set. The archive bit is not cleared when you complete the backup. If you have to restore data, you need only your last full backup and your last differential tape.

Digital data
Data consisting of a sequence of discrete elements.

Digital signal
A signal composed of two energy states (on and off or positive and negative current). Digital signals are used by computers to transmit data. The pattern of the current state represents individual bits of information.

DIP Switch
Stands for Dual In-line Package switch. It contains parallel rows of contacts that can configure computer components and peripheral devices.

Direct Memory Access
The method of directly transferring data from a device, such as a storage device, to memory without involving the processor.

Directory
A logical portion of disk space identified by a name.

Directory Services Network Model
Uses a hierarchical database to logically organize the network resources. This model scales well to small, medium, or large enterprises networks.

Disk Controllers
Manage floppy and hard disks. Disk controllers can be a separate piece of hardware, or they can be integrated with the hard drive.

Disk Duplexing
A mirrored set with two disk controllers and two hard drives.

Disk Mirroring
A mirrored set with one disk controller and two hard drives.

Disk Operating System
An operating system developed by Microsoft. DOS predominately uses command lines to manage the operating system.

Disk Partitioning
The process of creating logical disks from a physical disk. You can then format the logical disks and use them to store data.

Disk Stripe Set
A disk drive configuration that combines several logical partitions of the same size into a single logical disk. Stripe sets stripe data evenly over the entire set.

Distributed processing
The ability of network nodes to execute shared network applications, or parts of network applications, independently of other nodes.

DNA
Digital Network Architecture. A network designed by Digital Equipment Corporation.

DNS
Domain Name System. A system that resolves domain names to IP addresses using a domain name database for address resolution.

Domain Model
Used in NT Networks to logically group computers, users, and groups into a domain. Users log on to the domain and have access to any resources within the domain to which their user account has permission.

DOS
Disk Operating System.

Dot Pitch
Measures the distance in millimeters between two dots of the same color on the monitor.

DRAM
Dynamic Random-Access Memory

DTE
Data Circuit-Terminating Equipment. Equipment at the source and the destination allowing communications to take place. It establishes, maintains, and terminates connections and performs signal conversion and coding between the transmission medium and the DTE.

Dual Booting
Having two or more operating systems on your computer. At system start-up, you can select which operating system you will boot.

Dynamic RAM
A type of memory that uses capacitors and trnsistors to store electrical charges representing memory states. The capacitors that make up this type of memory need to be refreshed every millisecond and are unreachable by the processor during that time.

E

EBCDIC
Extended Binary Coded Decimal Interchange Code. An eight-bit code set developed by IBM.

ECP
Extended Capabilities Port. The standard developed for parallel communication by Hewlett-Packard and Microsoft to allow for data transfer rates of more than 2MBps. In addition to the high data transfer rates, it allows for bidirectional operation.

EEPROM
Electrically Erasable Programmable Read-Only Memory. A chip that maintains its contents without the use of electrical power. The stored contents of an EPROM chip are erased and reprogrammed by removing the protective cover and using special equipment to reprogram the chip.

Echoplexing
A crude form of error checking where the receiver repeats all signals it receives from the sender. The sender then checks for accuracy.

EIA
Electronics Industries Association. A standards organization comprised of electronic manufacturers in the United States.

Electron Gun
The device that shoots electrically charged particles called electrons toward the back of the monitor screen.

Email
Short for electronic mail. Email is probably the most commonly used application. At its heart, email is basically text messages transmitted and

stored over communication networks. It has evolved to be able to send varied media images, such as pictures, audio files, and video files.

Emulation
The ability of one device to mimic the operations of another. A common use involves running software on a microcomputer that allows it to operate as a terminal attached to a mainframe computer.

Encryption
Modifications of a bit stream so it appears to be random. Encryption is used for security reasons. The sender and the receiver agree on a encryption method prior to data transmission.

Enhanced Parallel Port
The standard developed for parallel communication by Intel, Xircom, and Zenith Data Systems to allow for data transfer rates of more than 2MBps. It supports bidirectional operation of attached devices and an addressing scheme.

Enterprise network
A network (usually very large) that connects all sites of a particular organization.

Ethernet
A popular network protocol and cabling scheme with a transfer rate of 10 mega bits per second, originally developed by the Xerox Corporation in 1976.

Extended Partition
A type of DOS partition created within logical partitions. You can have multiple extended partitions within a single logical partition.

F

FAT
File Allocation Table

FCS
Frame Check Sequence. An error detection mechanism used in bit-oriented protocols.

FDDI
Fiber Distributed Data Interface. A network specification that defines a logical ring topology of fiber transmitting at 100Mbps. FDDI provides similar network connectivity as Ethernet and Token Ring, and functions at the same layers of the OSI model.

FDM
Frequency Division Multiplexing. A technique used by a multiplexer to allow shared use of a single channel based on differences in frequency.

Fiber optics
Glass fibers that can carry information as light signals.

File Allocation Table
A type of file system that stores files and folders and keeps track of where files are stored on the disk. DOS made this file system widely available. Most operating systems support the FAT file system.

File server
A device providing shared access to files and data.

File Transfer Protocol
A protocol that transfers files between an FTP server and FTP clients. Most Web browsers use FTP client software to download and upload files to Internet servers running the FTP service.

Finder
The finder is what Macintosh users run in lieu of an operating system.

Flag
A bit field or character used to delimit data on either side of it. The term "flag" is sometimes used to reference a single bit indicating the presence or absence of a condition.

Floppy Disk
A removable plastic disk that stores small amounts of data. This is a popular media because of its low cost and wide availability.

Footprint
The amount of space a computer takes up on the desktop.

Format
The structure of a message or data that allows it to be recognized.

Formatting
The process of initializing a floppy disk or logical drive and preparing it so that you can store data on it.

Frame
A data block in a bit-oriented protocol.

Freeware
Software that you can use without payment.

Frequency
The number of cycles of a signal per second.

Frequency modulation
Changing the frequency of a carrier frequency to transmit digital or analog information.

FTAM
File Transfer, Access and Management. The Open Systems Interconnection (OSI) protocol for transferring and remotely accessing files on different makes and models of computers also using FTAM.

FTP
File Transfer Protocol. The TCP/IP protocol used to log-in to a network, list files and directories, and transfer files.

Full-duplex transmission
A channel allowing simultaneous transmission in both directions.

Full Duplexing
Means that simultaneous two-way communication can take place.

G

Gateway
A hardware/software combination that allows communications between dissimilar systems.

Global network
A computer network extending over a very large geographic area, often to various countries and continents.

GOSIP
Government Open Systems Interconnection Profile. A suite of standards based on the OSI reference model. Intended for use in government projects. Both the United States and United Kingdom GOSIP exists.

Graphical User Interface
A graphically based interface that presents information in a user-friendly manner. Windows and Macintosh operating systems both use GUI (pronounced "gooey") interfaces.

H

Half-duplex transmission
A channel allowing transmission in only one direction at a

Half Duplexing
Means that two-way communication can take place, but only one device can communicate at a time. time.

Handshaking
Synchronization message sent between devices.

Hard Drives
Store data. They consist of a series of magnetically coated disks. Data is stored on the disks as ones and zeros. A positive charge indicates a one, and the absence of a charge indicates a zero.

HDLC
High-Level Data Link Control. Standard bit-oriented communication line protocol developed by the ISO.

Hertz
International unit of frequency. The number of cycles per second. It is abbreviated "Hz."

HFS
Hierarchical File System.

Home Directory
A special folder that is assigned to a user where personal files can be stored.

Hop count
In routing, the number of links that must be crossed to get from any given source device to any given destination device.

Host
A computer system on a network.

HTTP
Hypertext Transfer Protocol

Hub
A central point to and from which communications flow.

I

IDE
Integrated Drive Electronics. A drive technology that integrates the drive and controller into a single piece of hardware. IDE drives are an inexpensive data storage solution.

IEEE
Institute of Electronic and Electrical Engineers. A standards organization dealing with electronics.

Impedence
An electrical property of a cable that combines capacitance, inductance, and resistance, measured in OHMs.

Incremental Backup
A backup of only the files that have the archive bit set. After the incremental backup is complete, the archive bit is cleared. If you have to restore data, you must use your last full backup and each incremental backup that you have done.

Input/Output Channel
The channel between the computer and a peripheral device. If you have more channels for data transfer, you have better performance.

Internal Cache RAM
Internal high-speed memory included on a memory chip.

International Standards Organization
An international standards organization dedicated to defining global communication and informational exchange standards. ANSI is the American representative to the ISO.

Internet
The world-wide public network consisting of millions of nodes.

Internet Browsers
The media through which users navigate the Internet World Wide Web(WWW)

Internet Service Provider
A third-party company that provides Internet services.

Internetwork
A series of network segments connected by bridges, routers, or gateways.

Internetwork Packet Exchange/Sequenced Packet Exchange
A network communication protocol that is propietary to Novell and is used primarily in NetWare networks

Interrupt Request
The method a device uses for informing the microprocessor(CPU) that the device needs attention. Through this method of interruption, the microprocessor can function without needing to poll each device to see if it needs service.

I/O Memory
A memory address, called an I/O address, for a device. The address acts like a mailbox for the processor to send instructions to the device. The I/O address is also commonly called the port address.

ISDN
Integrated Services Digital Network. CCITT project for standardization of networks to allow mixed digital and transmission services.

ISA
Industry Standard Architecture.

ISO
International Standards Organization. A standards organization recognized for its development of the OSI protocols and the OSI Reference Model.

J

Jabber
A continuous and meaningless transmission generated by a network device, usually the result of an error or a hardware malfunction.

Jitter
A type of distortion found on analog communication lines that result in datSG-transmission errors.

Jumper
A small plastic and metal connector that completes a circuit, usually to select one option from a set of user-definable options. Sometimes referred to as a “shunt.”

K

Kermit
A file transfer protocol developed at Columbia University and placed in the public domain, used to transfer files between PCs and mainframe computers over standard telephone lines.

Keyboard
The most common type of input device. The keyboard takes in information in the form of letters and numbers. The letters and numbers are translated into instructions that the computer must perform. The computer translates literally what you enter, so any typing mistakes result in an error.

L

LAN
Local-Area Network. A collection of connected computers allowing users to share data and peripherals.

LCD
Liquid crystal display, used in flat-top monitors.

Leased line
A communications circuit or telephone line reserved for the permanent use of a specific customer.

Line
A communications circuit.

Line protocol
Consisting of both handshaking and line-control functions, line protocols perform data communications over network lines.

LINUX
A popular version of Unix, because it is offered as shareware and freeware. Many of the utilities distributed with Linux are also freeware or shareware. This makes Linux an attractive offer for people who want a powerful desktop operating system at little or no cost.

LocalTalk
The Macintosh built-in networking protocol.

Logical Link Control
A sublayer of the OSI model Data-link layer. The LLC sublayer contains information about service access points, which identify the higher-level protocol that will be used at the Network layer. Along with the MAC sublayer, the LLC sublayer provides physical access to the hardware to the upper-layer protocols.

Logical Partition
Part of the hard drive that is allocated as a logical drive.

Logon Script
A special script or batch file that is executed each time a user logs on to a computer or network.

M

Mark
Condition of the digital signal sending a binary

MAC
Media Access Control. A sublayer fo the OSI model Data-Link layer. The MAC sublayer contains information about the physical address of the network adapter and, along with the LLC sublayer, provides physical access to the hardware to the upper-layer OSI protocols."1."

MAN
Metropolitan-Area Network. A communication network that serves an urban area.

MCA
Micro Channel Architecture. (IBM proprietary 32-bit design)

Member Server
A special type of server in the NT environment that does not contain a copy of the domain user accounts database.

Message
Information communicated from one location to another. It is usually composed of a header, the body of the information, and the trailer.

Message switching
Data transmission in which there is no need to establish a dedicated physical path between the sender and receiver. Sometimes referred to as a "store and forward" network.

MHz
Megahertz; unit of measurement. (Millions of cycles per second.)

Microwaves
Very short radio waves used for unbounded transmission.

Mirrored Set
A disk drive configuration that contains a primary partition and a secondary partition. Anytime data is written to the first partition, it is automatically written to the second partition. You use a mirrored set for fault tolerance.

Modem
MOdulator/DEModulator. A device that converts digital signal to analog for transmission and then converts it back to digital after the reception.

Monitor
The most common type of output device. The monitor allows the human eye to interact with the computer. Without a monitor, the computer's output capabilities would be very limited.

Mouse
A common type of input device. You use the mouse for navigating, selecting, or drawing in the user environment. The mouse movements are translated into computer instructions by motion and button selection.

Multimedia Extension
A processor technology that dramatically improves the response time of games and multimedia-based applications. The technology was introduced through the MMX-equipped line of Intel Pentium chips. MMX processors contain additional instruction code sets that increase the processing speed of audio, video, and graphical data by up to 60 percent, compared with traditional processors.

Multiprocessor Computer
A computer that uses more than one processor installed in a single computer. Computers that contain more than one processor can scale to meet the needs of more demanding application programs.

Multiplexer
(MUX) An electronic device that accepts several signals and combines them into one high-speed data stream.

N

NDIS
Network Driver Interface Specification. A device driver specification developed by Microsoft and 3COM in 1990.

NetBEUI
Net BIOS Extended User Interface. A network device driver for the transport layer supplied with *Microsoft* Windows and Windows NT suite.

NetWare
A popular network operating system from Novell and a competitive product to NT.

Network
A collection of devices that can communicate with one another.

Network Drive
A mapping to a network path that appears to the user as a drive letter. You access it the same way you access a local drive.

Network Layer
The layer of the OSI model responsible for moving packets over an internetwork so that they can be routed to the correct network segment.

New Technology File System
NTFS is a file system used on NT computers that supports features such as local security.

NIC
Network Interface Card. A printed circuit board installed into a network device. When the card is connected to a common cabling system, the NIC allows the device to communicate with the other devices on the network.

Node
Any device on the network.

Noise
Unwanted signals on a channel.

Nondedicated
A term used to describe a file server that can be used simultaneously as a workstation.

Nonproprietary
A specification or implementation that was not created by a single private organization.

Numeric Coprocessor
A secondary processor that speeds operations by taking over some of the main processor's work. It typically performs mathematical calculations, freeing the processor to tend to other tasks.

O

OEM
Original Equipment Manufacturer. The original manufacturer of equipment.

Offline Storage
A storage method in which data is not immediately available without user intervention. You use offline storage for large amounts of infrequently accessed data or to store computer backups.

Online Data Storage
A storage method in which data is readily available at high speed. You do not need to do anything special to access online storage.

Open Systems Interconnection Model(OSI Model)
A theoretical model that defines how networks work from the ground up. The OSI model defines seven layers and the function of the data flow within each layer.

Open System Interconnection
A term used to refer to a set of protocols as well as a communication reference model created and promulgated by the ISO.

P, Q

Packet
See data packet

Packet switching
Data transmission where packets are divided into packets, each with a destination address.

Parallel Communication
The process of transmitting and processing data 1 byte (8 bits) at a time.

Parity bit
A bit added to character bits to make the total number of bits odd or even. It is used in error checking schemes.

PC Card
A device to enhance the capabilities of a computer. Adding a card to your computer allows you to customize it for your needs. Without this feature, the computer would not be as modular and would not allow you to add devices chosen to meet your specific needs.

PDS
Processor Direct Slots.

Peer-to-Peer Networks
Do not use dedicated network servers for authenticating users and providing secure access to network resources. In this network model, clients share resources, and other clients have access to whatever has been shared.

Peripheral device
A device attached to a computer to perform a task such as printing or data storage.

Peer-to-peer communications
Communications between similarly capable network devices.

Phase modulation
Modifying the phase of a signal to transmit digital data.

Physical Layer
The layer of the OSI model responsible for the transmission of data over a physical medium.

Plotter
A special type of print device that draws high-resolution diagrams, charts, graphs, and other layouts

Plug-and-Play
A technology that automatically configures hardware devices for you.

Point-to-point
Physically, a channel that runs from one point to another point without passing through intermediate devices. Logically, communication between two devices.

Polling
Sequentially contacting several network devices to see if they wish to transmit or communicate.

Portable Operating System Interface(POSIX)
A standard interface for UNIX implementations.

PowerPC
A type of microprocessor designed by Apple, Motorola, and IBM.

Presentation Layer
The layer of the OSI model responsible for formatting and translating data.

Primary Domain Controller
Used in an NT domain, the PDC contains the read/write copy of the domain accounts administration database, called the Security Accounts Manager, or SAM.

Primary Partition
The first logical partition you create on a hard drive.

Print Device
In NT terminology, the actual physical printer or hardware device to which you will print.

Print Processor
Processes a print job into language that the printer understands so that the job is formatted as the application specified.

Print Queue
In a print environment, a special directory that resides on print servers and stores print jobs until they are sent to the print device.

Print Server
In a print environment, the computer on which the printer has been defined. Print jobs are sent to print servers before they are sent to the print device.

Print Spooler
In NT terminology, the service responsible for managing incoming print jobs and passing the print jobs to the print device.

Programmable Read-Only Memory
A special type of chip that is manufactured without any configuration. Manufacturers can then "burn in", or program, the PROM chip to contain whatever configuration is needed.

Proprietary
A specification or implementation created by a single organization.

Protocol
A formal set of rules that governs message exchange and communication.

PSTN
Public Switched Telephone Network.

R

RAID
Redundant Array of Inexpensive Disks.

RAM
Random Access Memory. Storage area that is initialized after a reboot or power cycling.

RAS
Remote Access Service. Allows computers to access the network remotely; for exampel, through a phone, ISDN, or Internet connection.

Repeater
A device that amplifies and improves the quality of signals on a network.

Ring Topology
A physical topology that is circular. It is similar to a bus topology, except the two ends are connected to form a ring.

RISC
Reduced Instruction Set Computing. A reduced set of instructions used by a processor. PowerPC and Alpha processors are manufactured using this standard. RISC allows a microprocessor to operate at higher speeds.

ROM
Read Only Memory. A type of memory that can only be written to with a special device.

RS-232
Communications interface developed by the EIA. It is commonly used between electronic devices such as computers, modems, and printers.

Router
A device capable of sending information along various paths through an internetwork.

S

SAM
Security Accounts Manager

SCSI
(Pronounced "scuzzy.") Stands for Small Computer System Interface.

SDLC
Synchronous Data Link Control. A bit-synchronous data communication protocol developed by IBM.

Separator Page
In a print environment, a special page that identifies a print job by owner and name.

Serial Communication
The process of transmitting and processing data 1 bit at a time.

Server
The computer on the network that provides network services.

Session
A logical connection between network addressable units.

Session Layer
The layer of the OSI model responsible for managing communication sessions between service requesters and service providers. This layer manages communications by establishing, synchronizing, and maintaining the connection between sender and receiver.

Shareware
Software that is generally available for trial use. If you like the software, you should pay a small licensing fee.

Shielded twisted pair
Twisted pair cable surrounded by a metallic or foil shield.

Signal splitting device
A device used in a network to distribute signals from node to node. An example is an active hub.

Silicon-On-Insulator
The microchip manufacturing innovation that IBM invented. SOI is based on the ability to enhance silicon technology for improved performance through a new generation of chips manufactured using this technology.

Simplex transmission
Channel that allows communication in only one direc

Single-Edge Cartridge
An advanced packaging scheme that the Intel Pentium II uses. The SEC processor is encased in a cartridge module with a single edge that plugs into a 242-pin slot on the system board, much as an expansion card plugs into the system board.tion.

SNA
System Network Architecture. A network blueprint developed by IBM.

Software Drivers
Special programs that tell the computer's operating system how to communicate with and control hardware device. Each device has a driver that allows it to communicate with the computer. The driver is written to operate only within a certain operating system. For instance, a Windows 3.1x driver will not work for that device if Windows NT is installed.

Spreadsheet
An application that keeps track of data and performs mathematical calculations based on data organized within rows and columns. Spreadsheets appear as a series of cells, which are the boxes at the intersection of a row and a column.

SRAM
Static RAM. A type of computer memory that retains the information within it as long as power is supplied, allowing it to refresh. SRAM chips can store only about one-fourth the information a dynamic RAM chip can store. The typical application for SRAM is in cache memory.

Start bit
A bit added in synchronous transmission that indicates the beginning of a character.

Station
An individual device on the network.

Stop bit
Bit added in synchronous transmission to indicate the end of a character.

Stripe Set with Parity Drive
A disk drive configuration that is similar to a stripe set with a parity stripe, except that the parity information is stored on a single drive as opposed to being striped.

Stripe Set with Parity Stripe
A disk drive configuration that is similar to a stripe set, but it contains a parity stripe across all drives. This gives you the benefits of a stripe set while also offering fault tolerance.

Synchronous transmission
Method of transmission where the messages are sent as continuous bit streams. Each block of data is preceded by a synchronous character or character sequence and is followed by an end-of-message sequence.

T

Tape
A magnetic media that you commonly use for backup. It is a slow media for accessing data, but its large capacity and low cost make it ideal for backup.

T-connector
Hardware used to connect coaxial cable to a computer's network interface card.

TCP/IP
Transmission Control Protocol/Internet Protocol. Two protocols developed by the Department of Defense.

Terminator
A device needed to terminate a linear bus; It marks the beginning and end of the cable segment.

Throughput
A measure of the productivity of a computer, network or device.

Token
A special packet that signifies that a user can transmit data to a Token Ring network.

Token Ring
A networking protocol that is specified at the Physical and Data-Link layers of the OSI model. Token Ring uses a token-passing scheme to transmit data within a logical ring topology.

Topology
The physical arrangement of the network nodes and links. Examples are ring, star, and bus.

Transport Layer
The layer of the OSI model usually associated with reliable end-to-end connections. This layer responsible for managing connections, error control, and flow control between sender and receiver.

Trunk
A multiple line-circuit connecting switching or distribution centers.

Twisted pair
A cable consisting of four or more pairs of copper wires, twisted together in pairs. Telephone wire is an example of twisted pair cable.

U

UMA
Upper Memory Area. The area of memory between 640KB an 1MB in and IBM-compatible computer.This area of memory was originally reserved for system and video use.

Uniform Resource Locator (URL)
Specifies the location of TCP/IP resources.

UNIX
A popular operating system that is 32-bit, multiuser, and multitasking.

V

VAX
The Virtual Address eXtension technology built by Digital Equipment Corporation to run the VMS platform computers.

Video Display Adapter
The adapter inside your computer that connects to the monitor.

Virtual Circuit
A logical connection between two devices. Both devices share a logical connection that transmits and receives data.

Virtual Memory
A method of emulating physical memory on the hard disk.

Virus
Software that affects the way your computer works without your permission or knowledge. Viruses do not exist naturally and are written by programmers with specific agendas. Viruses have two main characteristics. The first is that they spread without user knowledge from one file to another through a technique called self-propagation. The second characteristic is that the virus has some action that it performs, which is called the payload. The payload may be something fairly harmless, such as displaying a message, or it might be more malicious, such as erasing your entire hard drive.

Virus Scanner
A special application that scans your computer for the presence of computer viruses. Most virus scanners also can remove viruses.

Voice grade
Media suitable for voice or analog data.

Volt
A standard unit of electrical potential.

Volume Set
A disk drive configuration that extends the size of a partition beyond a single physical drive.

W

WAN
Wide-Area Network. Large network formed by connecting LANs or MANs.

Warm Boot
Reloading a computer's operating system through the use of reset keys on the keyboard.

Watt
A standard unit of power.

Windows Internet Name Service
In NetBIOS networks, resolves NetBIOS names to IP addresses. NT requires NetBIOS network services

Word Processor
A fully featured application that creates, edits, and prints documents.

World Wide Web
The name of the network of links consisting of hypertext documents.

WYSIWYG
(Wiz-ee-wig) What you see is what you get.

Workstation
An individual personal computer attached to the network with a network interface card. Sometimes referred to as a node on the network.

X, Y, Z

X.25
Transmission protocol standardized by the CCITT for packet switching networks.

Index

Index

Symbols

A

B

C

D

INDEX

E

F

G

H

I

INDEX

J

K

L

M

INDEX

N

O

P

Q

R

INDEX

S

T

U

INDEX

V

W

X, Y

Z

A+ CERTIFICATION COURSE

MINDWORKS LAB MANUAL

VERSION 5.X

MINDWORKS
4141 N. Granite Reef Road, Suite 101
Scottsdale, AZ 85251
www.mindwork.com

Publisher: MINDWORKS
Executive Editors: Jim Gardner, Ron Brown
Editor: Carol Hartwig
Technical Editor: Dan Waldo
Page Layout/Design: Carol Hartwig
Layout & Graphics: Jim Knott
Cover Design: Tom Hagen, Jim Gardner
Author: Tom Hagen
Supported By: The Entire Staff at Mindworks

THIS BOOK IS DEDICATED TO ALL OF OUR VALUED STUDENTS AND CUSTOMERS WITHOUT WHOSE SUPPORT THIS BOOK WOULD NOT BE POSSIBLE.

THANK YOU!

CORE HARDWARE EXERCISES

Exercise 5.1: Avoiding Conflicts

OBJECTIVE

Configuring a network interface card for non-conflicting IRQ and I/O address.

PREPARATION

You are installing a 3COM 509 network board in your PC which has the following equipment:

- Standard disk controller
- Serial ports COM1 and COM2
- Parallel port LPT1
- Standard VGA monitor

Using the charts from the previous pages, determine what IRQs and I/O Addresses are currently in use.

	IRQ	I/O Address
Standard Disk Controller		
COM1		
COM2		
Parallel Port LPT1		
Standard VGA Monitor		

Available IRQs____

Available I/O addresses________________________________

Exercise 5.2: Installing and Configuring Peripheral Cards

OBJECTIVE

Configure and install one of the following: modem, network interface card or sound card into your PC.

PREPARATION

Obtain a peripheral device as listed above with the required software and documentation necessary to complete the exercise.

Step 1: Determine what IRQs and I/O addresses are currently in use and which ones are available.

- Boot your PC to DOS.
- Change to the MS DOS directory by typing **cd\dos**
- Locate and run the **MSD** program (Microsoft Diagnostic Program).
- Determine what IRQs and memory I/O addresses are currently available.

Step 2: Using the board and documentation provided, configure the board with nonconflicting settings.

Step 3: Install the board into any open Bus slot.

Step 4: Test the board by using the diagnostics that came with it.

Step 5 (Optional): Set the board for a conflict.

(*For example*, you might configure the board for IRQ 7, which is the printer port.) Run the diagnostics again and review the resulting message.

This page intentionally left blank.

Exercise 8.1: Formatting Diskettes

OBJECTIVES

When you've completed this exercise, you will be able to:

- Format a blank diskette.
- Create a boot disk using the format system option.
- Unformat a diskette.
- Create a volume label on the diskette.

PREPARATION

Obtain a blank, high-density diskette.

Part One: *Formatting a diskette using the* FORMAT *command.*

Step 1: Change to the root directory.

- Type **cd**
- Verify your location by typing **dir**

  You should see the **AUTOEXEC.BAT** and **CONFIG.SYS** files.

Step 2: Format the diskette in drive A.

- Insert the blank diskette in drive A.
- Type **format A:**
- Press **Enter**.
- When completed, you will be asked to supply a volume name. Type in your first name. (It cannot exceed 11 characters.)
- Answer **No** to *not* format another diskette.

Step 3: **View the volume label on the newly-formatted diskette.**

- Type **dir a:** at the DOS prompt
- Press **Enter**.

Step 4: **Copy the DOSKEY.COM file from your hard disk to the floppy diskette in drive A.**

- Change to the DOS directory by typing **cd\dos**
- Press **Enter**.
- Locate the Doskey program by typing **dir doskey.com**
- Press **Enter**.
- Copy the file to a floppy diskette in drive A by typing **copy doskey.com a:**
- Verify that the file is on the diskette by typing **dir a:** Is the file listed?

Part Two: *Formatting a diskette using the quick formatting option.*

Step 1: Change to the DOS directory.

- Type **cd\dos**
- Type **format a: /q**
- Press **Enter**.
- When prompted for a label, type **quick**
- Press **Enter**.
- Answer **No** to *not* format another diskette.

  NOTE: The quick format should have been much faster than the previous format.

- Type **dir a:**
- Examine the directory. The file that you copied to the diskette will no longer be there. Formatting a diskette erases all files on the disk.

Part Three: *Using the* UNFORMAT *command to recover data erased by the* FORMAT command.

Step 1: Verify your location in the DOS directory.

- Type **cd\dos**
- Press **Enter**.
- Type **unformat a:**
- Press **Enter**.
- Answer **Yes** to update the system area.
- After the disk is unformatted, type **dir a:** The **doskey.com** file should be restored.

Part Four: *Creating a DOS bootable diskette.*

Step 1: Format the diskette in drive A using the /s system option.

- Type **format a: /s**
- Press **Enter**.
- When prompted for a volume label, type **bootable**
- Press **Enter**.

Step 2: Boot the system using the newly formatted bootable diskette.

- Restart your PC with the diskette in drive A.
- Press the **Enter** key when prompted for the date and time.

Step 3: Verify the system files on the diskette.

- Type **dir a: /a**
- Press **Enter**.
- Examine the directory. What files did the **format /s** put on the disk?

NOTE: You now have a bootable diskette that could be used to boot your PC in case something caused the boot files on your hard drive to become corrupted.

Part Five: *Formatting a diskette using the unconditional* FORMAT.

Step 1: **Remove the diskette from Drive A and reboot.**

Step 2: **Format the diskette using the /u option.**

- Type **format a: /u**
- Press **Enter**.
- When prompted for the volume label type **format.**
- Press **Enter**.
- Answer **No** to *not* format another diskette.

Step 3: **Attempt to unformat the disk.**

- Type **unformat a:**
- Press **Enter**.
- View the resulting message. Was the unformat successful?

  NOTE: The unconditional format command does not allow for unformatting later.

Exercise 8.2: Creating a Directory Structure

OBJECTIVES

When you've completed this exercise, you will be able to:

- Use the DOS **md** command to create directories and subdirectories.
- Use the **rd** (remove directory) command to delete directories.
- Use the **tree** command to view DOS directories and subdirectories.
- Use the **cd** (change directory) command to move into a directory.
- Copy files to a DOS directory.

PREPARATION

Change into the root directory of your hard drive by typing: **cd**

Step 1: View the current directories on the hard disk.

- Type **dir** to view the current directories.
- Press **Enter.**

Step 2: Create a directory using your first name as the directory name.

- Type **md joe** *(type in your name).*
- Press **Enter.**
- Type **dir** and confirm that the new directory is listed.

Step 3: Move into the newly created directory.

- Type **cd joe** *(type in your name).*
- Press **Enter.** What does your prompt display?

Step 4: **Create two subdirectories under your directory. Name them** DATA **and** GAMES.

- Type **md data** to create a new directory named DATA.
- Press **Enter.**
- Type **md games** to create a new directory named GAMES.
- Press **Enter.**
- Type **dir** to view the list of directories.
- Press **Enter** to verify that the new directories are listed.

Step 5: **Use the DOS** cd **command to move one level up the directory tree.**

- Type **cd..** to move one step up the directory tree; in this case, all the way up to the **root** directory.
- Press **Enter.**

Step 6: **Use the** cd **command to move into the newly created** DATA **directory.**

- Type **tree**
- Press **Enter** to find the data directory.
- Type **cd\yourname\data**
- Press **Enter.** What does your prompt display? It should show that you are now in the **data** directory.

Step 7: **Use the** rd **(remove directory) command to delete the** GAMES **directory.**

- Type **rd games** to remove the **GAMES** directory.
- Press **Enter.** What happened? You should get an error message telling you this is an invalid path. This is because you need to be in the directory which contains the subdirectory you want to remove in order to use the **rd** command.
- Type **cd..**
- Press **Enter**.
- Type **rd games** again.
- Press **Enter**.
- Type **dir**
- Press **Enter** to view the directory's contents. The **games** directory should no longer be listed.

Step 8: **Make a directory named** backup **and copy the** AUTOEXEC.BAT **file from the root to this directory.**

- Type **md backup** to create a new directory named **Backup**.
- Press **Enter**.
- Type **cd backup** to change to the **backup** directory.
- Press **Enter**.
- Type **copy c:\autoexec.bat** to copy the file to the **backup** directory.
- Press **Enter**.
- Type **dir** and verify that the **AUTOEXEC.BAT** file was copied to the **backup** directory.

Exercise 8.3: Creating a DOS Batch File.

OBJECTIVES

When you've completed this section, you will be able to:

- Describe the use of DOS batch files.
- Create a DOS batch file.
- Execute a DOS batch file.

PREPARATION

DOS batch commands can be very useful and can save you time. For example, let's say that as part of your job you need to create multiple directories and subdirectories on every new machine that comes into your office. You also have to copy files to these directories. You could use the **md** and **copy** commands repeatedly each time you configure a new system, or you could create a batch file that will do this for you.

In this exercise, you will create a batch file to do the following: create five directories, copy your current **AUTOEXEC.BAT** and **CONFIG.SYS** file to a directory called **backup**, and copy all DOS files to a directory called **c:\save.**

Step 1: **Change the root directory and view the directory.**

- Type **cd** to change to the root directory.
- Press **Enter**.
- Type **dir** to display the contents of the directory.
- Press **Enter**.

Step 2: Create a DOS batch file called repeat.bat.

- Type **edit repeat.bat**
- Press **Enter**
- Enter the following commands:

```
cd\
md backup
md save
md word
md common
md test
copy c:\dos\*.* c:\save
copy c:\autoexec.bat c:\backup
copy c:\config.sys c:\backup
```

Step 3: Now exit and save the file.

- Press the **ALT** key.
- Press **Enter**.
- Press **X** to exit.
- Press **Enter** again when the system asks if you want to save.

Step 4: Run the batch file you just created and view the results.

- Type **repeat.bat** to run the batch file.
- Press **Enter**.
- Type **tree** to verify that the directories have been created.
- Move into the **save** directory.
- Type **dir** to view the contents of the directory.
- Press **Enter** to verify that you have a backup of the DOS files.

This page intentionally left blank.

Exercise 8.4 (Optional): Installing and Partitioning a Hard Disk

(Note: This is done as a group exercise)

OBJECTIVES

When you've completed this exercise, you will be able to:

- Install an additional hard disk drive.
- Edit your **CMOS** settings to accurately reflect system configuration.
- Use the **fdisk** utility to create primary and extended partitions.
- Create logical drive assignments.
- Format a hard disk drive partition.
- Use the **fdisk** utility to delete a primary partition.

PREPARATION

DOS must be available on the student machines' hard disk or through a bootable DOS diskette that contains at least the following files: **FDISK.EXE, FORMAT.COM** and **SYS.COM.**

Obtain additional hard disk drive from your instructor.

Part One: Installing an additional Hard Disk Drive.

Step 1: **Power down your system.**

Step 2: **Install hard disk drive.**

- Set jumpers on new drive to **SLAVE.**
- Place hard disk drive in an available drive bay, and fasten in place with appropriate screws.
- Connect HDD ribbon cable and power connector.

Step 3: **Power up your system.**

- During the boot process, observe hardware information displayed on computer screen. Were both drives discovered?

Part Two: Updating CMOS settings.

Step 1: **Reboot your system.**

Step 2: **Enter the CMOS Setup Screen.**

- Ask your instructor for the appropriate key sequence to access the CMOS Setup Screen on your computer.

Step 3: **Select Standard CMOS Setup.**

- Observe current hard disk drive configuration.
- Press **Esc** to return to main CMOS menu.

Step 4: **Select IDE HARD DISK DETECTION.**

- Select **Primary Master Option**.
- Type **Y** and press **Enter.**
- Select **Primary Slave Option**.
- Type **Y** and press **Enter.**
- Select **Secondary Master and Slave Options**.
- Type **N** and press **Enter** for each one.

Step 5: **Select Standard CMOS Setup**.

- Observe updated hard disk drive configuration.
- Press **Esc** to return to main CMOS menu.

Step 6: **Save and Exit CMOS Setup.**

- Select **Save and Exit Setup.**
- Type **Y** to confirm save and press **Enter.**

  (System will re-boot.)
- After boot process completes, observe hardware information displayed on computer screen. Are both drives now displayed?

Part Three: Creating new partitions.

Step 1: View the existing partitions on your hard disk.

- At the **C:** prompt type **fdisk** and press **Enter.**
- Choose **Option 5** from the **fdisk** main menu. How many partitions currently exist?
- Make sure Disk Drive Number **1** is selected.
- Press the **Esc** key to return to the **fdisk** main menu.

Step 2: Create an Extended DOS partition and two Logical DOS drives.

- From the **fdisk** main menu, select **Option 1** to create a DOS partition or Logical DOS drive.
- Select **Option 2** to Create an Extended DOS Partition.
- Press **Enter** to accept the default size in megabytes.
- Press **Esc** to continue.
- After a short pause, you will see the command: **Create Logical DOS Drive in the Extended DOS Partition.**

No Logical drives defined

- Type **50%** in the total space field and press **Enter** to create the first logical drive. Note which letter is assigned to the first logical drive.
- Press **Enter** to accept the total space and create the second logical drive. Note which letter is assigned to the second logical drive.
- Press **Esc** to return to the main menu.

Step 3: Create a primary DOS partition.

- Select **Option 5** from the **fdisk** main menu.
- Select disk **2**.
- Press the **Esc** key to return to the **fdisk** main menu.
- Select **Option 1** to create a DOS partition.
- Select **Option 1** again to create a primary DOS partition.
- When prompted with **Use the Maximum Size**, click **No** and press the **Enter** key.
- Enter **50** megabytes for the size.
- Press the **Esc** key to return to the main menu.

Step 4: Exit the fdisk **program.**

- Exit the **fdisk** program by pressing the **Esc** key until the system re-boots.

Part Four: Format a new partition.

Step 1: Format the new primary partition (D).

- From the **C:** prompt type **format D:**
- Press **Enter.**

Step 2: Verify that you can access the newly formatted drive.

- Type **D:** to switch to the D drive.
- Press **Enter.**
- At the warning message, type **Y** and press **Enter.**
- When prompted for a volume label, press **Enter.**
- Type **dir** to view the contents of the D drive.
- Press **Enter.**
- Type **C:** and press **Enter** to return to the root partition.

Part Five: Deleting a Primary DOS Partition.

Step 1: View the existing partitions on your hard disk drive.

- At the **C:** prompt, type **fdisk** and press **Enter.**
- Select **option 5** from the **fdisk** menu.
- Select **Disk Drive Number 2** and press **Enter.**

Step 2: Delete a Primary DOS Partition.

- Select **option 3** from the **fdisk** main menu.
- Select **option 1** to delete a Primary DOS Partition.
- Press **Enter** to select the default partition.
- Press **Enter** to accept the volume label.
- Confirm by typing **Y** and press **Enter.**
- Press **Esc** to return to the **fdisk** main menu.

Step 3: Confirm partition has been deleted.

- Select **option 5** from the **fdisk** main menu.
- Observe changes to partition table information.
- Press **Esc** until system restarts.

Exercise 9.1 : Viewing and Optimizing System Memory

OBJECTIVE

View and optimize system memory usage with the DOS **mem** command and the DOS Optimize Program (**MEMMaker**).

PREPARATION

Rename your current **AUTOEXEC.BAT** and **CONFIG.SYS** to **AUTOEXEC.BAK** and **CONFIG.BAK**.

- Type **ren autoexec.bat autoexec.bak** to rename your current **AUTOEXEC.BAT** file.
- Press **Enter.**
- Type **ren config.sys config.bak** to rename your current **CONFIG.SYS** file.
- Press **Enter.**

Part One

Step 1: Create a new AUTOEXEC.BAT **file.**

- Type **edit autoexec.bat** to modify your **AUTOEXEC.BAT** file.
- Press **Enter.**
- Enter the following commands:

  echo off

  path c:\;c:\dos

  prompt PG
- Save the new file by pressing the **Alt** key.
- Press **Enter.**
- Type **X** to exit.
- Press **Enter** to save.

Step 2: Create a new CONFIG.SYS **file.**

- Type **edit config.sys**
- Press **Enter.**
- Enter the following Remark (REM) Statement **rem This is my config.sys file**
- Save the **CONFIG.SYS** file by pressing the **Alt** key.
- Press **Enter.**
- Press **X** to exit.

Step 5: **Exit the** MSD **program by pressing function key F3.**

Step 6: **Edit your** CONFIG.SYS **file:**

- Type **edit config.sys**
- Press **Enter.**
- Add the following line by typing:
  device=c:\dos\himem.sys
- Save the file.

Step 7: **Reboot your computer by pressing** CTRL + ALT + DEL **simultaneously.**

Step 8: **Run the** MSD **program and record the amount of Available Extended Memory.**

- Type **msd** to start the MSD utility.
- Press **Enter.**
- Press **m.**
- Record the amount of Available Extended Memory ____________.
- Exit **msd** by pressing the function key **F3**.

Step 9: **Add the Expanded Memory Manager (**EMM386.EXE**) to your** CONFIG.SYS **file.**

- Type **edit config.sys**
- Press **Enter.**
- Add the following line to your **CONFIG.SYS**, immediately following the **HIMEM** line by typing **device=c:\dos\emm386.exe**
- Save the new file by pressing the **Alt** key.
- Press **F**
- Type **X** to exit.
- Press **Enter** to save.

Step 10: **Reboot your computer and note the addition of Page Frame in the Upper Memory Area.**

- Type **msd** to start the MSD utility.
- Press **Enter.**
- Press **m** and notice Page Frame Memory.
- Exit **msd** by pressing the function key **F3**.

Step 11: Load DOS into High Memory by adding dos=high **to the** CONFIG.SYS **file.**

- Type **edit config.sys**
- Press **Enter.**
- Add **dos=high** as the last statement in the **CONFIG.SYS** file.
- Save the changes.

Step 12: Reboot your computer to view the changes.

Step 13: View the effects of the dos=high **statement, using the DOS** mem **command.**

- Type **mem /c |more**
- Press **Enter.**
- Record the amount of **Total Conventional Memory** ____________.
- Compare this to the results of Step 4.

Step 14: Add the noems **command to the end of the** device=c:\dos\emm386.exe **statement in the** CONFIG.SYS **file.**

- Type **edit config.sys**
- Press **Enter.**
- Add **noems** to the end of the **emm386.exe** line. The line should read:

  device=c:\dos\emm386.exe noems
- Save the changes.
- Reboot your computer.

Step 15: Run the MSD **Program to see your changes and note that the Page Frame is now gone.**

- Type **msd**
- Press **Enter.**
- Press **m** and notice that the **noems** prevented **Page Frame** from being created.
- Exit **msd** by pressing the function key **F3**.

Step 16: Add the umb **statement to the** CONFIG.SYS **file to create Free Upper Memory Blocks.**

- Type **edit config.sys**
- Press **Enter.**
- Add the **umb** statement to the **dos=high** statement. The line should read **dos=high, umb**
- Save the changes and reboot your PC.

Step 17: Run the MSD **Program and look for the creation of Upper Memory Blocks. (These are the areas designated by FF.)**

- Type **msd**
- Press **Enter.**
- Press **m** and look for the Free Upper Memory Blocks.
- Exit **msd** by pressing the function key **F3**.

Step 18: Loading a program into the umb **area.**

- Type **lh doskey**
- Press **Enter.**. (This will load the **DOSKEY** Program into Upper Memory.)
- Type **msd**
- Press **Enter.** View where the **DOSKEY** Program was loaded. (You should see four U's in the Upper Memory Area. This is the **DOSKEY** Program.)
- Exit **msd** by pressing the function key **F3**.

Part Two: *Running the* MEMMaker Program *to optimize memory.*

Preparation

Rename your **AUTOEXEC.BAT** and **CONFIG.SYS** files to **autoexec.xxx** and **config.xxx**.

Step 1: Create a new AUTOEXEC.BAT**.**

- Type **edit autoexec.bat**
- Press **Enter.**
- Add the following lines:

```
echo off
path=c:\;c:\dos
prompt=$P$G
vsafe
doskey
```

- Save the new **AUTOEXEC.BAT** file.

Step 2: Create a new CONFIG.SYS **file.**

- Type **edit config.sys**
- Press **Enter.**
- Add the following line:

```
device=c:\dos\setver.exe
```

- Save the new **CONFIG.SYS** file.

Step 3: Reboot your computer.

Step 4: Using the mem **command to view and record the location (conventional or Upper Memory area) and size of the following** doskey **and** vsafe **programs.**

- Type **mem /c /p**
- Press **Enter.**

	LOCATION	SIZE
DOSKEY:	__________	__________
VSAFE:	__________	__________
SETVER:	__________	__________

How much Conventional Memory is Available?_________

How much Extended Memory is Free? _________

How much Upper Memory is Free? _________

DOS MEMORY OPTIMIZATION

Part Three : ***Running the* MEMMaker Program *to optimize the system. Compare the results with the information listed above.***

Step 1: **Run the MS DOS** MEMMaker **Program.**

- Type **memmaker**
- Press **Enter.**
- Choose **Custom Setup**.
- Respond **No** to **EMS Support.**
- Respond **No** to **Support Windows**.
- Toggle all the rest of the **Advanced Options** to **Yes**
- Press **Enter** to accept the **Windows Default Directory.**
- Respond **Yes** to optimize **setver** and **doskey**.
- Respond **No** to optimize **vsafe**.
- Press **Enter** to allow **MEMMaker** to **Optimize System.**

Step 2: **The computer will automatically reboot twice.**

- Press **Enter** after the first reboot.

Step 3: **If the computer boots the second time, respond** Yes.

Step 4: **Note any changes that MEMMaker has made.**

- Press **Enter** to exit.

Step 5: **View the** AUTOEXEC.BAT **and** CONFIG.SYS **and note the changes that were made.**

- Type **type autoexec.bat**
- Press **Enter.**
- Note changes.
- Type **type config.sys**
- Press **Enter.**
- Note changes.

Step 6: **Use the** mem **command to compare this to the results that you recorded in Part Two.**

OPERATING SYSTEM TECHNOLOGIES
EXERCISES

Important Note: If you are working in an existing Windows 95 environment, refer to Exercise 12.1 to perform an upgrade. Otherwise, refer to Exercise 12.2 to conduct a clean installation of Windows 98.

Exercise 2.1: Performing a Windows 98 Upgrade

OBJECTIVES

Upgrade an existing Windows 95 system to the Windows 98 operating platform.

PREPARATION

This exercise assumes that you will be running setup from the Windows 98 CD. If not, check with your instructor for the location of the source files and setup program.

Secure from your instructor a copy of the Windows 98 CD-ROM software and the CD-ROM product key number.

Ensure that your Windows 95 computer is running correctly!

Step 1: Start Windows 95.

- From the desktop, insert the Windows 98 CD.
- If it autostarts, click on the **Install Windows 98** button. If it does not autostart, click on the **Start** button.
- At the **Start** menu, click on **Run**.
- At the **Run** menu, click on **Browse.**
- At the top of your **Browse** menu go to the top where it says **Look In** and click on the down indicator.
- Now select your CD-ROM drive (most likely the **D** drive).
- Locate the **Win 98** folder and double-click it.
- Locate the **Setup** folder and double-click it.
- Then click on the **setup.exe** file and click **Open**.
- This should now take you back to the **Run** menu window with the **setup.exe** file selected.
- Now click **OK** to proceed.

Step 2: Windows 98 Setup **window opens and the system starts to copy files for the setup process.**

Step 3: **The** Microsoft License Agreement **window appears.**

- You can scroll down to the end of the agreement.
- To continue, you MUST click the **I Accept the Agreement** statement.
- Click **Next** to continue.

Step 4: **The** Product Key **window appears.**

- Enter the product key number supplied to you by your instructor.
- Click **Next** to continue.

Step 5: **The** Select Directory **window appears.**

- Accept the default of **C:\Windows.**
- Click **Next** to continue.

Step 6: **The** Preparing Registry **window opens and checks the current Windows 95 Registry and the disk space available.**

Step 7: **The** Save System Files **window opens.**

- This will allow you to save the files necessary to return to Windows 95 if for some reason Windows 98 is not right. If **Yes**, it will take approximately 50 MB of disk space for these files.

Step 8: **The** Setup Option **window opens and asks what kind of setup you want.**

- Typical
- Portable
- Compact
- Custom

NOTE: Choose **Typical** *for this installation.*

- Click **Next** to continue.

Step 9: **The** User Information **window is displayed.**

- Enter your name and company or other identification here.

  NOTE: This information will be used for identification in the future.

Step 10: **Check for Windows components.**

- This will allow Windows to check for your components and load the necessary drivers.
- Click **Next** to continue.

Step 11: **Establish your location.**

- Select your location
- Click **Next** to continue.

Step 12: **Create a Windows Startup Disk.**

- This will allow you to create a Startup Disk, used to boot your system in the event of a Windows 98 boot failure.
- Click **Next** to continue. It will load the files for the startup disk. If you want a startup disk, insert a clean floppy diskette in your **A** drive at this time. If you choose not to create a startup diskette, click **Cancel** at the **Insert disk** prompt.
- Otherwise, click **OK**. It will copy the necessary files.
- When completed, click **Next** to continue.

Step 13: **Windows will now start the copy process.**

NOTE: This may take a little time, so be patient.

Step 14: **When the file copy is complete, the system reboots.**

Step 15: **After the system restarts, it displays the Windows Password Dialog Box.**

- If you don't want a password, just click **OK**. If you enter a password, the system will ask you to verify it by entering it again.

Step 16: Windows 98 continues to load.

- The setup program may ask you to load drivers (depending on your PC configuration and installed devices).
- Click **Next** to continue.
- If Setup ask you where you would like to search, select CD-ROM. *NOTE: If you have the manufacturer's disk with the necessary drivers, you can specify it as the destination.*
- Click **Next** to continue.
- When the drivers have installed, click **Finish**.

NOTE: Windows 98 should load with the new desktop and display the Welcome Screen.

Exercise 2.2: Performing a Windows 98 Installation

OBJECTIVES

Perform a Windows 98 Installation from a DOS-based computer.

PREPARATION

This exercise assumes that you will be running setup from the Windows 98 CD. If not, check with your instructor for the location of the source files and setup program.

Secure from your instructor a copy of the Windows 98 CD-ROM software and the CD-ROM product key number.

Step 1: Launch the Windows 98 setup program.

- Insert the Windows 98 CD.
- Change to your CD-ROM drive (typically drive "D").
- Type **setup**.
- Press **Enter**.

Step 2: Accept the Microsoft License Agreement.

- Click the **I Accept the Agreement**.
- Click **Next**.
- Enter and verify the **CD Product Key**.
- Click **Next**.

Step 3: Select an Installation Directory.

- Accept the Default **C:\Windows**.
- Click **Next**.

NOTE: Be patient. This may take a few minutes.

Step 4: Choose an Installation Type.

- Select the **Typical** option.
- Click **Next**.

Step 5: Enter User Information.

- In the name field insert your student ID **(studentx)**.
- Enter **Company name** (be creative, but nice).
- Click **Next**.

Step 6: Select Windows Components.

- Accept the **Default** (recommended).
- Click **Next**.

Step 7: Enter Location Information.

- Choose your location from the drop down box.
- Click **Next**.

Step 8: Create a Startup Disk.

- Click **Next** to continue.
- Insert floppy disk when prompted.
- Click **OK**.

  NOTE: Notice the progress report in the lower left side of your screen.
- Remove the floppy when prompted and click **OK**.

Step 9: Copy the Windows files.

- Click **Next** to begin file copy.

  NOTE: Be patient. This may take awhile.

Step 10: Restart the PC.

- Allow Windows to restart the PC.

  *Make sure that the floppy diskette has been removed.

  NOTE: The setup program will detect your hardware and search for Plug-and-Play devices. Be patient.

Step 11: Restart the PC again.

- Allow Windows to restart after the hardware has been detected.

Step 12: Configure the network.

NOTE: You will need to provide the Computer and Workgroup names to identify this PC to the network.

- Click **OK**.

  Computer Name ____________________

  Workgroup ____________________

  Computer Description ____________________
- Click **Close**.

Step 13: **Set Time and Date Information.**

NOTE: Use the drop down window to select your time zone

- Click on the **Time and Date** tab.
- Enter your Time and Date.
- Click **Apply** then click **OK**.

NOTE: Be patient. The setup program will now configure your PC.

Step 14: **Restart the System.**

NOTE: You may be asked for a password if one was entered, if not click **Cancel** *to continue.*

- Click **Begin** at the **Welcome Screen**.
- Click **Register Later** at the **Registration Window.**
- Close the **Welcome Window**.

The Windows 98 Installation is now complete.

This page intentionally left blank.

Exercise 2.3: Configuring the Desktop

OBJECTIVES

Modify the Windows 98 desktop. Change the wallpaper settings, enable the screen saver and modify the task bar and mouse properties.

Step 1: **Change the wallpaper settings.**

- Place the pointer to any open area on the desktop.
- Click the alternate mouse button.
- Click **Properties**.
- Select a wallpaper and mark the tile box
- Click **Apply**.
- Click **OK**.

Step 2: **Modify mouse properties to display pointer trails.**

- Double-click on the **My Computer** icon on the desktop.
- Double-click on **Control Panel**.
- Double-click the **Mouse** icon.
- Click on the **Motion** tab.
- Click the **Show pointer trails** box.
- Click **Apply**.
- Click **OK**.
- Close **Control Panel**, by clicking on the **X** in the upper right-hand corner.
- Close **My Computer**.
- Move your mouse and notice the trails.

Step 3: **Modify the task bar options, to** Auto Hide

- Place the pointer anywhere on the **Taskbar** and alternate-click.
- Click **Taskbar Properties**.
- Click the **Auto Hide** box.
- Click **Apply**.
- Close the **Properties** box

Notice that your **Taskbar** is now hidden from view. Move your pointer toward the bottom of the screen to display **Taskbar**.

Step 4: Enable the Screen Saver program.

- Place the pointer anywhere on the open desktop and click the alternate mouse button
- Select **Properties**.
- Click the **Screen Saver** tab.
- Select a screen saver.
- Set the **Wait Time** to 1 minute.
- Click **Apply**.
- Click **OK** and wait 1 minute, without touching the keyboard or mouse.

Exercise 2.4: Windows 98 Explorer Lab

OBJECTIVE

Use Windows 98 Explorer to create, view, rename and move files and folders.

PART 1: Creating, renaming and deleting folders (directories).

Step 1: Create a Folder.

- Click **Start**.
- Click **Programs > Windows Explorer**.
- Highlight the "**C**" drive (click on it)
- Click **File >New**.
- Select **Folder**.
- Name the new folder with your first name and press **Enter**.
- Repeat the above procedure to create another folder called **Sub1**.
- Highlight the **Sub1** folder in the left pane of **Explorer**
- Click **File > New > Folder**.
- Name it **Sub2** and press **Enter**.

  NOTE: Notice the plus (+) sign next to the **Sub1** *folder indicating that it now contains a sub-directory or folder.*
- Double-click the **Sub1** folder.

  NOTE: Notice that the plus (+) sign now changes to a minus (-) and displays the **Sub2** *folder.*

Step 2: Rename a Folder.

- Locate the folder corresponding to your first name.
- Alternate-click that folder, select **Rename.**
- Change the name to **Copytwo**.
- Press **Enter**.

  NOTE: This folder will be used in the copy exercise.
- Locate the renamed folder.

Step 3: Delete a Folder.

- Locate the **Sub1** folder in the left pane in **Explorer**.
- Double-click the **Sub1** folder.
- Alternate-click on the **Sub2** folder and select **Delete**.
- Click **Yes**.

NOTE: Notice that the **Sub1** *folder no longer has a* **+** *sign next to it.*

PART 2: Creating, renaming and moving files.

Step 1: Create files in your SUB1 Folder.

NOTE: To view the DOS (.txt*) extensions, you must unhide the DOS file extensions.*

- Highlight the **Sub1** folder.
- Alternate-click in any open area in the right pane of **Explorer**.
- Select **New, Text Document**.
- Name it **RED.TXT**.
- Repeat the above procedure creating two more files named **WHITE.TXT** and **BLUE.TXT**.

Step 2: Rename a file.

- Alternate-click the **WHITE.TXT** file.
- Choose **Rename** and name it **BLACK.TXT**.
- Press **Enter**.

Step 3: Copy a file (BLACK.TXT).

- Alternate-click the **BLACK.TXT** file.
- Click **Copy**.
- Alternate-click the **COPYTWO** folder.
- Click **Paste**.
- Double-click the **COPYTWO** folder to verify that the file was copied into the folder.

Question: Is the original **BLACK.TXT** file still located in the **SUB1** folder?

Step 4: Move a file.

- Click on the **Sub1** folder in the left pane of **Explorer**.
- Alternate-click the **RED.TXT** file and choose **Cut**.
- Alternate-click the **COPYTWO** folder and choose **Paste**.
- Double-click the **COPYTWO** folder to verify that the file was copied into the folder.

Question: How many copies of the **RED.TXT** file exist?

Question: What is the difference between the **Copy** and **Cut** commands?

PART 3: View long file names.

Step 1: Create a file and name it LONGFILENAME.TXT

- Open the **SUB1** folder by double-clicking it.
- Alternate-click any open space in the right pane of **Explorer**.
- Select **New, Text Document**.
- Name it **LONGFILENAME.TXT**

  NOTE: Notice that the full file named is displayed.

PART 4: View long file name attributes.

Step 1: View file attributes.

- Open **Windows 98 Explorer**.
- Open the **SUB1** folder.
- Alternate-click on the **LONGFILENAME.TXT** file.
- Choose **Properties**.

  NOTE: Notice that file attributes are now displayed and can be changed or modified. This box also displays both the DOS and long file names.

Exercise 2.5: Configuring File Type Associations

OBJECTIVE

Use **Folder Options** to configure file type associations.

Step 1: Change the .txt file association.

- Click **Start > Settings > Folder Options.**
- Select the **File Types** tab.
- Scroll down and select **Text Document**.
- Click **Edit** to open **Edit File Type** dialog box and select **Edit** again.
- In the **Editing action for type: Text Document** dialog box, select **Browse**.
- Select the **C:** drive and open **Program Files.**
- Find and open the **Internet Explorer** folder.
- Locate and select **Iexplore.exe.**
- Click **Open**.
- Click **OK** and close the **Edit File Type** dialog box.
- Select **Close** at the **File Types** tab.

Step 2: Test the file type association.

- In **Windows Explorer,** navigate to the **C:\Program Files\Internet Explorer** folder.
- Locate and open the **readme.txt** file.

  Question: What program does **Windows Explorer** use to open the **.txt** file?

Step 3: Revert the .txt file association back to the default setting.

- Click **Start** > **Settings** > **Folder Options**.
- Select the **File Types** tab.
- Scroll down and select **Text Document**.
- Click **Edit** to open **Edit File Type** dialog box and select **Edit** again.
- In the **Editing action for type: Text Document** dialog box, select **Browse**.
- Select the **C:** drive and open the **Windows** folder.
- Locate and select **Notepad.exe**.
- Click **Open**.
- Click **OK** and close the **Edit File Type** dialog box.
- Select **Close** at the **File Types** tab.

Step 4: Test the file type association.

- In Windows Explorer, navigate to the **C:\Program Files\Internet Explorer** folder.
- Locate and open the **readme.txt** file.

Question: Now what program does Windows Explorer use to open the **.txt** file?

Exercise 2.6: Adding and Deleting a Printer

OBJECTIVE

Add and Delete a Printer using the **Printers** Folder.

Step 1: Add a printer with the Printer Wizard.

- Open **My Computer** from the desktop.
- Select **Add Printer** to open the Printer Wizard.
- Click **Next** at the **Add Printer Wizard** introductory screen.
- Accept the default local printer selection by clicking **Next**.
- Wait for a moment while Windows prepares a driver information database.
- In the Manufacturers list to the left, scroll down and select **HP (Hewlett-Packard)**.
- In the Printers list to the right, scroll down and select **HP LaserJet 4**.
- Click **Next**.
- Make sure that the **LPT1: Printer Port** is selected as the port to use with this printer and click **Next**.
- Accept the default name **HP LaserJet 4** and select **Yes** to configure this printer as the default printer for Windows-based programs.
- Reject the option to print a test page by selecting **No** in the **Print Test Page** dialog box and clicking **Next**.

  Note: A new icon named **HP LaserJet 4** should appear in the **Printers** folder. The icon should display a check mark in the upper left-hand corner indicating that this is the default system printer.

Step 2: Delete a printer from the Printers folder.

- Right-click the **HP LaserJet 4** icon and select **Delete**.
- Click **Yes** at the dialog box that asks whether you are sure you want to delete the printer.

  Note: Windows will now delete the printer and uninstall its drivers. The **HP LaserJet 4** icon should now be removed from the **Printers** folder.

This page intentionally left blank.

Exercise 2.7: Installing and Uninstalling a Program with the Add/Remove Programs Tool

OBJECTIVES

Install and uninstall the MindWorks Prelim™ Test Preparation Software using the **Add/Remove Programs** tool.

PREPARATION

Locate the Prelim™ Test Prep CD in the back of your A+ Courseware.

Step 1: Install the MindWorks Prelim™ Test Preparation Software using the Add/Remove Programs tool.

- Insert the Prelim™ CD into the CD drive of your system.
- Select **Start > Settings > Control Panel**. Double-click on **Add/ Remove Programs.**
- Select the option to install a program from a CD or floppy.
- When prompted to insert the products first disk or CD-ROM, click **Next.**
- The **Add/Remove Programs** tool should find the **setup.exe** on the Prelim™ CD. If it does, click **Next.**. If for some reason it doesn't find the **setup.exe** file, click on **Browse** and locate it on the CD and then select **Finish.**
- At the Prelim™ **Setup** screen, select **OK**. Click on the icon to install to the default directory.
- Click **OK** when the Setup windows appears notifying that the Prelim™ setup was successful.
- Test the installation by selecting **Start >Programs > Prelim™**. The Prelim™ splash screen should appear along with the **Log on** dialog box. Select **Cancel** to exit Prelim™.
- Close the **Add/Remove Programs Wizard** and then close the **Control Panel.**

Step 2: Uninstall the MindWorks Prelim™ Test Preparation Software using the Add/Remove Programs **tool.**

- From the **Control Panel**, open **Add/Remove Programs**
- At the **Add/Remove Programs, Install/Uninstall** tab, scroll down and select **Prelim**.
- Click the **Add/Remove** button.
- Select **Yes** when Windows asks whether you are sure you want to remove Prelim and all of its components.
- Click **OK** at the **Program installation removed** dialog box.
- Click **OK** to close **Add/Remove Programs**.
- Close **Control Panel**.
- Select **Start >Programs** and confirm that Prelim has been uninstalled.

Exercise 4.1: Windows NT Version 4.0 Installation

OBJECTIVES

Perform a Windows NT 4.0 CD-ROM installation from a DOS-based computer.

Part 1: Text Based Portion of the Windows NT 4.0 Installation

Step 1: **Change to the I386 directory on the installation CD**

- Type **CD\I386**

Step 2: **Start the installation program**

- Type **Winnt /b**

Step 3: **Enter the location of the installation files**

- Press **Enter** to except the default location (I386)

  NOTE: The setup program will now start to copy installation files to your hard disk. When the file transfer is complete remove any floppies and press enter to reboot your computer.

Step 4: **Windows NT Setup**

- Press the **Enter** key at the initial setup screen

Step 5: **Load additional adapters**

- Press **S** at the hardware identification screen if you need to load additional adapters.

Step 6: **Continue Installation**

- Press the **Enter** key to continue

Step 7: **Accept the NT license Agreement**

- Scroll through the license agreement
- Press **F8** to accept and continue

Step 8: **Accept the default device list**

- Select **The above list matches my computer**
- Press **Enter** to continue

Step 9: **Selecting an NT Partition**

- Select the primary partition

Step 10: **Convert the Partition to NTFS**

- Press **C** to convert to NTFS

NOTE: Read the ***Warning Message*** *and continue with the NTFS conversion.*

Step 11: **Select the NT Directory**

- Press **Enter** to accept the default directory location (WINNT)

Step 12: **Disk scan**

- Press **Enter** for an examination of the hard disk

NOTE: *Remove any floppy disks or CDs and press the* **Enter** *key to reboot the system.*

Part 2: Graphical Portion of the Windows NT 4.0 Installation

Step 1: **Begin the NT 4.0 Graphical Portion of the Installation**

- Click **Next** to begin the Graphical portion of the Installation

Step 2: **Enter your Name in the Dialog box**

Step 3: **Enter your Company Name in the Organization field**

Step 4: **Continue the Installation**

- Click **Next** to continue

Step 5: **Enter the License Number**

- Enter the CD key information
- Click **Next** to continue

Step 6: **Choose License Mode**

- Select Per Seat License
- Click **Next** to continue

Step 7: **Enter the Computer Name**

- Type in the computer name in the Name Field
- Click **Next** to continue

Step 8: Select the Server Type

- Choose **PDC**
- Click **Next** to Continue

Step 9: Create the Administrator Password

- Enter the Administrator password (twice)
- Click **Next** to continue

Step 10: Create an Emergency Repair Disk

- Choose **Yes** to create Emergency Repair Disk
- Click **Next** to continue

Step 11: View Components List

- Accept default components list
- Click **Next** to continue

NOTE: Click on the Next button to bypass the initial configuration dialog screen.

Step 12: Configure Network

- Select **wired to the network** box

Step 13: Remote Network Access

- **Do NOT** check the Remote Access box
- Click **Next** to continue

Step 14: Install Network Adapter

NOTE: Ask your Instructor for the name of the adapter installed in your computer or choose **MS Loopback Adapter**.

- Select your adapter type from the list
- Click **OK**
- Now click **Next** to continue the installation

Step 15: Select Network protocol

- Select **NetBEUI** protocol (deselect any others at this time)
- Click **Next** to continue

Step 16: Default Services

- Accept the Default Services
- Click **Next** to continue

Step 17: Install Selected Components

- Click **Next** to install selected components

NOTE: *Respond to request to configure components and click* **Continue** *to finish the NT installation.*

This page intentionally left blank.

Exercise 5.1: Performing a Windows 2000 Professional Upgrade

OBJECTIVES

To perform a Windows 2000 Professional Upgrade from a Windows 98 Based computer.

PREPARATION

See **INSTRUCTOR** for the following information:

User Names________________________________

Passwords________________________________

Step 1: Launch the Windows 2000 Upgrade Program

- Boot to the current operating system (Windows 98).
- Insert the Windows 2000 Professional CD.

  NOTE: The CD should auto-start.
- Click **Yes** to upgrade to Windows 2000.

Step 2: Accept the Windows 2000 Setup Defaults.

- Click **Next** to accept defaults (recommended).

Step 3: Accept the License Agreement.

- Click **I Accept This Agreement.**
- Click **Next.**

Step 4: Prepare to Upgrade to Windows 2000.

- Click **Next** to continue.

Step 5: Select Upgrade Packs default settings.

- Click **Next** to accept defaults.

Step 6: Upgrade to Windows 2000 NTFS file system.

- Click **Next** to accept the default.

  NOTE: Be patient. This may take a while.

Step 7: Accept Upgrade Report.

- Click **Next** to continue.

Step 8: **Begin to Install Windows 2000.**

- Click **Next** to continue.

Step 9: **Create a Password.**

- Enter New Password________________________
- Confirm Password __________________________
- Press **Enter** to continue.

Step 10: **Logon to Windows.**

- Enter User Name __________________________
- Enter the Password from Step 9.
- Press **Enter** to continue.

NOTE: Windows will now launch the desktop environment.

Step 11: **Get Started with Windows 2000.**

*NOTE: To prevent this window from coming up each time you load Windows, click on the check box in the lower left corner. Then click **Exit** in the lower right corner of the **Getting Started** screen.*

The Windows 2000 Upgrade is complete.

Exercise 5.2: Performing an Attended Installation

OBJECTIVE

To successfully perform a Windows 2000 Professional Installation

PREPARATION

Ask your Instructor for the Windows 2000 CD and product key code number and record it here ____________________.

Step 1: Begin the installation.

Start the installation by booting from the CD-ROM (this is accomplished on most systems by choosing to boot from the CD-ROM drive in the system BIOS) or by connecting to the i386 directory on the CD and typing **winnt** at the command line.

You can also use the Windows 2000 Professional Setup Disks or connect to an installation directory stored on the network. If the Setup Disks are not available, they can be created by executing **MAKEBOOT.EXE**. This program is located in the **BOOTDISK** folder on the setup CD-ROM. This Exercise assumes the Setup Disks are used.

Step 2: Access the i386 folder.

Use one of the several methods mentioned to access the **i386** folder and run **winnt** or **winnt32**.

Step 3: Copy Windows 2000 files.

At the **Setup Notification** screen, press **Enter** to continue as Windows 2000 performs the real-mode portion of copying the files to the hard disk.

Step 4: Restart the computer.

Take out the disk before restart #1.

Step 5: Windows 2000 begins.

Windows 2000 loads files and starts Windows. Hit **Enter** to begin, **R** to repair, or **F3** to quit.

Step 6: Accept the Windows Licensing Agreement

Select **F8** at the **Windows 2000 Licensing Agreement** screen.

Step 7: Select a partition.

Select a partition for the installation of Windows 2000 Professional and press **Enter**. In order to setup Windows 2000 Professional on the selected partition, press **C** to convert to NTFS.

Step 8: Format the partition.

Select **Format the partition using the NTFS file system** and press **Enter**, then **F**.

Step 9: Copy files to the Windows 2000 Installation Folder.

To format the partition, press **F**. Setup then copies files to the W2K installation folders.

Step 10: Restart the computer.

Remove any floppy disk from your system and reboot when prompted. Setup does the file system and disk check then performs the actual conversion to NTFS.

Step 11: Enter user settings.

This GUI mode Setup Wizard then performs a hardware detection and installation checks for Regional Settings and takes name and organization input.

Step 12: Complete the information requested.

Complete the product key boxes.

Step 13: Enter computer information requested.

Complete the Computer name field at the Computer Name and Administrator Password window. Also, choose an administrator password and confirm this password. Choose **Next** when finished.

Step 14: Enter Date and Time information.

Select the Date and Time settings.

Step 15: Select networking type.

From the **Networking Settings** window, choose **Typical** or **Custom** then select **Next**.

Step 16: Configure network.

Configure the networking settings and install software typical or custom settings.

Step 17: Choose Workgroup or Domain.

Choose between a **Workgroup** or **Domain** and select a computer name or accept the default that Windows 2000 gives you.

Step 18: Install components.

Windows installs components and performs final tasks.

Step 19: Restart the computer.

Remove the CD and restart.

Step 20: Enter user names and passwords.

In the **Network Identification Wizard**, configure the user names and passwords of the users that will logon to this machine.

Windows 2000 Professional runs for the first time.

Exercise 5.3: Creating A Customized Microsoft Management Console

OBJECTIVE

Create a customized MMC which includes the **Computer Management, Event Viewer** and **Performance Monitor** tools.

Step 1:

- Select **Start > Run**
- Type **mmc**
- Click **OK.**

Step 2:

- Click **Console** and select **Add/Remove Snap-in**
- Click **Add.**

Step 3:

- At the **Add Standalone Snap-in** dialog box, double-click **Computer Management.**

Step 4:

- Accept the default that **This snap-in will always manage: Local computer** by selecting **Finish.**

Step 5:

- At the **Add Standalone Snap-in** dialog box, double-click **Event Viewer**

Step 6:

- Accept the default that **This snap-in will always manage: Local computer** by selecting **Finish.**

Step 7:

- At the **Add Standalone Snap-in** dialog box, double-click **Performance Logs and Alerts.**

Step 8:

- Accept the default that **This snap-in will always manage: Local computer** by selecting **Finish**.

Step 9:

- Close the **Add Standalone Snap-in** dialog box
- Click **OK** at the **Add/Remove Snap-in** screen.

Step 10:

- Click **Console** and select **Save**.
- Name the console **Console1** and save it to the desktop.

This page intentionally left blank.

Exercise 5.4: Adding A Local Printer

OBJECTIVES

Manually add a local printer without the help of Plug-and-Play. Configure the printer as the default printer for the local system and make it available as a shared printer.

PREPARATION

Make sure to log off and log in if you are not currently logged in as an Administrator:

- Press **Ctrl+Alt+Del** and select **Log off.**
- Select **Yes** at the **Log Off Windows** dialog box.
- At the **Log On to Windows** dialog box, enter **Administrator** as user name, enter the password provided by your instructor and press **Enter**.

Step 1:

- Click **Start** >**Settings** >**Printers**.

Step 2:

- Double-click **Add Printer** to start the **Add Printer** wizard.
- Select **Next.**

Step 3:

- Select **Local Printer**
- Click the box to uncheck the option to **Automatically detect and install my Plug-and-Play printer.**

Step 4:

- Accept the default **LPT1:** printer port by selecting **Next** in the **Select Printer Port** window.

Step 5:

- In the **Manufacturer's** window on the left-hand side of the **Add Printer Wizard** dialog box, scroll down and select **HP**.
- In the **Printers** window, scroll down and select **HP LaserJet 6L.**

Step 6:

- Accept the default printer name in the **Name Your Printer** dialog box by clicking **Next**.

Step 7:

- Select the **Share as** option in the **Printer Sharing** dialog box and name the shared printer **HP LaserJet 6L**.
- Click **Next**.

Step 8:

- In the **Location and Comment** dialog box, type **Studentx** (where x is the student number assigned you by your Instructor.)
- In the comment area, type **HP LaserJet 6L attached to Studentx**.

Step 9:

- Reject the option to print a test page by selecting **No** in the **Print Test Page** dialog box
- Click **Next**.

Step 10:

- Review information in the **Completing the Add Printer Wizard** window to ensure you have input everything correctly.
- If all settings are accurate, click **Finish**.

Note: Windows 2000 will now copy the necessary driver files and an icon will appear in the **Printers** folder which will be named **HP LaserJet 6L**. The icon should be supported by a hand verifying that the printer is shared and a check mark should appear in the upper left corner of the icon indicating that this is the default printer.

This page intentionally left blank.

Exercise 5.5: Configuring Desktop Settings

OBJECTIVES

Customize the Desktop using **Active Desktop** and create a password-protected screen saver.

Step 1:

- Right-click anywhere on the Desktop and select **Active Desktop.**
- Then select **Customize My Desktop.**

Step 2:

- On the **Background** tab, scroll down and select the **Windows 2000** background.
- Click **Apply**.

Step 3:

- Windows 2000 will tell you that in order for this wallpaper to be applied as the background, **Active Desktop** must be enabled. Choose **Yes** to enable the **Active Desktop**.

Step 4:

- On the **Screen Saver** tab, scroll down and select the **Channel** screen saver.
- Check the **Password protected** box.
- Click **Apply**.
- Select **OK** to exit the **Display Properties** screen.

Note: In order to exit the screen saver, you will need to enter the Windows password of the user currently logged on to the system.

This page intentionally left blank.

Exercise 5.6: Installing An Application Using Windows Installer

OBJECTIVE

Install the MindWorks Prelim™ Test Preparation Software using the Windows Installer.

PREPARATION

Locate the Prelim™ Test Prep CD in the back of your A+ Courseware.

Step 1:

- Insert the Prelim™ CD into the CD drive of your system.

Step 2:

- Select **Start > Settings > Control Panel.**
- Double-click on **Add/Remove Programs**.

Step 3:

- Select the option to install a program from a CD or floppy.

Step 4:

- When prompted to insert the products first disk or CD-ROM, click **Next**.

Step 5:

- **Windows Installer** should find the **setup.exe** on the Prelim™ CD. If it does, click **Next**. If for some reason Windows Installer doesn't find the **setup.exe** file, click on **Browse** and locate it on the CD and then select **Next**.

Step 6:

- Click **Finish** at the **Windows Installer** screen to begin the Prelim™ setup.

Step 7:

- At the Prelim™ **Setup** window, click **OK**.
- Click on the icon to install to the default directory.

Step 8:

- Click **OK** when the **Setup** window appears indicating that the Prelim™ setup was successful.

Step 9:

- Test the installation by selecting **Start > Programs > Prelim™**. The **Prelim™** splash screen should appear along with the **Log on** dialog box.
- Select **Cancel** to exit **Prelim™**.

Step 10:

- Close the **Add/Remove Programs** wizard
- Close the **Control Panel**.

Exercise 5.7: Using Windows 2000 Backup

OBJECTIVE

Use the Windows 2000 **Backup** tool to backup System State data.

Step 1:

- Select **Start > Programs > Accessories > System Tools > Backup.**

Step 2:

- At the **Windows 2000 Backup** screen, select **Backup Wizard.**

Step 3:

- Click **Next** at the **Backup Wizard Welcome Screen.**

Step 4:

- At the **What to Backup** dialog box, choose **Only back up the System State data.**

Step 5:

- Enter **c:\Backup.bkf at** the **Where to Store the Backup** screen and click **Next.**

Step 6:

- At the **Completing the Backup Wizard** screen, select **Advanced** and accept the default **Normal backup** by selecting **Next.**

Step 7:

- Select **Verify data after backup** at the **How to Back Up** screen and click **Next**

Step 8:

- At the **Media Options** screen, select the **Replace the data on the media with this backup** option and click **Next.**

Step 9:

- Accept the default labels at the **Backup Label** screen by clicking **Next.**

Step 10:

- Select **Next** at the **When to Back Up** window to run the backup immediately.

Step 11:

- Click **Finish** to begin the backup and wait for it to complete.

Step 12:

- When backup is complete, click **Report** to review.
- Close the **Report** window
- Close the **Backup Progress** window
- Close the **Backup Welcome** window.

This page intentionally left blank.

Exercise 5.8: Creating an Emergency Repair Disk (ERD)

OBJECTIVE

Create an Emergency Repair Disk to use in case of system failure.

Step 1:

- Select **Start** > **Programs** > **Accessories** > **System Tools** > **Backup**.

Step 2:

- At the **Windows 2000 Backup** screen, select **Emergency Repair Disk**.

Step 3:

- When prompted, insert a floppy disk into drive **A:**
- Select the option to backup the Registry.
- Click **OK**. Wait while System Data is copied.

Step 4:

- After a few seconds you should receive a message stating that the Emergency Repair Disk was saved successfully. Remove the disk from the drive and label it **Emergency Repair Disk for Studentx** and write in the appropriate date.

Step 5:

- Click **OK** to close the **Emergency Repair Diskette** dialog box and then close the **Backup** screen.

This page intentionally left blank.

Exercise 5.9: Starting Windows 2000 in Safe Mode

OBJECTIVE

Start Windows 2000 in Safe Mode in order to troubleshoot system problems.

Step 1:

- Press **Ctrl+Alt+Del** and select **Shut Down**.

Step 2:

- At the **Shut Down Windows** screen, select **Restart**
- Click **OK**.

Important Note: Make sure to pay attention to the system restart so that you do not miss the **Please select the operating system to start** message.

Step 3:

- Press the **F8** key when prompted to select the operating system to start.

Step 4:

- Press **Enter** to select **Safe Mode**.

Step 5:

- Press **Enter** to select Windows 2000 as the operating system to start and wait for Windows 2000 to start up.

Note: When Windows 2000 has completed the start up process in Safe Mode, you should notice that the desktop is slightly different and that the words **Safe Mode** appear in each corner of the screen.

Step 6:

- Type in the user name and password at the **Log On** screen and click **OK**.

Step 7:

- An alert message should appear to inform you that you are running in **Safe Mode**. Read this screen and click **OK** to close.

  Note: If you had actually experienced problems with the system you would now troubleshoot based on recent changes to the system. For example, if you had just installed a new Network Interface Card and its driver before experiencing problems, you would now troubleshoot the card and its driver, perhaps using the **Device Manager** as we learned in the Windows 98 section.

Step 8:

- Press **Ctrl+Alt+Del** and select **Shut Down**.

Step 9:

- At the **Shut Down Windows** screen, select **Restart** and click **OK**.

Step 10:

- Press **Enter** when prompted to select the operating system to start to begin Windows 2000 in normal mode.

Step 11:

- Enter username and password and click **OK** to log back on to Windows 2000.

Exercise 6.1: Working With User Accounts, User Profiles and Printer Objects

OBJECTIVES

Use Windows 2000 to create user accounts, user profiles and to add and configure Windows printer objects.

PREPARATION

Ask your Instructor for the Administrator account password____________________.

Part 1: Creating a local user account and user profile

Step 1: Logon to the Windows 2000 PC as Administrator.

- Enter the User Name **Administrator**.
- Enter the administrative **password**.
- Click **OK**.

Step 2: Add a new local user account.

- Double click the **My Computer** icon.
- Open the **Control Panel**.
- Double click the **User and Password** icon.
- Click on the **Add User** button.
- Enter your first name in the user name field.
- Click **Next** to continue.
- Enter the user account password and confirm.

  NOTE: ***Remember this password...****write it down here*__________________________

- Click **Next** to continue.
- Accept the default **Standard User**.
- Click **Finish**.
- Click **OK** to close screen.
- Close the **Control Panel** window.

Step 3: Logon as the new user.

- Click **Start, Shutdown.**
- Click **OK** to log off administrator.
- Log on as new user.
- Click **Exit** to close **Getting Started** screen.

Step 4: Create a custom desktop environment.

- Right click any open space on the desktop.
- Click **Properties.**
- Select a background picture for your wallpaper.
- From the drop down box **Picture Display** choose the **Stretch** option.
- Click the **Apply** button.
- Click **OK** to continue.
- Click and drag your desktop icons to random positions on your screen.

Step 5: Verify your desktop settings.

- Log off and log on again as the new user.

*NOTE: Did you get the same desktop settings?*______________________________

Step 6: Delete the user profile.

- Log on as Administrator.
- Open **My Computer**.
- Open **Control Panel**.
- Locate and double click the **System** icon.
- Click on the **User Profile** tab.
- Click on the **New Users** profile.
- Click on the **Delete** button.
- Confirm delete, click **Yes**.
- Click **OK** to close.
- Close the **Control Panel** and log on as the new user.

*NOTE: Did you get the user's custom desktop?*______________________________

Why or Why Not?

____

Part 2: Troubleshooting an existing Device

Step 1: **Log on as the Administrator.**

Step 2: **Open the Add/Remove Hardware applet.**

- Click **Start >Settings > Control Panel.**
- Double click **Add/Remove Hardware** icon.
- Click **Next** to continue.

  NOTE: The **Add/Remove Hardware** *applet has the following two options: You can add and troubleshoot a device or uninstall a device.*

- Select **Add/Troubleshoot,** then click **Next** to continue.
- Click on and highlight **Default Monitor**.
- Click **Next** to continue.

  NOTE: Notice the device status.

- To start the troubleshooter option, click **Finish**.
- Click the **Next** button to view help screens.
- Close the **Help** screen window.
- Close the **Control Panel.**

Part 3: Install local and default printers

Step 1: Add printer objects

- Click **Start > Settings > Printers.**
- Double click **Add Printer**.
- Click **Next** to continue.
- Select **Local Printer**, deselect the **Plug-and-Play** option
- Click **Next** to continue.
- Select **LPT2: Printer Port**, click **Next** to continue.
- Select **HP** from the manufacturer drop down box.
- Select **HP Color LaserJet** printer from the right window.
- Click **Next** to continue.
- Name your printer **My Second Printer**.
- Answer **No** to **Default**, then click **Next** to continue.
- Share as: **My Shared Printer**, click **Next** to continue.
- Click **Yes** to accept **Warning Message**.
- Enter location information and click **Next** to continue.
- Answer **No** to print test page, click **Next** to continue.
- Click the **Finish** button.

Part 5: Selecting a Default printer

Step 1: Change the Windows default printer.

- Right click the second printer icon.
- Select **Set as Default Printer**.

NOTE: Notice that the check mark is now attached to the second printer icon, indicating that this is now the default Windows printer.

Exercise 9.1: Installing and Configuring TCP/IP

OBJECTIVES

- Install TCP/IP
- Configure IP address and subnet mask
- Test installation and configuration using the Ping command

PREPARATION

Obtain an IP address and subnet mask from your instructor.

IP Address ________.________.________.________

Subnet mask ________.________.________.________

Step 1: Install TCP/IP

- Right-click on the **Network Neighborhood** icon
- Select **Properties**
- Select the **Configuration** tab
- Click **Add**
- Select **Protocol**
- Click **Add**
- Select **Microsoft** from the Manufacturer's List in the left side of the Window
- Scroll down and select **TCP/IP** from the Network Protocol list in the right side of the Window
- Click **OK**

Step 2: Configure TCP/IP

- Select the TCP/IP which is bound to the Network Interface Card (NIC)
- Click on **Properties**
- Select **Specify an IP Address**
- Enter the IP address provided by your instructor
- Enter the subnet mask provided by your instructor
- Click **OK**

Windows will ask you to specify a source directory The files are located in **c:\Win98**.

- Click **OK** again to close the Window
- Your machine will now ask you if you would like to restart to implement changes. Answer **Yes**

Step 3: Test TCP/IP installation and configuration using the Ping command

- After restarting your machine, select **Start > Programs > MS-DOS Prompt**
- At the DOS prompt, type: **Ping** followed by your IP address, and press **Enter**
- View reults

* You should see a reply message. This means that you have correctly installed and configured TCP/IP.

- Repeat the above steps, entering another student's IP address after the Ping command in the DOS prompt

* Again, if you receive a reply message this means that TCP/IP has been installed and configured correctly and that you are communicating on the network.

Exercise 10.1: Configuring Internet Explorer Options

OBJECTIVES

- Change the **Home Page** setting
- Modify the **Temporary Internet files** setting
- Change the **History** setting

Step 1: Open the Internet Options window

- Launch Internet Explorer
- At the top of the screen select **Tools** > **Internet Options**

Step 2: Change the Home Page setting

- Highlight the current default home page URL
- Replace URL by typing **http://Instructor**

Step 3: Modify Temporary Internet files setting

- Select **Settings**
- Set amount of disk space to use to **100 MB**
- Select **OK**

Step 4: Change History setting

- Highlight default **Days to keep pages in history** setting
- Replace default by typing **30**
- Select **Apply**
- Select **OK**

Step 5: Test modifications to General settings

- Close Internet Explorer
- Open Internet Explorer

Note: *The Instructor website should appear as the default Internet Explorer web page.*

Exercise 10.2: Using Basic FTP Commands

OBJECTIVES

- Open an FTP session
- Download a file using the "get" command
- Upload a file using the "put" command
- Close an FTP session

PREPARATION

Ask your instructor for the FTP server IP address and name.

Server IP Address:

_________._________._________._________

Server Name: ________________________________

Ask your instructor for your FTP user name and password.

User name: ________________

User password: ________________

Part 1: Using the get *command to download a file*

Step 1: Create an FTP Session

- Click **Start**
- Choose **Programs > MS-DOS Prompt**
- Type **ftp** <FTP Server Name>
- Press **Enter**
- Enter User Name and press **Enter**
- Enter Password and press **Enter**

Step 2: Use the get command to download a file

- Type **get** and press **Enter**
- Type **exercise32.txt** and press **Enter**
- Type **c:\My Documents\exercise32.txt** and press **Enter** to indicate the name of the local path and file name where the document will be saved

Step 3: Verify file download

- Minimize the MS-DOS Window
- Open **Windows Explorer**
- Locate the **My Documents** folder
- View contents of the folder
- Open the **exercise32.txt** file to verify download
- Close the **exercise32.txt** file

Part 2: Using the put *command to upload a file*

Step 1: Use the put command to upload a file

- Maximize the MS-DOS Window
- At the FTP prompt type **put**
- Type **c:\My Documents\exercise32.txt** to indicate local path and file name
- Type any name you choose to designate new file name on the FTP server
- Ask instructor to verify upload on FTP server

Step 2: Close the FTP session

- At the FTP prompt type **quit** and press **Enter**
- Type **exit** to close MS-DOS Window

Exercise 10.3: Accessing an FTP Server Using Microsoft Internet Explorer

OBJECTIVES

- Use the correct syntax for accessing a secure FTP server
- Download a file using Internet Explorer

PREPARATION

Refer to Exercise 10.2 for FTP server name and for User Name and Password

Step 1: Login to FTP server using Internet Explorer

- Open Internet Explorer
- In the Address Box type the following URL address: **ftp://<username>:<password>@<servername>**
- Press **Enter**

Step 2: Copy a file from the FTP server to your local hard drive

- Right-click on file **exercise33.txt**
- Select **Copy** to folder and browse to the **My Documents** folder.
- Copy the file.

Step 3: Verify file download

- Open **exercise33.txt** file in **My Documents** folders
- View contents

Exercise 11.1: TCP/IP Utilities

OBJECTIVE

- Use TCP/IP command-line utilities

PREPARATION

Open a MS-DOS-based session and record your IP Address.

Hint: Try typing **IPCONFIG** *at the DOS prompt.*

Your IP Address_______________________

Step 1: Ping local host

- Type **Ping 127.0.0.1** then press **Enter.**
- View results.

* This will test your TCP/IP installation. A reply would indicate a successful install.

Step 2: Ping your IP Address

- Type **Ping <your IP Address>** then press **Enter.**
- View results.

* A reply would indicate a successful IP configuration.

Step 3: Ping a remote host (computer)

- Type **Ping <your neighbor's IP Address>** then press **Enter.**
- View results.

* Note: If reply was successful, this would indicate valid connectivity between your local machine and the remote host.

Step 4: Use the ARP command

- Type **ARP** then hit the **Enter** key.

* This will display the **ARP** help screen

- Type **ARP -a** then press **Enter.**

* If no entries are found, the local ARP cache is empty. To create the ARP cache, ping your neighbor's computer and try the **ARP -a** command again. The ARP cache table is automatically deleted after a short period of no use.

Step 5: **Using the tracert command to display the route to Instructor's computer**

- Type **tracert Instructor** then press **Enter**.

* Notice the results displaying the HOP and TICK count.

Step 6: **Using NETSTAT to display active connections to local machine**

PREPARATION

Connect to a neighbor's shared folder.

Connecting to a shared network resource

- Double-click **Network Neighborhood** icon on your desktop.
- Select a computer other than your own and double-click on it.
- Double-click on their folder.

Using NETSTAT

- Type **NETSTAT** then press **Enter**.

* Notice what computer (WHO) is connected and the protocol typc

Step 7: **Using the WINIPCFG utility to view local TCP/IP configuration**

- Type **WINIPCFG** then press **Enter**.

* This same information can be viewed by typing **IPCONFIG**. Try it! **IPCONFIG** will only work on Windows 98 and Windows NT/2000 machines.